Never Throw Rice at a *Pisces*

Also by **STACEY WOLF**

- *Get Psychic!*
- *Love Secrets of the Signs*
- *Psychic Living*
- *Secrets of the Signs*

Stacey Wolf

Never Throw Rice at a
PISCES

The Bride's Astrology Guide to

- Planning Your Wedding,
- Choosing Your Honeymoon,
- and Loving Every Second of It,
- No Matter What Your Sign

Thomas Dunne Books ▪ St. Martin's Griffin ♏ New York

THOMAS DUNNE BOOKS.
An imprint of St. Martin's Press.

www.thomasdunnebooks.com
www.stmartins.com

Design by Gregory P. Collins

Library of Congress Cataloging-in-Publication Data

Wolf, Stacey.
    Never throw rice at a Pisces : the bride's astrology guide to planning your wed-
ding, choosing your honeymoon, and loving every second of it, no matter what
your sign / Stacey Wolf.—1st ed.
        p. cm.
    ISBN-13: 978-0-312-35918-8
    ISBN-10: 0-312-35918-7
    1. Astrology.   2. Weddings—Planning.

BF1711.W83 2008
133.5'839522—dc22

2007038324

First Edition: January 2008

10 9 8 7 6 5 4 3 2 1

To my tender Taurus husband, **Ed Lamadrid,** whose Sagittarius Rising makes our life together a wonderful heartfelt adventure!

Contents

■ **Introduction** 1

1. Using Astrology to Plan Your Big Day 5

Busy brides: Read up on the basics of astrology and discover why it's the perfect tool to use to plan your wedding!

5 ■ Astrology: A *Really* Brief History

7 ■ A Little Astrology Goes a Long Way

8 ■ Sun Signs: A Tour of the Zodiac

13 ■ The Four Personality Types: Nature's Organization System

15 ■ The Three Qualities: Your Modus Operandi

20 ■ Planning by the Stars: Choosing the Perfect Wedding Day

2. Bridal Signs 33

Discover the bride you are born to be. Learn how to use your strengths and avoid your weaknesses. Uncover your secret desire, your biggest pet peeve, and exactly what you need in a bridal party.

33 ■ Fire Elements: Aries, Leo, Sagittarius

42 ■ Earth Elements: Taurus, Virgo, Capricorn

49 ■ Air Elements: Gemini, Libra, Aquarius

59 ■ Water Elements: Cancer, Scorpio, Pisces

3. Getting Started:

Where Astrology and Weddings Meet 69

Discover how your sign tackles projects, tasks, and budgets. Meet brides of different signs that have been in your shoes and see how they handled their big day!

70 ■ Organize Yourself

73 ▪ Getting Your Groom Involved

78 ▪ Bringing Up the Budget

80 ▪ Setting Your Priorities

84 ▪ Number of Guests

85 ▪ Making Early Decisions

88 ▪ The Gift Registry

92 ▪ The Invitations and the Printing

96 ▪ Tackling the Legalities

4. The Look of the Bride, Groom, and Bridal Party   101

Uncover your inner personality and find the perfect dress, shoes, and accessories to suit your style. Discover a great look for your groom that you *both* love. Plus, read up on dress disasters you can avoid.

101 ▪ The Wedding Dress

107 ▪ Completing the Look: Shoes, Accessories, Hair, and Makeup

112 ▪ The Groom's Attire

116 ▪ Dressing the Bridal Party

5. Prewedding Parties   122

From the theme to the decor, you want these events to reflect your signature style—even if you're not completely in charge of planning them.

123 ▪ The Bridal Shower

130 ▪ The Bachelorette Party

136 ▪ The Rehearsal Dinner

6. Designing an Unforgettable Ceremony   146

Create a ceremony that honors your astrological essence. Choose the perfect officiant, design an unforgettable ambience, and get to your ceremony in style. Topping off this chapter is a list of tips to avoid those last-minute freak-outs that can turn a mere mortal into bridezilla.

146 ■ Officiant and Ritual

150 ■ Readings and Vows

155 ■ Creating the Perfect Ambience

158 ■ Flowers

162 ■ Music

166 ■ Photography and Videography

169 ■ Transportation

171 ■ The Morning Of

7. A Reception That Suits Your Sign   177

With the zodiac as your guide, create a party that perfectly reflects who you are, from the hors d'oeuvres to the last dance. Grooms, pay attention: Read the tips for her sign and give her the support she *really* needs—something only you can do!

177 ■ Setting the Tone

180 ■ Seating Your Guests

184 ■ Food and Drink

186 ■ Flowers

189 ■ Music

193 ■ First-Dance Selections and Styles

196 ■ The Cake

199 ■ Toasts and Speeches

202 ■ Favors and Crafts

8. Your Honeymoon   208

Discover where to go and what to do on this romantic getaway. Peek into the honeymoons of previous brides and grooms of the zodiac and make your honeymoon come alive!

208 ■ Choosing the Perfect Destination

213 ■ Practical Decisions

217 ■ Romantic Activities for Day and Night

221 ■ Adding the Perfect Surprises!

■ **Happily Ever Afterword: Being Mrs. Right!** **225**

Use the strengths of your astrology chart to have a wonderful life. Plus, a few juicy tidbits from the experts on how to make it through the ups and downs!

225 ■ The Aries Newlywed

226 ■ The Taurus Newlywed

227 ■ The Gemini Newlywed

227 ■ The Cancer Newlywed

229 ■ The Leo Newlywed

229 ■ The Virgo Newlywed

230 ■ The Libra Newlywed

231 ■ The Scorpio Newlywed

233 ■ The Sagittarius Newlywed

233 ■ The Capricorn Newlywed

234 ■ The Aquarius Newlywed

234 ■ The Pisces Newlywed

■ **Acknowledgments** **237**

Once upon a time, a Pisces bride was getting ready to celebrate her wedding. She wanted the fairy tale, the "walk out of the church surrounded by guests throwing rice" photo op. But this sensitive sign knew that it would be harmful to the innocent birds singing in the trees. "Birdseed!" this animal lover exclaimed. "That's what the guests will toss!"

As she and her bridesmaids sat over tea, one of them asked why they were wrapping little bundles of *seeds* in pretty pink pouches. With a smile she replied, "Geminis may like their guests to blow bubbles and Libras may like them to cast rose petals, but *never throw rice at a Pisces.*"

Never Throw Rice at a *Pisces*

Introduction

■
■

Congratulations, **bride-to-be!** You are newly engaged, you've flashed your ring to all your neighbors and you've called all your friends and family with the exciting news—now what do you do? Read your horoscope, of course!

You've been following the stars ever since you can remember, learning about your sign in *Teen* magazine, sneaking away with your mother's *Vogue*. Now you can use astrology as a tool to plan the biggest day of your life! The catch? You can't just pick up *any* astrology book for bridal guidance. No other book, bridal or astrological, combines insightful information about your unique personality and the special needs of a bride planning a wedding.

For the first time, instead of reading the great suggestions in the latest wedding magazines and wondering if they'd work in your real life, you can be sure. With this guide in hand, you've got sign-specific advice on everything from invitations to ceremonial readings to honeymoon activities. *Never Throw Rice at a Pisces* cuts through the massive amount of options with words of wisdom tailored to suit your sign.

After doing astrology for many years and encountering numerous new brides and newlyweds, I can say with certainty that in addition to the various personality types laid out in the stars, there are distinct patterns that emerge from a bride's chart that will play a part in her big day. Yes, it's true, whether you are aware of it or not—the type of wedding you have is guided by the unseen forces at work around us!

For instance, Sagittarius brides are much more likely than any other sign to plan their wedding as an adventure. Of the three Sag brides whose stories are reflected in this book, one got married in Jamaica, one on a cruise, and the one who got married close to home created an elaborate religious adventure combining two unique cultures.

Talk to a Cancer or Pisces bride, the emotional signs of the zodiac, and you'll learn that they have distinct motivations for *every* choice. From the dress down to the colors of the favor-gift wrapping paper, nothing is chosen arbitrarily.

Where other brides may include elements to appease family, the powerful Scorpio bride will almost *never* incorporate anything she considers meaningless into her ceremony or reception—no matter how popular a tradition it seems to others. All three Scorpios highlighted within these pages drove their mothers to distraction over their willful independence and freethinking!

This book goes farther than most other astrology books, delving past your Sun sign to reveal the hidden elements of your chart that equally drive your personality and emotions. You will discover your Rising and Moon signs and the often overlooked role they play in your big day. This will be especially eye-opening if you are one of those brides that reads your horoscope and feels like it never really speaks to you. When you've got the total picture at your fingertips, navigating the world becomes a snap.

With a road map like this available, why take your chances? Wedding planning can be stressful enough without trying to figure out what would make your wedding perfect for you in the process. With its myriad of choices, and busywork that can keep you occupied for months, a young woman can too easily lose herself in the process if she's not careful.

Never Throw Rice at a Pisces is a wonderful reminder of what's truly important to your spirit, but it's also a realistic guide to help you stay grounded and focused during what can often be chaotic interpersonal exchanges.

We've all heard the horror stories about parents overstepping their boundaries and opinionated friends giving their unsolicited, unwelcome advice. We're equally aware of what unprofessional vendors, incompetent wedding planners, and last-minute weather changes can do to your plans.

Every bride knows there are some elements (and people) she can control and some elements (and people) she cannot—that's part of planning a big elaborate celebration. Emotional outbursts and bad behavior are bound to happen, but you now have powerful, sign-specific ways to address, minimize, and solve these all-too-common problems before they become too hot to handle.

Finding your soul mate and getting married is a wonderful thing. Let's not overlook your significant other in the whirlwind of all the activities. Revealed within these pages are some great sign-specific suggestions to get your groom involved and to have his emotional support.

Astrology is not only a great wedding planning tool, it's a light that guides your relationship as well. As you plan your wedding, you are planting the seeds of a good marriage. Start off a lifetime of communication and cooperation with a better understanding of each other now. This will be just the first of many milestones ahead for you as a couple.

As you journey into the world of weddings, it's a pleasure to bring you a truly unique perspective. An astrologer for many years, I had the opportunity to plan my wedding by the stars several years ago. As a Pisces marrying a Taurus, I searched many hours to find the perfect day to fulfill all our dreams, and crafted a romantic, down-to-earth wedding and honeymoon that we will remember for the rest of our lives.

Within the myriad of wedding planners and bridal guides, you're holding the one that shines light on all the others. It's a wedding book, an astrology book, and a psychology book all rolled into one!

Leave the freak-outs to the other brides—you've got the ultimate guide to planning your wedding! May your special day be a wonderful reflection of you and your new mate, and the love you share for each other. May *Never Throw Rice at a Pisces* assist you in fulfilling that dream and creating a wonderful life together.

Chapter *One*

For as long as humans have been on the planet, they have been looking up to the heavens for guidance, using the movement of the stars to plan events and peek into the future. This same search for guidance continues even today. You hold right now the ideal wedding planning guide for your modern life, but before we take off on our wedding journey through the stars, here's a one-minute history of the science and lore of nature's own planning software in the sky.

■ Astrology: A *Really* Brief History

Astrology has been around for a very, very long time. The earliest known astrological artifacts date back to 20,000 to 15,000 B.C. Simple charts of the sun and moon were used to determine the planting and harvest seasons.

Later practiced in temples in ancient Babylon and Egypt, astrology became infused with religious symbolism and an amazing amount of superstition (every eclipse was a bad omen waiting to happen).

The planets were worshipped as gods by the Greek and Roman civilizations between 900 and 300 B.C., and elaborate myths were created to explain the heavenly bodies as they flirted and chased one another around the sky. Life, death, war, riches, famine—the astrology of the time was one part mathematics, one part soap opera.

Over eons of observation, these ancient civilizations created a system to convey the passage of time. It was the Babylonians who set up the 360-degree horoscope wheel based on the movements of the sun, with the twelve different pieces of pie we call astrology signs that we still use today. By attributing various personality traits to the movement of the stars, not only did they create a calendar, but they created the modern study of astrology—four thousand years ago!

In other societies, the astrologers began monthly cycles at the appearance of the new moon (that tiniest sliver of light we see when the rest of the moon is in shadow). This is how the Chinese, Hindu, Hebrew, and Arabic calendars still count time today.

Eventually they figured out that the twenty-eight-day cycles of the moon and the 365-degree cycle of the sun don't fit into a neat little sum and they were left with a few extra days to play with when the sun came back around for its next run. Some of these civilizations devised interesting ways to fix the problem, others just left it. By adding even more myths to their history, they were able to introduce a whole month every so often or an extra handful of days to the end of their lunar year to make up the difference.

The astrology of ancient Egypt, Greece, and Rome, based on the movements of the sun, wasn't a perfect fit either. Let enough years go by at 360 days and the seasons fall out of harmony. The drama of our modern calendar begins in 45 B.C. when Julius Caesar's astrologer cleared up the muckety-muck and created a leap year every four years—which worked well until after his death when the Romans minding the store inserted a few too many extra days. It was Pope Gregory who eventually skipped eleven days in 1582 just so that, 106 leap years later, you could get to the church on time!

With no Internet and no calendar police to enforce the pope's decree, it took a few centuries before everyone got on board with the modern calendar. Set up to parallel the tropical year (the length of time it takes for the earth to cycle around the sun), the Gregorian calendar's calculations are so precise that almost 500 years later it can be accurately used by modern astrologers and laymen alike to reveal character traits, predict key events, and express the passage of time.

■ A Little Astrology Goes a Long Way

Nowadays we don't have to get our horoscope fix from studying the sky, we just turn on our computer and the daily 'scopes are waiting for our consumption. The end product is wildly fascinating and oddly accurate—but how?

The elaborate picture of the heavens at the moment of your birth depicts the astrological makeup of who you are. The location of the sun, moon, and the planets, the constellation rising on the eastern horizon, all came together to create the totally unique person you are today.

The relationships of the planets at that one moment creates a truly once-upon-a-time scenario. The force that creates high tides is the same push-pull that acts among planets to bring forth the different aspects of your personality that we see in your chart; your greatest gifts just waiting to shine through in your life.

The number one personality indicator, your Sun sign, is the constellation the sun was passing at the time you were born—your special thirty-degree section of the sky. The Sun sign is the most important aspect of your chart, and that's the one we'll be focusing on in this book.

If you look at a zodiac wheel, you see that each of the twelve signs corresponds to one of the twelve pie slices—or *houses* as they are traditionally called—each signifying the twelve different aspects of life we experience on our journey. From our individual personalities to our home life to our relationships and career, it's all there on the wheel. What Sun sign you were born under and what house it rules tells you a lot about what's important to you.

Below is a quick journey through all the signs, their natural houses, and their approximate dates on the calendar. Most of us follow the sun's movement by counting days but astrologers go by *degrees*. The following dates for each sign are the most common, but occasionally the calendar can be off by as much as a day or two in some years compared to the sign's actual degree. If you are born on or close to the first or last dates in a sign, find a free online astrology site and plug in your birth information just to make sure you are reading the right 'scopes. I've seen a fair share of surprised clients and friends who had thought they were born at the end of one sign only to find out they were born in the early degrees of another.

▪ Sun Signs: A Tour of the Zodiac

Before Julius Caesar came along and decreed January first the beginning of a new year, there were a few different acceptable days to celebrate that event, including the popular spring equinox. That's why the beginning of the zodiac's new year is the birth of spring on March 21, making Aries the first sign.

Aries

MARCH 21 — APRIL 19

♈ *Birthing new energy for all the zodiac, the Ram says, "I am!"*
Our journey around the wheel begins with birth and the first house of self and personality. Aries gals always explode onto the scene, expressing themselves, sharing their ideas, their tastes, and their style with an innate sense of urgency.

Taurus

APRIL 20 — MAY 20

♉ *Claiming a piece of the world, the Bull says, "I have."*
The next stop on life's road is the second house of money and possessions, where Taurus rules the roost.

Taureans work hard in order to ensure the stability of their life, their friends, family, their homes, and their cherished collections.

Gemini

MAY 21 – JUNE 20

Learning and discerning, the Twins affirm, "I think."

The Twins are at home in the third house, which is the house of communications. They are master talkers (writers, readers, and thinkers). They always seem to know everything and have a very charming manner. Indeed, Geminis win admirers simply with words.

Cancer

JUNE 21 – JULY 22

Exploring new emotions, the Crab's mantra is, "I feel."

Crabs rule the fourth slice of heaven, home life. Cancers love to create their own private hideaways. They decorate, garden, and throw intimate dinner parties for those they let into their inner circle. Get inside their shell and you'll find they are the most tender friend and fiancée.

Leo

JULY 23 – AUGUST 22

Commanding center stage, the Lion sings, "I will!"

Leos are born to rule in the fifth house of creativity, sex, romance, fun, and children. The Lion has a larger-than-life attitude, always surrounded by a whirlwind of drama and fun. Natural attention-grabbers, they are born entertainers and presidents of the zodiac.

Virgo

Working hard on self-improvement, the Virgin states, "I analyze."

The sixth house of work, service to others, pets, and health belongs to the security-minded Virgo. This house lies in early fall and the sign is aptly named for the virgin harvest. Virgos love to help others. Whether a friend, coworker, or fiancée, they've got inexhaustible energy for you, and in return they love to feel needed and appreciated.

Libra

SEPTEMBER 23 – OCTOBER 22

Seeking harmony, fairness, and order, the Scales say, "I balance."

The next step on the journey of life: The house of partnerships. Libra loves a good pairing; romantic, friendship, or work-related. The scales of justice naturally experience life in graceful, fair balance. This sign is all about beauty, elegance, and cooperation.

Scorpio

OCTOBER 23 – NOVEMBER 21

To fulfill destiny, the Scorpion cries, "I desire!"

This intense creature is at home in the eighth house of other people's money, taxes, death, and transformation. They love to delve into the mysteries of life and will stop at nothing to understand the subtle forces at work in our lives.

Sagittarius

NOVEMBER 22 – DECEMBER 21

Exploring new concepts, the Archer says, "I see."

As we make our way around the wheel to the house

opposite of Gemini, communication, we see Sagittarius and the ninth house of higher education, law, religion, and foreign cultures. The Archer loves learning, traveling, and understanding human nature.

Capricorn

DECEMBER 22 – JANUARY 19

Ingeniously striving to become the best, the Goat declares, "I use."

Next we visit the driven Goat and the tenth house of fame, career, and success. Capricorns love to work hard to achieve positions of power. While Leos like to be admired for their charm, Capricorns prefer to win kudos for their efforts and abilities.

Aquarius

JANUARY 20 – FEBRUARY 18

Determined to improve the issues of the world, the Water Bearer's motto is, "I know."

Aquarius rules the eleventh house of friendships, group activities, and secret wishes. Aquarians express themselves best by working toward a common goal with like-minded (and offbeat) people. Their lofty ideals always have a humanitarian bent!

Pisces

FEBRUARY 19 – MARCH 20

Using intuition and self-awareness, the Fish echoes, "I believe."

The twelfth house, where Pisces resides, is the place where the mystical meets the mind. Some say that Pisces, in the last house, is a sign that encompasses a little bit of every sign that came before it. No wonder Pisces is the queen of intuition, deep-seated feelings, and dreamy romance.

Our trek through the stars is just beginning. Now that you understand how the different signs interact with one another on the journey through life, we can move on to the naturally forming groups within the circle.

Here is where it gets interesting. Yes, we understand our individual signs, but astrology is more complicated than twelve signs running loose around a wheel.

The ancient astrologers who set up the system noticed that certain signs around the zodiac related to one another in special ways, creating different groupings of three and four kindred spirits—or in our case, bands of brides! Understanding your Sun sign is one thing, but knowing how it relates to other signs takes your planning skills to a whole new level.

Let's take a look at the most well known of these groupings first, the four elements, then we'll uncover the little known, but very important groupings of qualities.

The Marriage Generation:
From October 1971 to October 1983

If you were born between the fall of 1971 and the fall of 1983, when Pluto was traveling through Libra, the sign of marriage, then you have an innate need to settle into a committed relationship early in your life. You are built for marriage. People born under this aspect like their partnerships to be superharmonious, balanced, and fair. They naturally think in pairs and know they are more powerful working as part of a team.

Taking responsibility for the welfare of your partner is second nature, as is your understanding of human justice. You dislike it when things are unfair or unbalanced—whether it's an in-law taking advantage of you or a natural disaster halfway around the world. You have a strong need to correct inequitable situations; diplomatically, of course. Together, as a generation, you can change the course of history, demanding fairness and equality in all relationships—partners, friends, and nations.

■ The Four Personality Types: Nature's Organization System

The most well-known division of the horoscope is the four personality types, named after the four elements of nature that relate to the individual temperaments. The four elements are the natural characteristics shared by groups of three signs, making them cousins and soul sisters.

Fire signs start the chart by being the leaders and hams of the zodiac. Their warmth and glow attracts people, guaranteeing them a spot at center stage. Earth signs follow by being the practical managers, born with the uncanny ability to use their resources to pull off anything they set their minds to. Air signs are focused on the intellect; they love to learn, to know. As astrology's social butterflies, they thrive on their interactions with others. Lastly we come to the Water signs, whose primary motivations are their feelings and intuition, which can run as deep as an ocean, as calm as a lake, or as turbulent as Niagara Falls.

Take a look at the following chart—are you in *your* element?

FIRE: Aries, Leo, Sagittarius
EARTH: Taurus, Virgo, Capricorn
AIR: Gemini, Libra, Aquarius
WATER: Cancer, Scorpio, Pisces

Fire sign brides have all the energy in the world to plan their big event; they want to take advantage of every opportunity to party, and include all their friends and family in the mix—they like a large group of admirers! An Aries does best coming up with the ideas and passing the details to a wedding coordinator. Leos like the best of everything and have a supernatural power to get their way. Then there's the Sags, who love the fun, but like their freedom so much that it may be hard for them to commit to a huge wedding, perhaps choosing an offbeat adventure instead.

Earth sign brides are made for planning and organizing big events, using their ingenuity to work around budgets and set backs. Taureans, ruled by Venus, are more likely to choose a quiet, outdoor springtime affair than a big showy shindig. Virgo likes perfection from start to finish—she's the one with the latest planning software and notebooks full of checklists. Capricorns, on the other hand, are the most outward-focused of the Earth signs. They like every public event to reveal their ambitious, traditional nature. Leave it to the Goat to choose brunch at Tavern on the Green for their bridal shower.

Air sign brides love to learn all the facts, compare them, and make judgments. They are going to make sure they've seen every interesting location before choosing their venue and will interview every florist, looking for that perfect nuance and style. Geminis are the trendsetters, look to the Twins for an eclectic mix of vintage, modern, and funky styles. Libra, ruled by Venus, is all about beauty, elegance, and tradition from the invitations to the desserts, everything has to be aesthetically just so. And then there's independent Aquarius, who likes to buck trend and tradition and just make one big statement. You'll definitely know what's important to an Aquarius on her big day.

Finally we have the Water signs, full of sentimentality and compassion. Whether it's big or small, they want their weddings to ooze with the sense of love and romance. Cancer, the most down-to-earth of the three, wants a gazebo by a lake with every friend they've ever loved on hand for the occasion. The mystical Pisces desires the ultimate fairy-tale affair—from the horse-drawn carriage to the glass slippers. And Scorpio will make sure the day is infused with a humanitarian bent—donating the leftovers to a homeless shelter and recycling the decorations.

You will learn to use the natural power of your element more in chapter 2 when you discover how to be the bride you are born to be, but for now let's move on to our next astro-secret revealed, the three qualities.

The Marriage Revolution:
From November 1968 to November 1974

If you were born between the end of 1968 and the end of 1974, then it's an innate part of your nature to transform the institution of marriage. These are the years that Uranus, the mighty planet of reform, passed though Libra, the sign of partnerships, and changed tying-the-knot forever.

Marriage is more than just a commitment when Uranus comes to town; it's a way of being, an otherworldly expression of all that is. Soul mates and nonconformists, there is nothing traditional about how you approach wedlock. You need a lot of freedom to explore new ways of doing everything matrimonial. From the ceremony to your parenting techniques, it's all about expressing your values and ideals—and if that means scrapping the establishment in the process, well then, *buh-bye.*

This need to upgrade the system goes beyond your own marriage. With deep insight into human nature, you are passionate about all of us working to create fair and honest interactions. It's the spirit behind the laws of marriage that matters most to you, a generation of innovators, re-creating partnerships better suited to our modern world.

■ The Three Qualities: Your Modus Operandi

Everyone knows their Sun sign these days, and most people know their element—but do you know your quality type? Just as the elements are four groups of three signs each, qualities are three groups of four—one of each element to be exact.

Your Sun sign and element determine your style, but your quality determines the way you operate in the world. Why is this important to know when you are planning a wedding? Because your quality tells you a lot about how you focus your energies, interact with people, and deal with obstacles, last-minute issues, and emergencies. Hello—*wedding?*

The three qualities are Cardinal, Fixed, and Mutable. Cardinal signs are self-starters, they have an active way of moving through life and engaging with others. They take each situation into account, listening to others before they make up their mind; always knowing the appropriate actions to take for any circumstance.

The meanings of Fixed and Mutable are exactly as they sound. People with a Fixed quality are *stubborn.* They have a lot of force, drive, and will. It's not always about getting what they want (not *always!*) but they are not going to give in easily unless they feel like they are getting something in return. Mutable signs, on the other hand, are flexible gymnasts. They compromise well and can easily handle any challenging situation with grace. All this adaptability can be hard for firm decision making—and if they don't watch out, their dreams and wishes might get lost in all the bargaining.

Get ready for your first big aha moment. Now that you know all about the secret of *qualities,* which category do you fit into?

> **CARDINAL:** Aries, Cancer, Libra, Capricorn
>
> **FIXED:** Taurus, Leo, Scorpio, Aquarius
>
> **MUTABLE:** Gemini, Virgo, Sagittarius, Pisces

Let's look into these a little further. Cardinal signs (Aries, Cancer, Libra, and Capricorn) take a hands-on approach to everything they do; they love putting ideas into action and trying new things along the way. An Aries, with her Fire action, is always going to have more energy than her Cancer, Libra, and Capricorn Cardinal sisters, but their initiative and take-charge attitude is the same. As a bride, these signs have bold, creative ideas and want to mix it up along the way, asking tough questions, listening to the experts, and looking for win-win solutions, all while not losing sight of the finish line.

The difference is in the sign. Fiery Aries may have too many great ideas and need to focus on one task at a time. A Cancer will always get the best results when she feels safe—lest she get moody and clam up. The Libra wants elegance and will have no problem being gracefully assertive in order to achieve her goals, and a Capricorn brings her ambitious nature to the job, "Whatever I have to do to get the job done," is her mantra.

The one thing the Cardinal signs can keep in mind is setting good boundaries. Each sign has their tipping point, that one moment they want to hide, run, or tune out. When you've had enough with the busy-work, walk away. Stop doing wedding planning when it stops being fun and do something to nurture yourself instead.

Elements:
The Secret Ingredient in Your Bridal Party

Friendships aren't random affairs in astrology. Fire and Air signs have a natural affinity for each other, as do Earth and Water. It's logi-cal when you think about it, air fans a fire, and water nourishes the earth. But they don't quite work the other way around, earth gets scorched by fire, water puts it out, and air doesn't do much for either earth or water.

Take a moment to think of all your friends' birthdays; you'll proba-bly find that most of them fit into the same element as you or its partner affinity. If you know your Rising sign or your friend's Rising sign (that's the constellation on the eastern horizon at the time of birth which we'll discuss in detail later in the chapter), compare those as well. Don't be surprised to find out that those signs make a neat fit, too!

Fixed signs (Taurus, Leo, Scorpio, and Aquarius) are the immov-able objects of the zodiac. They have a vision and they must see it through to reality. They have no desire to make it easy on their vendor-partners. To these strong brides where there's a will, there's a way. They are great at inspiring others to come into their corner, but they can ap-pear a bit domineering on a bad day. Don't ever say, "Just trust me," to a Fixed sign bride, they might not want to do your job themselves, but they'll definitely be making sure you're doing it according to their high standards!

In this category, power rules. Leo, queen of the jungle, uses her warm and generous nature to ensure the assistance of her loyal followers. Tau-rus girls have a down-to-earth, friendly vibe that disarms but doesn't back down. Watery Scorpio almost hypnotizes others into submission, while the Aquarius comes up with a million reasons why her way is actually the best, most effective, and humanitarian.

They do share one thing in common, though: If they feel disrespected, they will dig in their heels and not give an inch! It's wonderful to be so focused, but sometimes it really is in a Fixed sign's best interest to listen and compromise. In this business, it may save you time and money to find win-win solutions (not to mention avoid some potential bridezilla-style clashes!).

The Mutable signs (Gemini, Virgo, Sagittarius, and Pisces), are the easygoing, nonconfrontational-types. They are open-minded, easily swayed, and tend to shy away from absolutes—unlike their Fixed counterparts, they never need anything to be exactly the way they see it *or else*. When it comes to a wedding, they can use this flexibility to their advantage. After listening to all their options, they can easily let go of ideas that aren't working or are too expensive, and make different choices without compromising their ideals.

Because Virgos are born to organize, this sign is the most driven of the four. Staying busy with little projects and keeping on top of vendors is fun for this sign. The Gemini does a lot of talking as she tries to figure out the best way to go, charming her vendors into good deals along the way. Sagittarius gals are so busy planning their hip-hop-around-the-globe honeymoon that they might just let someone else take care of the wedding details. Then there's the Pisces princess, who wants the most sentimental day—yet won't even be able to choose the color of the tablecloths without consulting her friends and family.

Mutables need to make sure there is someone on their side who completely understands them—a best friend, fiancé, or wedding coordinator. Someone who can be their gatekeeper when things get nuts and can help them make the choices that truly reflect their innermost desires.

Whether you are Cardinal, Fixed, or Mutable, now you understand why you behave the way you do—it's in your nature! When you start visiting bridal salons and asking the serious questions, you'll now be able to use your quality to your advantage!

As you can see, your individual sign, element, and quality all add up to make a very unique astrological combination. Brides with the same Sun sign aren't automatically going to choose the same flowers. Not everyone in the same element is going to respond to their mother-in-law the same way, and not everyone in the same quality is going to choose the same main course for dinner. Before we move on to uncovering even more secrets for each sign, let's first discover the secret to using astrology to choose the perfect date for your wedding.

Using Your Rising and Moon Signs: Astrology 2.0

These days there are a lot of astrologically savvy brides out there, so let's push the envelope a bit. Your Rising sign, the thirty-degree chunk of stars that was rising on the eastern horizon at the time of your birth, is a major factor in who you are, as is the sign the moon was in when you took your first breath. Your Rising sign determines your outward personality, the first impressions people get when they meet you, and your Moon sign determines how you feel and express your emotions.

Your Sun sign has the starring role, with your Rising and Moon following closely behind as supporting cast members. Mixed together, your Sun, Moon, and Rising signs are a more accurate account of who you are, inside and out—thinking, feeling, and expressing.

These tidbits of helpful information once were available only to people willing to shell out the big bucks to visit a pro, but these days it's easy to find out your Rising and Moon signs and to incorporate that knowledge into your daily planning. Simply find one of the many free astrology sites available on the Internet and plug in your date, time, and place of birth. Within seconds you will uncover the secrets of your astrological chart.

If this sounds like something you are interested in learning more about, you can visit my Web site for a current list of free astrology sites on the Internet where your time, date, and place of birth will reveal your Moon and Rising signs in a jiffy. Visit staceywolf.com and just click on "my books."

Of course, you don't need to know either of these pieces of information to read this book and have it be accurate for you. They're just
another tier on the wedding cake. If you do know, then you can work
your way through the chapters and discover how these signs play their
own parts in creating the celebration of your dreams! If not, just keep
applying all the sections of your Sun sign to the different aspects of
your special day.

■ Planning by the Stars: Choosing the Perfect Wedding Day

Astrology isn't just about understanding your personality. People have
been using astrology to plan and predict key events for longer than any
of us have been breathing. Astrologers use many tools to map out the
best and worst days for their clients, but you can use a simplified ver-
sion to plan your wedding date, bridal shower—even the groom's
bachelor party.

The Moon sign of any given day tells us a lot about how people will
feel and interact, what type of ceremony will inspire them, and what
kind of mood they'll be in at the party. It is also what connects you as a
couple emotionally, so the Moon sign on your wedding day will cement
how you will feel in your marriage and how you express those feelings
for the rest of your lives.

Since the moon moves around our planet very fast, changing signs
every two to three days, it's impossible to know what sign the moon is
in by just looking at a standard calendar. But right now I'll teach you a
little secret about how you can quickly find out what sign the moon is
in for any day on your short list.

All you have to do is find one of those wonderful astrology Web
sites I mentioned earlier and plug in all the dates, times, even potential
locations you are considering for your wedding, as if you are creating a
birth chart for the first day of your marriage. Identify the Moon sign for

each day and skip the rest. (If you are really serious about this, you can even buy a special calendar with the Moon signs already printed on it.)

Realistically, there are lots of things to consider when setting a date. Modern brides are juggling their choice of seasons, the availability of the reception hall, even other family events. I know it's not so easy to choose a day based solely on the stars, but this is a great opportunity to set some priorities, do some juggling, and come up with a day for the perfect party that will also serve your emotional sides. Here's how.

First, read the chart on page 22. Decide what qualities are most important to you and your fiancé, as well as what qualities conflict with your ideal marriage.

At this point, knowing your own Moon sign can be helpful. When you get married, you become an emotional mix of you and your groom's Moon signs and the Moon sign of your marriage. You may want to explore a Moon sign that will give you both individually and as a couple some qualities you might feel you have been missing from birth. If you are full of fun and flighty Air signs, you might look into choosing an Earth sign for stability or a Water sign for more emotional connection. On the other hand, if you both have down-to-earth Moon signs, you may wish to choose one that brings you a little spontaneity, travel, and fun.

Write a list of all the potential dates and their Moon signs. Take the time to read about each sign in depth and separate them into two categories—a yes group and a no group. There are no rules here; you may be attracted to more than just one Moon sign and that's fine. It just gives you more choices to work with.

Put the perfect I-do dates in an order that feels right to you and begin to work with that list in your planning. Block the no-no dates off in your calendar and pass on them *no matter what.*

You ultimately want to choose a day whose Moon sign best enhances your emotional nature as a couple—or, when everything is taken into consideration, one that doesn't conflict with who you are just because the venue is available. You'll be creating the perfect mood for your special day and a solid foundation for a successful, healthy marriage.

A Quick Look at Moon Signs and Your Marriage

Aries	A spicy, fun life together with a dash of independence
Taurus	Stability is paramount—along with lots of hugs and thoughtfulness
Gemini	Someone to talk to, to read the paper with, and chat about your day
Cancer	A big family and a loving, secure home
Leo	Big parties and larger-than-life experiences
Virgo	A lifetime of healing and working together
Libra	Love and partnership mean everything to you
Scorpio	Passion and intensity, sex and romance
Sagittarius	Redefining your roles and embarking on big adventures
Capricorn	A traditional marriage with very ambitious careers
Aquarius	Leaders in the community with a large, extended family
Pisces	Sentimental coupling with home as a safe haven

Now that you've got a feel for each sign, let's look into these Moon signs more deeply before you make your ultimate choice. Aries Moons are wild fun with big expressions of emotion. If you are looking for a lifetime of spontaneity, this sign may be perfect. On the other hand, when emotions run hot there can be some minor explosions in your house. That's not as bad as it sounds, because once the eruptions are over, they are quickly forgotten.

Aries is a good sign to choose if you are a reserved couple looking to come out of your shell. Although you might want to skip it if you're already mixing it up and you're not even married yet!

As far as the day of the wedding goes, choose an Aries Moon and you will have a great, spontaneous party. Guests will dance all night, there will be many outward gestures of emotion, but people can also get a little headstrong at times and won't be into sitting for a long-winded, mystical ceremony. If you've already got a fun family bordering on the nutty, you won't be able to count on them being on their best behavior. Buyer beware!

Taurus Moons are one of the classic choices for couples wishing to create a large home and family. This is a very fertile moon—you will have many kids and work hard to have a sizable, stable home filled with nice things. This Earth sign moon is rich in warmth, love, and thoughtfulness. If you like to have growing collections around your home, whether it be sentimental photos or plates from different nations, this is the moon for you. Your sweetie will bring you little presents often and take you out for nice meals.

On the flip side, you might have a hard time letting go of your issues, and this moon can make for an obstinate pairing. This moon spends a lot of time at home. If you need some stability this is terrific, if you like travel and adventure or enjoy a big social scene, skip this moon; you may be a little bored.

Choose a Taurus Moon if you want a traditional wedding; a church ceremony, and a classic reception. The day of a Taurus Moon will be filled with lots of quiet, sentimental moments; the groom hugging the best man, the bride's dance with her father. But no one can be rushed on a Taurus Moon, so try to keep things as simple as possible and don't stick to a rigid schedule. You may also find your guests more stubborn than usual, if Aunt Mary isn't seated next to Aunt Bea, she may just move someone out of the place next to her no matter what you planned.

It's all about communication under a Gemini Moon. If you'd love to laugh and chat with your best buddy for the rest of your life, and have the freedom to mix it up about everything from world news to family gossip, then this is your match. You're more likely to analyze your feelings than argue about them, and want things to blow over as quickly as possible. This is a light and airy moon, which can bring levity to an intense couple, but may not be enough to hold a lightweight pairing together. If you need sweeping, dramatic expressions of love and tons of hugs and kisses, you might be left hungry by a Gemini Moon.

Everyone will be a little spacey the day of a Gemini Moon wedding. Make sure you've gone over every detail with your vendor a million times because chances are, something is going to get left undone and a last-minute scramble will ensue. Guests of honor will give great speeches, but don't hold them to a heavy-duty ceremony; no one is going to have a particularly long attention span—not even you. You'll be in the mood to say a quick "I do," and then party, laugh, and mingle with your guests all night long!

Next on the list is the Cancer Moon. The marriage of a Cancer Moon couple is sweet and sentimental. If you desire a strong emotional bond and large close-knit family, this is the best moon to choose. Cancer Moons create a home that is a loving, romantic sanctuary to escape the business of the world and farther down the road will be doting parents to boot. They enjoy their privacy and express themselves best in small groups.

If you like your independence, you're not going to get very far inside Cancer's emotional grip. Although if you like going on adventures as a couple (and one day a family), then Cancer is the sensitive home you've been looking for. If deep, emotional conversations turn you off, run for the hills.

A Cancer Moon is perfect for a small, heartfelt wedding, maybe at home or in a beautiful yard by a lake. Guests will be loving and affectionate, enjoying the quiet beauty of the day. With this Water sign Moon you are free to write the sappiest vows you can and express yourself in the most tender of ways, just don't expect everyone to crowd onto the dance floor and do a jig. And if you try to take on too much, your nerves can get the best of you. Looking for an exciting wedding? Pass this one over.

If creativity and self-expression are on top of your list, then you're a perfect fit for a Leo Moon. Leo Moon couples have a regal air about them, always walking with a little dramatic flair. They like things grand, going to expensive restaurants and shopping at luxury stores. Warmth, joy, and optimism abound with a Leo Moon. If you like large-scale romance and spontaneous affection, you may have found your match.

The downside: With two healthy egos, who is going to back down in a fight? If you're both a bit hotheaded, this sign may put you over the top. If you're on the introverted side, this Fire sign will bring more power to you.

If you want your wedding to be the best party you've ever been to, then Leo is the obvious choice for the day. Guests will enter a theater where you create a show full of sweeping romance and drama. They will dance, drink, eat, and have the time of their lives! Again the ego issues can arise; how many peacocks showing off their feathers would you like hanging around on your special day?

Next up is Virgo Moon, a tough sell for most couples. Virgo's detailed energy in a marriage can make for a nitpicky pair. It's good if you have a working partnership, own a business together, and maybe even want to conquer the world, but in most relationships a Virgo Moon can make for two people who are too cautious to really express themselves. However, if you've won a long, hard battle to be together, done a tremendous amount of healing together, and are dedicated to the service of humanity, then this is your special moon.

Not only is a Virgo Moon hard on most marriages, it isn't so great for the day of the wedding, either. Your guests will be examining the smallest details for imperfections in the plan—and do you really care how the napkins are folded? Instead of going with the flow and enjoying the day, you'll be too busy thinking of all the things that have already gone wrong. Unless you are a very mature couple, my suggestion is, don't play with fire.

Thankfully, we now come upon the gracious Libra Moon. Since Libra is the sign of marriage, any couple married under this moon will be blessed with a deep appreciation for love and beauty. If you like being half of a pair, and like everything you do to be beautiful and elegant, then this is your choice. Being diplomatic and tactful is of the utmost importance to a Libra Moon pairing; to them even just arguing borders on vulgar.

If you like to express yourself with passion and have a strong need to share your emotions, then you will feel quite frustrated by this moon. If you want to have children, be aware that they will always come second to you and your partner in this relationship, which is not necessarily a bad thing, but something you should know.

The day the moon is in Libra is every astrologer's dream of perfection. The wedding will be absolutely breathtaking. The food will be graciously prepared; the music elegant; the guests well dressed. Everyone will get along better than you ever thought they could. If a beautiful wedding is all you've ever wanted, then you can't ask for a better day. Now, if you can't wait to gush over your groom, don't expect everyone else to be overtaken by emotions and sentiments. There will be no crying at this affair, for that might seem a bit impolite.

Moving on to the mysterious Scorpio Moon. If romance, sex, and children are on top of your list, if you are passionate about your ideas and values, and enjoy expressing them to your significant other, and if you take commitment *very* seriously, then marry under a Scorpio Moon. This is a juicy, intense sign that demands a lot and is very rewarding.

The negatives? Scorpio Moons are prone to jealousy and guard their privacy intently. There may be no independence and freedom to speak of unless you both have plenty of that built-in to your charts already. If the idea of being possessed by your love for each other scares the pants off of you, you'd be smart to pass.

Do not plan for a big wedding on a day that Scorpio rules, you'll wake up in the morning and feel as if you want to hide under a rock. But it's a perfect day to choose when you wish to have a meaningful, spiritual ceremony in front of those you care most deeply about. People will be inspired by your vision and grateful for your love in their lives. Make sure you don't invite any exes, as the smallest thing can cause a huge amount of tension.

On to the Sagittarius Moon. As a couple, if you love personal freedom, enjoy traveling, and learning about foreign cultures, a Sag Moon is it for you. Sag Moons marry their best friend and lover and live life as one big exploration. They dislike being tied down by big extended families and being overloaded with obligations. Sag Moon couples work hard to liberate themselves from tradition, preferring instead to redefine marriage in a way that best works for them.

Choose this moon and you have to be ready to embrace the unconventional; even raising your children will have a progressive flavor. How deep do you want your love to grow? You may find your need for freedom getting in the way of settling down into a solid, emotionally stable relationship. If feeling unsafe is an issue you have now, it may just get magnified under this moon.

Are you thinking about having a destination wedding? A Sagittarius Moon may create the perfect wedding day for you. All your guests will be open-minded and up for anything, just keep the ceremony short or their attention may wander. There will be a playful quality to the day for all to enjoy. If you plan to have many children involved in your wedding, everyone will delight in the laughing, crying, and fun spontaneous behavior they bring to their roles.

Moving along to Capricorn. If you value tradition above all else, this Earth sign Moon may interest you. Capricorn couples enjoy working together to create a safe, secure home. If life's been rocky for you in the past and you wish to build a new foundation, or have mutual ambitions to create a dynasty rather than a mere marriage, then a Capricorn Moon will bring you solid support.

On the flip side, this coupling isn't known for spontaneity and fun, as it will always be tempered by the considerable responsibilities you both enjoy taking on. And if you both like to wear the pants in the relationship, you could turn into a pair of control freaks under a Capricorn Moon.

A Capricorn Moon is perfect for a big wedding in a church or synagogue followed by a classic reception, one where you've taken your time planning all the details to perfection. Your guests will be well dressed, well behaved, and enjoy all the traditions your special day has to offer. On the other hand, forgive the key players—your parents, bridal party, even your wedding coordinator—if they get controlling under the pressure. Everyone's different ideas of perfection can dampen the emotion and enthusiasm.

Next up, Aquarius Moon. If your ideal partnership includes being leaders in the community, then this Air sign Moon is the right choice for you. Couples with Aquarius Moons are aware of their place on the planet, they love their large group of friends and family, and keenly understand that you are not just marrying each other, but are marrying two families as well. This is a wonderful choice for a second marriage where there are stepchildren, as there is plenty of room for everyone to grow into their new roles.

This large community can come at the expense of a traditional intimate marriage. If you want to create your own private Idaho where you and your significant other can live in relative peace, unencumbered by the world, then think twice about choosing Aquarius as your moon.

This is such a big sign that on the day of an Aquarius Moon wedding, as with the Gemini Moon, people can be a bit spacey. You might be too aware of the party, the family, and the fun, and not that focused on the ceremony, the vows, and the commitment. Everyone will have a great time, but take lots of pictures and hire a videographer so you can catch all the little details after the show is over.

Bringing up the rear is the sensitive, yet otherworldly Pisces Moon. If you and your partner feel that you've finally found your soul mate, that you've finally found that someone who is completely simpatico with your ideals, then Pisces Moon is a divine choice. Pisces Moon couples like to express their emotions deeply and often, dealing with their vulnerabilities in the safe haven they have created together.

All this dreamy romance does have a downside. Pisces Moon couples are so supersensitive that they can easily get their feelings hurt if they don't learn to take things lightly. If you enjoy being mushy to the max then it'll work out just fine, but if you find tranquility a bit dull and doing everything together a tad restrictive, then this is not the moon for you. For a coupling that's all fun and adventure, it could add a lovely emotional element.

If a spiritual, sentimental wedding is your goal, you will do best with a Pisces Moon on your big day. Your guests will be moved by your inspiring ceremony and will freely express their love and affection to you and one another all night long. Everyone will be touched by the old photos, the heartfelt speeches, and the beautiful favors. On a Pisces Moon you can truly have the wedding of your dreams. If you're a fun-loving couple and don't want a day full of tear-jerking moments, pass this one up.

It Happened on a . . . Moon

ARIES An intense Scorpio bride, a laid-back Leo groom, and a beautiful, creative reception. Married by their brother-in-law, who was ordained for the day, their nontraditional ceremony included vows of not disturbing her *Oprah*-viewing and his NASCAR-watching.

GEMINI The Cancer couple created their ceremony with an ordained healer. Their own personal vows were very important to them, as were the many heartfelt speeches of friends and family. The evening's many elements happened so fast that it got away from their planner.

CANCER A low-key intimate summer affair at the mother of the bride's home. The ceremony was held in a lovely backyard, and the hostess prepared delicious food. All the planning brought the Virgo mother and Taurus daughter closer than they have ever been before.

LEO An opulent feast for 180 people in an exquisite reception hall where the Cancer bride invoked the elegance of Grace Kelly. A friend made out with a cousin in the closet and the priest sang "Can't Help Falling in Love" at the reception.

LIBRA A traditional ceremony in a 118-year-old church for a couple that mean everything to each other. The Capricorn groom recalls of his Aries bride, "You don't know until that moment . . . you always think she's beautiful, but she looks the most beautiful you've ever seen her, it really, literally takes your breath away."

SCORPIO A heartfelt, untraditional ceremony on the lawn of a big mansion in the country. The Virgo-Gemini couple arranged to have a private moment in their room to share their innermost feelings about the day before joining in the large celebration.

AQUARIUS My destination wedding in a castle in Scotland; the marriage of two large families from two different cultures. I wore a ball gown, the men all wore kilts. The bagpiper called me by the wrong name and our Capricorn and Libra fathers ended up showing a little too much leg after a little too much scotch.

PISCES   An elaborately crafted interfaith ceremony lit by lantern and candlelight. The friends and family of this Cancer-Leo pair still recall it as one of the most spiritual experiences they've ever had. They carried the theme throughout—even the favors were tied with ribbons reading, "We are all one."

As you can see, every Moon sign has its positives and negatives, as do all the Sun signs each one of us are born under. The great thing about being aware of this now, is that you get to consciously choose what qualities will serve you and your fiancé on your wedding day and into your future.

If after reading this, you're still not sure what Moon sign to marry under, choose a date with the moon in your Sun or Moon sign. It's my experience looking back on wedding charts that about half of married couples unknowingly choose the bride's Sun or Moon sign as the emotional element of their marriage. Proving two things (to me, at least!): one, that women are often the heart of the marriage, and two, that there are no coincidences when setting a wedding date!

Remember, Moon signs are important, but the date of the wedding isn't going to condemn you to a particular fate for the rest of your lives. There are so many other factors in your romance that matter that are too great to even list, including the makeup of your Sun, Moon, Rising, and the rest of your astrological chart. You'll be reading more about that in the next few chapters.

Before we move on, let's discuss setting the dates of all the other parties that go along with getting married. If you are choosing the perfect day for your bridal shower, choose one whose moon is compatible with your and the majority of your friends' Sun signs. An easy way to do this is to break down your list of guests into groups of the four elements

(Fire, Earth, Air, Water) on page 13. Once a clear pattern emerges, you'll know exactly what Moon signs to look for.

If you are like most brides, and you want your bachelorette party to be really fun and adventurous, then choose a date with a moon in Aries, Leo, Gemini, or Scorpio. On the other hand, if you want your groom's last party as a single guy to be fun but a little less wild than it can potentially be, choose a date with a Taurus, Cancer, Virgo, Libra, or Pisces Moon. He'll have warm memories of his awesome friends without getting too hot under the collar!

Heather's Leo Moon Wedding

No one obsesses more than an astrologer over choosing the perfect wedding day and Heather Roan-Robbins was no different. It was important to Heather, whose chart is full of earthy Virgo, to have a long, thoughtful ceremony out in the woods. Both she and her husband, Jamie, with a chart full of sensitive Pisces, wanted to create a quiet space to speak their vows, yet they also wanted a fun party that included their whole community of eclectic friends. Their solution? They started their day with a small ceremony in front of family and friends, followed by a large party for one and all.

After rejecting several other days, Heather settled on a Leo Moon, which loves ritual and pageantry, wild parties, and spontaneity. As a detail-oriented, analytical Virgo, Heather first needed to study the role of the bride. Once she learned everything there was to know about weddings, she spent nine months creating the perfect ceremony down to the last detail.

Anything goes with a Leo Moon. Their half Celtic-Wiccan, half Native American ceremony included quotes and poems from the Song of Solomon, Rainer Maria Rilke, Joseph Campbell, Thomas Moore, and the Sufi poet Hafiz. Not to mention their tenderly recited vows to each other.

The party for a hundred, held in the backyard of a friend, started with spicy tamales and chili sauce and ended with a *huge* cake, because

as Heather puts it, "It's a Leo Moon." She traded her astrological services for a band of belly dancers and had Middle Eastern music playing
all night. "We know so many introverts and we also know people who
don't get along with one another. We really wanted something to get
them outside themselves, to laugh, to dance, to have joy—and not to
have to talk to one another if they didn't want to."

And how has their Leo Moon served them throughout the last few
years? "We wanted our marriage to be about encouraging our self-
growth and self-expression," Heather explains. "The Leo Moon helps
us make sure we don't forget the romance."

As an astrologer she adds, "If we were settling down to work together, wishing to have children, or taking on the family farm, we
might not have chosen a Leo Moon. It's not a great sign to work out
ego issues under either, but we're mostly past that." With a little astrological know-how, Heather chose the right Moon for her relationship: "As it turns out, with all our Virgo and Pisces aspects, we're
enjoying a little Leo in our lives."

Now that you've got the basics down, let's take a look at you, the
bride. To use the stars to the fullest (and brightest!) it's important to
honor your Sun sign, element, and quality, to use your strengths and prop
up your weaknesses so that you can have the wedding of your dreams.

Let's dive right into chapter 2. Using the four elements as our guide,
we're about to get to know the bride you are born to be. Learn how to
stay true to your sign throughout this difficult and wonderful process.

Chapter  *Two*

If you're like most people, you've been reading your horoscope for a long time. You may know the characteristics of your sign like the back of your hand. Whether you are stubborn, flexible, outgoing, or private, it's hard to translate those everyday 'scopes into becoming a bride and planning your wedding.

With a little special knowledge, your sign's unique attributes, strengths, and weaknesses can be used to understand how you take to being a bride, what type of choices you'll make, and what your needs will be as you go through the wonderful and potentially hazardous job of planning your wedding.

Here's where we get to have some fun! Uncover the bridal side of your personality; bring out your inner party planner and let it shine. Organized by the four elements you read about in chapter 1, find your sign and see your horoscopes in a whole new light.

What does your sign reveal about you as a bride? You might just be surprised!

■ Fire Elements: Aries, Leo, Sagittarius

Fire sign ladies are born to be brides. You love to be the center of attention, to have everyone gushing over you. Fire signs take every opportunity to party—from the engagement party to the bridal shower, bachelorette

party to wedding, there is nothing more enjoyable to you than socializing with the people you love. Warm and gregarious, you have a
pretty wide net that includes a lot more than just your friends and family, so it's likely that you'll have little celebrations at work, at the gym,
and so on.

Fiery gals know how to throw a party, too. Aries and Leo like everything larger than life; the grand entrance, the flowing champagne, the
dramatic cake. Sagittarians are a bit different, their energy goes into
creating an elaborate adventure that no one has ever experienced before, rather than creating the big outward gestures, but the result is the
same "Wow!"

All Fire signs are known for their creativity; your wedding will be
full of personal touches, bold colors, and lavish surprises for all your
guests. Whether it's thirty people or three hundred, you'll find the time
to give each one special attention. Everyone will feel like a million
bucks and you will feel like royalty—just the way you like it!

If you choose to take on some do-it-yourself projects, make sure you
know what you're committing to. Fire signs don't like to get bogged
down in tiny details and you can easily get in over your head. Make
sure you have some Earth sign friends or family members around that
can finish what you start when it becomes too much to handle. You may
just make a snap decision to junk the whole thing and run out to purchase the expensive finished products instead, spending even more
money in the process.

Let's put the individual Fire sign brides under the microscope. First
we'll take a look at how your characteristics translate into being a
bride, then we'll uncover some tips on staying true to your sign, element, and quality, honoring who you are inside and avoiding some of
the pitfalls that nature gave you.

□ □ Aries

Being a bride is like being the CEO of your own company, the *perfect*
Aries role. You get to lead the pack, focus on the details you like, delegate

those that you don't—all while being surrounded by a gaggle of admirers. What could be bad?

Your independence is very important, being able to do what you want when you want is key to your happiness. You love coming up with new ideas, forever channeling your boundless energy in new directions—now you get to focus all that fire toward your many celebrations. From the engagement party and rehearsal dinner through the ceremony and reception, that's a lot of creative choices to make, a lot of exploring to do, and a lot of new people to meet along the way. You must be overjoyed!

Everybody knows Aries likes to have her way, but despite how it may seem to an outsider, this wedding isn't really *all* about you. You know it's as much for your friends and family. You thrive on constant excitement and your celebration will be no different. Throughout the different events, you'll make elaborate plans to ensure your guests will have a total blast. The food, music, entertainment, dancing—your wedding will be the most fun people have had in years.

Even though you'll do much of the decision making yourself, planning a wedding is much more fun when you have your best friends or family following you around. Visiting venues, bridal shops, craft stores, you need someone to laugh with along the way. It's a good thing people love being surrounded by the whirlwind of drama you create just by the way you dance through the world.

Let's talk about your weaknesses for a moment. We know Aries love to start things, but let's be honest, you don't love to finish them—it's too easy for you to lose interest when you've got the next exciting item to cross off your list. It's hard to force yourself to sit down and focus on small details when you're not in the mood. Even when you are ready to get down to business, you get restless pretty quickly.

The good news is, when you don't want to do something you have this great way of motivating other people to do it for you. After all, you are a wonderful friend, everyone knows you would do anything for them. Since you love taking advantage of all the good cheer around weddings, throw a few more wine and cheese parties for your pals when the invitations have to go out or the programs have to be finished. Miraculously, everything will get done on time.

You are also good at passing over the mundane minutiae as well. Yes, you've got a million great ideas, but you're not one to obsess over the particulars like some other signs. After you choose the music and the flowers you're not about to micromanage the entire song list or inspect every twig in the centerpieces. You've got better things to do!

We can't talk about Aries without mentioning the fact that you can get a little headstrong at times. Okay, maybe *very* headstrong at times— and this is especially true with something so important as your wedding. Your urgent need to express all these creative ideas makes you who you are, but what happens when you hit a roadblock? Eventually someone is going to tell you that something can't be done, it's too much money, they're not available, and so on.

Depending upon how you hear the dirty little word no, the reactions may vary from the innocent, "Let's figure out a way to do this," to the bridezilla, "What do you mean I can't have that!" When planning your big event, remember that even the most cooperative Aries have a force that can sometimes scare mere mortals.

Aries are action-oriented, competitive people, always out to prove their ideas and creativity in the world. As the perfect project, your wedding will be one for the record books, with everything reflecting your personality just so, the perfect amount of drama, fun, glitz, and glam. Even when it's over it's not over—you are such a great storyteller, you'll be reliving it for a lifetime!

❏❏ Leo

Leo is the royalty of all the zodiac, anyone who knows a Leo will attest to this. As a natural leader, you intuitively understand how to bring out the best in people. As a generous friend, you enjoy giving as much as you do receiving. With a flair for the dramatic, you always have something fun up your sleeve that ensures the spotlight will forever light your way.

These qualities will serve you well as a bride. You've surrounded yourself with a loyal group of friends (and followers) who are attracted to the warmth of your fire and will be there at every turn to admire your efforts and enjoy your largesse. They'll be there just when you need them the most—during your wedding. How fabulous!

Now that you are engaged, your first desire is to plan an event that befits your royal place in the stars. This larger-than-life affair must reflect your personality, highlight your fiancé, include the perfect amount of pageantry, and treat all involved as honored guests. It absolutely must be something you can be proud of for the rest of your life.

Leos have a strong distaste for anything mediocre. You believe if you are going to do something, you have to do it right or not at all. When it comes to your wedding, you want the best for you and your guests or you'd rather not invite them. This means a grand location with great food and great music all night.

You are programmed to like nice things. This will be all too clear as you start making the rounds—the reception sites, the florists, the print shops. You naturally gravitate toward the most pricey, top-of-the-line items. Unless you are Ivanka Trump, eventually someone close to you is going to try to put a stop to all the opulence. That should be interesting.

It's very hard for you to even think about compromising, your ideals and your integrity are big priorities. On top of that, you can be extremely stubborn and hotheaded. If you're put in a tough spot, you might have a downright temper tantrum, although those limitations can bring out your ingenuity: "How can I create this look within a budget" or "this space" or "this time frame," and so on. You're always up for a challenge.

You know exactly how to create the perfect amount of drama, setting a stage for a ceremony that will take people's breath away and a reception filled with all the trimmings. The extras are your props, the dramatic veil, the rich floral arrangements, the highbrow transportation. Everything dripping with romance; every choice illuminating your vision for the day.

Even with all this freedom to express yourself, you are distinctly traditional. You love the ritual of the church ceremony, the procession of flower girls, the exchanging of the rings, the drama of the vow, "'Til death do you part." You're a risk-taker by nature, but you'd never choose to get hitched in a hot air balloon. You want your bridal shower, rehearsal dinner, and reception to reflect those same ideals. You will want a gracious and dignified celebration where you can hold court.

Let's talk about your dark side for a moment. Leos are a powerful breed. When you lead through inspiration, you get cooperation; when you do it with a heavy hand, all that power comes across as domineering. Most of the time you are on your best behavior or you wouldn't be one of the most popular signs, but that bossy side does come out on occasion. Especially when there's a lot riding on getting your way, as in your wedding.

Loving drama makes for a lot of fun, but has its downside as well. When you've had a bad day, you blow off steam by doing the Leo's lament: "Oh, the injustice; oh, the indignity—oh, woe is me." If you weren't so entertaining, you might just drive people crazy. Thankfully your intense self-awareness and need to improve the situations you find yourself in are your saving grace. You never give up and admit defeat, and because of that you can move mountains.

Leo, this is the best time in your life. You've got a built-in audience who will applaud your every move, "Ooh" and "Ah" at all your finery, and treat you as royalty. Enjoy every minute of it, one day you'll happily play it forward to your next engaged pal, truly understanding the needs of the bride-to-be.

❑ ❑ Sagittarius

Sagittarians are the best friends of the zodiac. Always there to help a pal in need, giving your time and attention freely without a thought of what might be coming in return; a quality that will come back to you in spades now that you're the bride. How easy it will be to accomplish the impossible with helpers just one phone call away.

Everybody loves Sagittarians. Your energetic, optimistic nature infects everyone you come in contact with. Maybe that's why astrologers have given you the fun nickname, Sag (pronounced "Saj"), for short. You enjoy getting to know people from all walks of life, how they think and feel, what motivates them as they live their lives. You seem to know everyone in town. Not that you'll feel obligated to invite them all to the festivities, unlike some other signs; social conventions mean nothing to you.

Having such an expansive view of the world and an innate understanding of humankind makes you a very eclectic bride. You're not one to get caught up in the glitz and glam of the day. You love to have fun and you want a celebration, but you'll never lose sight of the fact that it's one day and that your marriage is the adventure of a lifetime.

Freedom is one of your most cherished possessions, every choice you make will reflect that ideal. Whether you are having a big event with tons of family or a small destination wedding, you're not going to do anything that seems constrictive—if you do, you'll automatically feel the pressure. How much time will planning this wedding require? How much will this reception burden me financially? How much energy am I willing to devote to each little creative project?

Your need for personal liberty translates to your family, friends, and fiancé as well. You want your wedding to give people a new experience; to give people something to think about and learn from. There has to be enough space for everyone to be who they are and for you to be the bride you are meant to be.

Sag's easygoing nature makes a very pleasant experience for those closest to you, you certainly know the difference between being in control of your day and controlling others. You'll skip the dress code, your bridal party can choose their outfits, and your gown will be easy to get on and off (a lot of buttons and laces can be *so* restricting). As long as everyone is comfortable, present, and in a good mood your most pressing needs will be met.

There are very few negatives that one can find in Sagittarius. The biggest and costliest is that you have a tendency to jump to conclusions, starting down a new path without all the facts and getting ahead of yourself. You don't even realize you've made some assumptions and filled in the gaps until it's too late and then you have to backtrack. Although being naturally lucky comes in handy, if you do need to be saved from a jam you always attract the right person at the right time to offer assistance.

Another personality trait that others may have a hard time with is your honesty; you are blunt and frank when it comes to speaking the truth. This is part of your idealistic nature and is in no way meant to be damaging. Sometimes you just don't get why someone's feelings would get hurt by the truth. No matter, once the shock is over, everyone knows you weren't being malicious; besides, you may have straightened it out with your friendly manner and have moved onto the next encounter already.

You love to travel far and wide, your honeymoon is often more important than the wedding. Whether you are planning to go to Bora Bora or a bed-and-breakfast in the countryside, you naturally create wonderful new experiences wherever you go. As independent as you are, you are looking forward to waking up beside your most precious friend and making every day a new adventure that you can share for the rest of your lives. Sounds positively exhilarating!

Your Biggest Pet Peeve

ARIES Anyone that says no to you. You believe that rules are meant to be broken—where there's a will, there's a way!

TAURUS Pushy vendors. If someone pressures you, you'd rather walk than deal with that person ever again!

GEMINI An uncreative person who doesn't *get it*. Nothing makes you steam more than someone who doesn't really hear you.

CANCER　A mother who misunderstands your needs. It's hard to drum up the courage to tell her your feelings are hurt.

LEO　Disrespectful salespeople. You'll demand an apology or leave that perfect dress on the rack with your head held high.

VIRGO　A frazzled wedding coordinator who misses the details. There is nothing worse than dealing with an inept person for nine months.

LIBRA　Loud, garish people who ask too much. I don't know what gets your goat more, unfair situations or brassy, tasteless ladies.

SCORPIO　Industry professionals with traditional beliefs. The last thing you want is a constant struggle to get the revolutionary wedding you desire.

SAGITTARIUS　Controlling family members who try to force their views on you. Can you say the word *elope?*

CAPRICORN　Anyone who thinks they know better than you. You've done the research, it's your wedding—*no one* is a greater expert than you.

AQUARIUS　Close-minded people. It's frustrating to try to explain your big ideas to those mere mortals who just can't keep up with the times.

PISCES　Realists. You have a mystical vision of how things should be—woe to the one who bursts your bubble and makes you cry.

■ Earth Elements: Taurus, Virgo, Capricorn

Planning a wedding is something Earth sign brides are born to do. Methodical, detailed, efficient, you love doing research, making lists, creating spreadsheets, it just comes naturally. You can spend all evening organizing your wedding notes and have a wonderful time.

You have a practical creativity that enables you to create a classic, beautiful affair on any budget. Money means a lot to you. You love all nice things, but you'll never make a spontaneous decision that wastes your precious cash—just the thought of it gets your juices boiling!

Earth girls are great bargain hunters, once you get your mind set on something, you'll find a way to get it done at a fraction of what other brides are willing to pay. It's simply no fun paying retail! The dress of your dreams? You'll turn over every rock until you find that one resale shop that stocks it. Ultimately, if you can't find *the* dress at your price, you'll take the copy as long as it's well made. If you can't be proud of the designer, you'll be proud of the price!

You love diving into special projects that reflect who you are—the more detailed, the better—instinctively knowing what you can accomplish with the amount of time, energy, and money you've got in the bank. If you decide to make your favors, they'll be practical gifts people will actually use (or eat!) that will be meticulously handmade.

Earth signs have no attachments to unrealistic schemes. You know what you want and you know how much you want to spend. If after doing the research you find that your perfect cake costs more than you're willing to shell out, you'll just drop that design for one that won't.

All three Earth signs prove that you can be realistic and romantic. Your wedding will be a day to remember, with beauty and budget rolled into one. Of course, there are differences between the Earth elements as well. Let's take a deeper look at Taurus, Capricorn, and Virgo's individual characteristics, and explore how you can honor who you are and avoid some of your astrological weaknesses as you move toward this big day.

□ □ **Taurus**

Taurus women are both strong and tender; creative and practical. As a bride, you will use these traits to design the wedding you've always wanted while making sure that your fiancé feels safe and that you don't compromise your plans as a couple. You'd never jeopardize your long-term goals of owning a home and having financial security in order to pursue a short-term over-the-top wedding.

You love being a bride, but it's very important to you to stay grounded in reality. While other brides are going into hock because they absolutely must have those out-of-season flowers, you are happy to pick a more available bloom. Taurus brides know you don't have to compromise beauty when you stick to a budget. Others may see limitation in the bottom line, you see a creative opportunity.

In fact, you'd much rather set the budget first, before shopping for locations, flowers, dresses, and so on. You just wouldn't feel secure doing it the other way around. Once you know what you have to spend, you can be free to enjoy being a bride, coming up with all sorts of projects to keep you busy for months to come!

Taureans love being surrounded by beautiful things. As a bride you lean toward tradition—the white gown with the train, the large bouquet of roses, the three-tier wedding cake topped with a bride and groom. You're not one to easily embrace change and are most at home with the trappings of the classic wedding.

Incorporate some sort of keepsakes in your big day; Taurus girls love to collect things. From preserving your flowers to keeping a satin box with hundreds of photos, you'll want mementos of your wedding close at hand to enjoy for years to come.

It might be hard for you to clean out your house or put away your wedding gifts after the whole thing is over. You love to be proud of your accomplishments and enjoy the fruits of your labor, after putting so much time and effort into something it's not that easy for you to let go. Everything from the brochures to the gift boxes is something special to you!

Bulls are driven people. All of that steadfast determination allows you to accomplish many things and never give up, but there is a downside to this as well; your stubborn nature. Once you've made a decision, you don't like to change it—even if it's in your best interest to do so! It just simply never crosses your mind that you can't will something into being because that is the way you envision it.

Feeling comfortable and secure is primal for you. You get especially uncomfortable when others act too quickly or try to change your plans. When you feel like someone is painting you into a corner, that's when your obstinate nature *really* shows itself. If you are approached the wrong way, there is absolutely *no way* you are going to back down. Get upset enough and you can potentially take this to the point of the ridiculous! You simply cannot allow yourself to walk away from a great catering hall because of an uncompromising sales manager.

Taureans cannot be rushed. From the planning to the honeymoon, leave yourself plenty of time to make decisions, pack, prepare, and enjoy. Whatever you do, don't surround yourself with a bridal party who doesn't understand this or every event can potentially turn into a nightmare for you. This goes for the morning of the big day as well. The last thing you need is a pushy mother or a high-strung bridesmaid running around your suite at breakneck speed trying to be helpful.

Loyal Bull, you would do anything for a friend in need; you are always there to lend your love and support to those closest to you. You'll use this down-to-earth good nature to create a wedding everyone will enjoy without having to give in too much. The truth is that behind that easygoing façade, there is a very determined girl who loves to get what she wants—especially as a beautiful bride-to-be!

❑❑ **Virgo**

Virgos love to observe, examine, and analyze *everything*. There is nothing you enjoy more than getting wrapped up in an extremely detailed project and to sort out every last piece of the puzzle.

No one brings a more thorough approach to planning a wedding than a Virgo. All the Earth signs enjoy working and accomplishing things, but Virgos are a cut above. Researching the tasks of wedding planning, organizing all of your information; practical and efficient Virgo, there is no end to all the analyzing. The spreadsheets, guest lists, seating charts—you think about the smallest details over and over. You can't help but want everything to be perfect, every scenario planned for. Your dream is to have the day unfold unlike any other before in the history of matrimony. It's the zodiac's Oscar-winning performance as bride and wedding planner.

The dark side of this analytical ability is your judgment. As a bride you'll be spending a lot of time meeting new people, comparing products and services, and deciding what works for your vision of the day. Noticing the difference between people, places, and things is something you do well, but be careful not to see things as right or wrong or you might unknowingly alienate your caterer or your in-laws.

You value hard work above all else. You have no desire to pawn little jobs off on your parents or your bridal party so that you can feel like a queen for the day, although you will expect them to do their part. You can't stand slouches, anyone you've asked to stand up for you better know they're signing up for some seriously detailed tasks. Slapping a stamp on an invite is for a Fire sign bride and her pals, you've got ribbons, tissue paper, and embossing on the list first. (Oh, and that stamp better be placed evenly or you might just throw the whole thing out and start again!)

Virgos like to be meticulously groomed as well. You are likely to choose a classic gown à la Audrey Hepburn in *Breakfast at Tiffany's*. The look of the wedding will have the same understated elegance. Fine quality, well-presented food is also a must. The perfect combination of regal and down-to-earth as only you can create.

It's a Virgo rite of passage to do all the work yourself, but you're probably juggling a job as well as planning your new life with your fiancé—how much can you handle at once? It's important to know the difference between the details that are absolutely necessary to have the wedding of your dreams and which items on the list make for trivial busywork.

Yes, diving into the small creative tasks is key to your happiness, but if you can't tell the difference, you may spend months perfecting napkin rings and not have enough time for the gilded flower girl baskets. Besides running out the clock, you tend to work yourself into the ground and the last thing anyone needs is a nervous or exhausted Virgo bride on their hands!

Your perfectionist tendencies give you the uncanny ability to see things other people just can't see. It's great for creating a flawless event, but can actually get you in trouble with your inner circle. On good days, your critical eye for details improves people's lives and inspires them to make changes, on bad days it seems like you are just being nit-picky. Worse still is when you turn that critical judgment on *yourself,* then it just seems as though you are making up problems that don't even exist!

Tender, loving Virgo, there is no role that is more suited to your natural gifts and talents than that of bride and wedding planner. I don't know which you will enjoy more, the months of planning leading up to your big day or watching that vision of perfection unfold before your very eyes! Just remember to stop analyzing for a few moments so you feel all the love your friends, family, and fiancé have for you!

❑❑ Capricorn

Capricorn, you were put on this planet to accomplish big things. There is no sign in the zodiac that feels this more deeply than the Goat. You love to set goals for yourself and do whatever it takes to get them accomplished. Long after other signs have given up, you are focused on the job at hand.

As a bride, this drive will serve you well. Once you decide how you want your big day to look, you will stop at nothing to make that vision a reality. Whether that means turning over every rock to find the exact dress of your dreams (at the perfect price) or spending extra hours at the office to pull in some extra dough, you will have the wedding of your dreams.

And Capricorns don't just want an ordinary affair. You want a traditional event full of class and elegance, something to show off your hardworking nature. You'll enjoy taking on ambitious projects such as making the favors, programs, place cards, even the flower arrangements. Doing things yourself not only fills you with pride for a job well done, but keeps down expenses and ensures things get done to your exacting specifications.

It's important for Capricorns to pay for their own wedding, or at the very least to share the costs, that way no one will be trying to tell you what to do. You intensely dislike being dependent on anyone, even those you love the most. The last thing you want is your wedding to turn into a battle of wills and you have no intention of curbing your independent ways.

You might be head over heels in love, but gaga bride you are not. Sensible, practical, and orderly, you'll spend just as much time devising new spreadsheets as you will going shopping and reading bridal magazines. You have a very grounded, commonsense approach to everything; asking the right questions, weighing all the options, negotiating good deals.

It's not easy for Capricorns to give up control. The only way you are going to let go is by surrounding yourself with a team of confident, competent people, giving them clear roles within the plan. You appreciate hard work and perfection. When you take on a job you give 100 percent and you expect others to do the same. It's vitally important that you choose vendors (and family volunteers) who have the same work ethic or you'll never feel comfortable that everything is being done correctly.

This is especially true the day of the wedding when you want to be a bride, relax, and enjoy the day. If your events planner is soft or sloppy, you will feel compelled to follow her around all day, keeping one eye on the schedule and missing out on the fun. Remember, just because you are good at managing everything doesn't mean you have to!

Your hardworking nature extends to your friends and family as well. Loyalty is one of your strongest character traits and something you

deeply admire in others. As a member of the clan you would do anything that's asked of you, quietly taking on huge responsibilities others
would balk at. You love being needed, but the best way someone can
show appreciation for your efforts is to do something important for you
in return. Capricorns have a reputation for being tough taskmasters;
you give a lot and ask a lot. When you are choosing your bridal party,
make sure to include people who can live up to your expectations or
you'll feel deeply hurt by their unreliable behavior.

Lucky Capricorn, as a bride, you get to use all your skills to complete the biggest project of your life. Just make sure you take a break
from all the hard work once in a while to remember your parents, in-
laws, and fiancé—after all, you do have to live with them for the rest of
your life!

Your Secret Desire

ARIES   To have your every wish granted, be catered to hand and
foot, lavished with tons of attention, and receive many generous gifts
with lots of bling-bling.

TAURUS   To have a beautiful wedding, great hair and makeup, lots
of flowers, hearty food—but it won't feel quite complete unless you
get the whole thing at a great price.

GEMINI   To have the hip, cool dress you design featured in an
episode of *Access Hollywood* and become the next overnight It girl.

CANCER   To have everyone close to you smother you with love,
while revealing how much you mean to them as they give you sentimental presents you'll cherish for the rest of your life.

LEO   For money to be no object, just once. You'd have the most majestic wedding and completely take care of your guests—jet planes,
private islands, and the most expensive favors you can imagine.

VIRGO To have all the time in the world to plan the perfect wedding down to the minutest detail, have the whole thing come off without a hitch, and have everyone tell you how wonderful it was (for the rest of your life).

LIBRA To create the most elegant ball any of your well-dressed guests have ever attended—and to have the cranky, ill-mannered invitees somehow stay home on *your* night!

SCORPIO To have every passionately chosen detail inspire your carefully chosen guests to realize the true meaning of love (whether they want to or not!).

SAGITTARIUS To quit your day job, drop the ridiculous planning routine, and travel the world on a never-ending honeymoon—Greece, Thailand, India, South Africa.

CAPRICORN To pull off the most ambitious wedding that anyone has ever seen, do it better than everyone else, and have them talking about your ingenuity and hard work forever.

AQUARIUS To have every square person you know drop their pretenses and understand what's truly important in love and marriage (and then tell you you were right all along).

PISCES To have your fiancé ride in on a white horse and save you from drowning in phone calls, contracts, and bills on your way down the aisle.

■ Air Elements: Gemini, Libra, Aquarius

Air sign gals are the intellectuals of the zodiac. You love to read, research, analyze, and draw your conclusions. How fun it will be to visit venues, read a gazillion brochures, compare locations, prices, and quality before making the decision that best suits you and your fiancé. Your head is swimming. You just have too many ideas to squeeze into one wedding, you absolutely must look at all the angles before you choose one path. Being hemmed into a plan too early is like taking the wind out of your sails.

You love to think, talk, and interact with just about everyone along the way. No doubt you'll chat up every location manager, wedding co-ordinator, receptionist, and caterer you find, learning more about the business of weddings than most newlyweds. You have a very cerebral vision of your day and you'll ask great questions in order to make that happen.

None of this is a waste of time, you instinctively know that the better you understand all the aspects of ceremonies and receptions, the better deal you will be able to arrange. Earth signs negotiate to decrease the bottom line, while Air signs just want to make sure they can get permission for that special aisle runner, or the unique food that's normally not on their menu.

Air signs don't get emotionally attached to plans that aren't working. Once you've done all of this thinking, analyzing, and communicating, if any of your ideas aren't feasible, you'll just let them go and move on to plan B without ever feeling as if you've compromised or lost a battle. Your church is too far away? You'll find another with the same cool spiritual vibe. Can't get baby blue butter cream for your cake? You'll take a pale fondant. Reception site doesn't have a gazebo for photos? You'll go to the local park. You see no problems, only creative solutions.

Air signs are not solitary brides, you love the camaraderie of pals and sweethearts; Libras focus on partnerships; Gemini and Aquarius on the gang of best friends. You'd hate doing all this alone and have a myriad of people you can sign up for every wedding adventure along the way. You need people to play with and discuss details with—what's the point of doing all this research if you can't talk about it with your friends, family, and fiancé?

As far as brides go, you are very easy to get long with. You were born with a natural charm and a great sense of humor that will serve you well as you navigate through tough meetings and awkward communications between two families. You seek cooperation with others. It's more of a priority for you to all get along than to constantly have your way. Although Aquarius is a little less flexible than your fellow Gemini and Libra, you make up for it by being so focused on the big picture that the little details most often escape your critical eye.

Now that we've covered some of the similarities between Gemini, Libra, and Aquarius, let's move on to some of the things that make each unique. Find your sign and discover more about the bride you are born to be.

❑ ❑ Gemini

Popular, charming, and people-oriented by nature, Geminis are always up for a good social occasion. Being a bride gives you lots of opportunities to do everything you love—hanging out with your friends, partying, shopping, chatting, laughing; you're in for the time of your life!

The Gemini mind doesn't rest. You've been thinking about this day since you attended your first wedding—except those plans have changed in your head a million times. If last year you wanted to get married in the hottest hotel in town, this year's plan is to get hitched in that celebrity-filled ski resort in Aspen you read about recently. The possibilities will have you contemplating forever!

Of course, there is a downside to all this thinking. With all the alternatives it's hard to make a firm decision, you can become almost paralyzed by all the choices. It's a good thing you can bounce ideas around with your parents, friends, and fiancé when things get tough.

Part of the problem is a Gemini's great need for freedom. You don't want to settle on any one idea too early or you fear you may be stuck with it. Once in a while it's so hard to commit to something that it's just easier to put it off until the last minute. Even though you think a lot, sometimes you are more comfortable with spontaneity than reason.

Eclectic and graceful, Twins have great taste. Everything from the

way you dress to the way you decorate your home is a unique combination of modern and vintage and you pull it off as no other sign can. No
doubt wherever you end up tying the knot will be totally hip and cool,
following the latest trends from food to favors.

Geminis are natural event organizers with a flexible and creative
style. From venue-hopping to cake-tasting, there is nothing more fun
than putting all the pieces together to design a fun and eclectic day that
reflects both you and your fiancé.

And you will enjoy crafting your ceremony just as much as the
party; choosing inspiring poems and readings that will make people
think. Your love of words will come across in the vows you craft, finding the perfect balance between humor and sentimentality, you will
leave people laughing and crying all the way to the hors d'oeuvres!

You love to read, watch, listen, analyze—Geminis are so *in the
know*. You'll totally immerse yourself in all things bridal—from watching every wedding show to reading every bridal magazine to perusing
every Web site.

It's hard to know what you love more: Having tons of information
at your fingertips or *talking* about all that juicy info. It might drive your
friends and family nuts, but talking, thinking, and changing your mind
is half the fun. You'll even have the latest gossip on rich and famous
couples to share at your bridal shower.

One of your greatest gifts is your ability to compromise. If your parents, in-laws, or fiancé feel strongly about something along the way, you
have a great way of finding a win-win solution that everyone can live
with. It's so easy for you to let go of ideas that aren't working and move
on without a second thought; other signs can learn a thing or two from
the Gemini adaptability.

All this mental energy makes you high-strung at times. Running
from appointment to appointment, overbooking your schedule, making a thousand phone calls—you thrive on the excitement, but at some
point your head can start spinning. You can either chatter out of control or learn to relax. Book a massage or find the newest yoga or Pilates
class and make it part of the routine.

Gemini bride, all this reading, writing, chatting, and organizing is time well spent—not only will you have a most unforgettable wedding, but after it's all over, newly engaged women everywhere will be asking your advice for years to come. Oh, good, more sharing, just what the Gemini ordered!

❑ ❑ **Libra**

Gracious, popular, and social by nature, companionship is an essential ingredient in the life of a Libra. Born under the sign of beauty and partnership, Libra girls are the natural brides of the zodiac. While other signs enjoy their independence, going it alone is unappealing to the Scales. You are keenly aware that relationships enhance who you are.

Why do something alone when you can do it with someone else? This is especially true when planning your wedding. Of all the signs, you most enjoy working in cooperation with others. You have a natural understanding of your fiancé's needs and your parents' wishes as much as your own and you will look to them to share in the experience. From the invitations to honeymoon, it simply would be no fun without their love and approval.

Refined and elegant, your two strongest desires for your wedding are that everything look beautiful and that everyone get along well. You will want a special harmony of all the elements—from the flowers to the music to the guests.

With impeccable taste, Libras have a natural elegance in the way they dress and decorate. Looking clean and neat is very important, you'd be mortally embarrassed to wear something wrinkled or have worn furniture in your home. On top of that, you're no bargain hunter. You'd rather spend more money on a classic look that you can have forever than own something that is made with shoddy workmanship.

As a bride, you will bring this same polish and elegance to the job. Seeking to create a traditional ceremony and reception with gracious appeal, you will choose the most romantic location, a beautiful dress, and quality food. Your taste runs on the expensive side, but this is your one and only day and you're not going to cheapen it by second-rate anything.

As the Scales, Libra has an exceptional understanding of fairness and a critical eye toward balance. You'll work hard to ensure that all of the choices you make and details you design work perfectly together and that everyone understands their role within this grand vision. Your biggest fear is that you get out of the limo and you spot something out of balance or that people are acting uncouth, ruining the delicate beauty you labored so hard to create.

As an Air sign, Libra has an intellectual approach to life. You observe, analyze, and dissect all sides of an issue, and your wedding is no different. When visiting potential venues you'll notice every last detail down to the color of the bathrooms, ask penetrating questions about their services, and pore over their brochures for hours. Not one to go by gut instinct, you need to think through all the facts and numbers before coming to the conclusion most in balance with your wishes and those of your inner circle.

The Libra is a pretty easy bride to live with mainly because you intensely dislike arguing; it disrupts the harmonious way you live your life. You'd much rather use your charm and grace to work through issues as they come up. The only time you'll fly off the handle is when something appears unfair and you are painted into a corner, then you will let loose on the offending partner. Whether that is your fiancé or your caterer is of no consequence to you.

On the other hand you love debating, so while you're trying to weigh and measure all the details, your mother, fiancé, and bridal party will be in for an articulate earful. Focusing your analytical ability on those closest to you, you end up dissecting their decisions and motivations. I hope for their sake they know why they prefer something one way and not another or you might exhaust them trying to figure it out!

Weddings were tailor-made for you, Libra. Take your time investigating, analyzing, and designing the most gracious, elegant event. Appreciate every opportunity to socialize and every partnership you make along the way. And most of all, enjoy sharing all of this with your fiancé and you will become closer than ever as you prepare for a harmonious, beautiful marriage!

❑ ❑ Aquarius

Aquarians are fun-loving and forward-thinking people who pride themselves on their individuality. Always pushing the envelope through new ideas and bold moves, the Water Bearer likes to live on the cutting edge. As a bride, you are the first to embrace new concepts in weddings. From the vows to the video to the seating arrangements, every aspect of your big day will be a new twist on an old tradition.

You value your community just as much as you do your independence. Aquarius is the sign of brotherhood and sisterhood, having like-minded people around you is vital to your happiness. There is nothing more fun for you than a good meeting of the minds. You greet everyone as an equal on your path, whether you've known someone since second grade or are just sitting on the same park bench, there is virtue in every exchange of ideas.

You'll take this same adventurous attitude to your role as bride, looking at every day as an opportunity to discover new things, meet new people, and express your creativity. Whether you are traveling around town or using the Internet, planning a wedding has never been more fun for the cutting-edge Aquarius.

The sign of Aquarius, represented by the Water Bearer, carries the life-sustaining element for all of humanity. It's in your blood to discover new ways to solve the problems of the world, large and small. One of your biggest goals is to reinvent the concept of *wedding* from the ground up. Taking a little piece from here and a little piece from there, your big day will be a unique reflection of you that all of your friends and family can enjoy.

Aquarians have such big ideas that they are rarely concerned with the tiny details, making you a very easy bride to work with. You want big band music and your fiancé wants jazz; you'll do a mix of both, no problem. You are considering a buffet but your mom is set on a sit-down dinner; you can go either way as long as your guests are well-fed. Whether someone wants beef or chicken is not your concern. What does matter to you is how your beliefs are incorporated into the main event.

The Water Bearer feels strongly about the ways of the world; you live by a very distinct set of spiritual beliefs and moral values. Whether you lean toward tradition or are a tried-and-true nonconformist, you need these core ideas to be a part of your wedding, from the vows you recite to where you donate the leftovers.

The things you are concerned with are not what the ordinary person has in mind. Because of this, your big ideas and forward-moving concepts may not always be well received. There is nothing more annoying to you than trying to explain how you want your ceremony to proceed to people who just can't keep up.

As stubborn as you are open-minded, when you feel you are being invalidated by square, old-fashioned people you just kick in your heels for a good debate. This is your wedding and you have no desire to roll over for small-minded people, even if they are your in-laws. You may be funny and charming, but sometimes you just like to stir people up!

On the outside the Water Bearer appears easygoing, but that can't be farther from the truth. All Air signs have a whirlwind of nervous energy pulsing through their bodies. You might be good at hiding it, but if you don't learn to take care of yourself, all that observing, analyzing, and moving about can throw your whole system into a tailspin. This is especially true now that you are planning a wedding. All this reading, meeting, shopping, and crafting can be quite stressful. If you burn the candle at both ends, you might be exhausted by your big day.

Independent, eccentric Aquarius, getting married enlarges your family and enriches your world. There is nothing more exciting to you than having a husband and best friend to share your views, your life, and your adventures with. Your wedding day is the first day of this special life together, make it one big celebration that everyone can enjoy and talk about for a lifetime!

Who You Absolutely Must Have in a Bridal Party . . . or Else

Everybody has great friends, but are they up for the task? Before you choose your maid of honor and your bridesmaids, consider what you need from them most during this highly emotional time.

ARIES People who know you best. Friends who will be around when you want them, who aren't going to be insulted if you don't, and won't take it personally if you have an explosion or two along the way. Conversely, don't choose someone overemotional or high-maintenance—you will pull your hair out if you have to baby-sit anybody.

TAURUS Generous, sensitive pals. Friends who can coax you out of your shell a bit, support your decisions, and yet still be honest when it's time to let something go along the way. Very often you're busy helping others; if you end up choosing friends who can't give back, you won't demand more, you'll just get very frustrated.

GEMINI Friends you can talk to. Surround yourself with people who have cell phones and are available to chat at all times of the day. You want to share all the latest details you've discovered and ask their advice before you make a decision. Stay away from people who want to appropriate all your time discussing their own dramas.

CANCER Friends who lend emotional support. You need close companions who will share in all the fun; from dress shopping to the bridal shower. Just being there for you is all you ask. You don't like feeling abandoned, so never choose a friend who lives in another city, is too busy with her own life, or who is emotionally unavailable.

LEO Admirers who appreciate you. Surround yourself with friends who will treat you the way a bride should be treated during this time in her life—with love, respect, and dignity. You love all your friends, but if you pick people who are out of touch with your needs, you'll be too proud to ask for something and you hate settling for less.

VIRGO Friends who are as fastidious and detailed as you are. You need people who understand your desires and can execute them in a way that makes you feel safe and secure. Choose pals who know the inner you; the last thing you need is a wild bachelorette party or a bridal shower in a restaurant with burnt food and dirty bathrooms.

LIBRA Like-minded companions. Choose friends who are looking forward to being your bridal partners, who will plan and attend all the social activities that go along with weddings. You may do the right thing and choose people your family approves of, just make sure they're not rough around the edges or you'll be sorry you did.

SCORPIO Your absolute best buddy. You do best with someone who knows you inside and out—your wishes, your secrets, everything. You need someone who takes this job seriously and passionately. Skip the pals that can't be tied down, even if it's only a trip to the craft store; not being able to count on people will drive you crazy.

SAGITTARIUS Unconventional fun-loving types. You only desire friends who can enjoy the experience and come with no agenda. You don't need emotional support, coddling, or hand-holding; if one friend isn't available, another will do just fine. The only thing you can't stand is someone who follows too many rules and regulations.

CAPRICORN Loyal, traditional friends. Truthfully, you can use someone who can loosen you up just a bit so you can take advantage of being a bride, but who respects you enough to avoid the stupid things like a visit to Chippendales. Pass up the pals who are too adventurous, domineering, or eccentric; you never know what they'll do.

AQUARIUS Your offbeat, entertaining friends. You love bucking the trend and making a social statement. A friend is a friend and that means everything to you. The one issue that will make your hair stand on end? Hearing that you *have to* choose someone because it's the customary thing to do; on that you will never cave.

PISCES Friends who intuitively understand your thoughts and wishes. You need people around you who can support and protect you without even asking, and can run interference with your family when things get tough. Stay away from friends who can potentially roll over your feelings like a bulldozer or you might be doing a lot of crying.

■ Water Elements: Cancer, Scorpio, Pisces

Water sign women specialize in feelings and instincts. You are known for your compassion, imagination, sensitivity, and selfless understanding of human nature. From the depth of your own emotions to the sympathy you have for the world, everything you touch has a distinctive intensity to it. Because of this, Water sign weddings are by far the most heartfelt and romantic of the zodiac. From the flowers to the readings, every detail is carefully chosen to set the mood and inspire your guests to feel something they've potentially never felt before.

Water sign brides have a special emotional expressiveness, being the best of all the elements at describing their decisions and motivations. Every member of the bridal party is vitally important to you; the colors have sentimental significance; even your jewelry and garter belt will be something borrowed or something blue.

Mermaids have no tolerance for anything superficial. You'd never repeat vows just because it's tradition or give out candied almond favors just because it's the trendy preference du jour—it absolutely must evoke meaning. If after reading up about weddings, you end up having a classic ceremony and reception, it's because that in itself is full of significance for you.

Your intuitions run as deep as the ocean and you rely on your impressions to navigate through the different planning stages. Even when you talk about your wedding with your best pals, you are more interested in analyzing how you feel about the invites or the menu; making your final decisions by those gut instincts, instead of more concrete facts and numbers.

Water sign gals are very devoted to their friends and family. You have a deep emotional bond with those you let into your inner circle, holding on to those you love with an intense grip—especially at such a sensitive time as this.

None of you like to take adventures alone. Pisces and Cancers can feel a bit emotionally insecure without a helpful presence near at hand and Scorpios are only comfortable moving around under the radar. Each of you would much prefer to take your best friend along dress shopping; you will spend the day at home reading bridal books if she's not available.

That's not to say you love having people around 24/7, but when you need the emotional support, you like to know it's there. Water signs have a very private side as well and need lots of alone time to figure things out, rest, and reenergize. Being the sensitive element of the zodiac can take its toll sometimes.

Spiritual Water sign, using your sensitivity to create an otherworldly wedding is written in the stars. First, learn more about the bride you are born to be as we explore the depths of the soulful signs: Cancer, Scorpio, and Pisces.

❑❑ Cancer

Sweet, sensitive, and loving, Cancer girls are the nurturers of the zodiac. You love nothing more than to spend the day at home with your fiancé, cooking a delicious meal, tanning in the yard, or sitting by a cozy fire. Hugs, kisses, and tender moments mean everything to the Crab. You'd much rather talk about your feelings with the ones you love than seek excitement or analyze facts like some other elements in the zodiac.

As a bride, you will have lots of opportunities to connect with your closest friends and share your innermost thoughts. You're excited about dress shopping with your mom, having lunch at potential reception sites with your groom, and poring over bridal mags with your maid of honor.

While some signs see a wedding as a big party, Cancers understand deeply that the commitment of their heart and soul is forever. Because of this, your most important goal is to create a wedding in a place you think of as your spiritual home, somewhere you feel comfortable sharing your emotions in front of your friends and family. Whether that be in a beautiful garden by a lake, an old mansion in the countryside, or a more traditional house of worship, you must choose a place where you feel safe to express yourself, your vows, and your commitment.

Crab girls hide a lot under their tough shell. On the outside, you often show the world your strong side. Friendly and caring, you are a wonderful listener and one of the best friends the stars have to offer. But the world can be a tough place for such a sensitive sign. You are easily hurt by the callous actions of others and can get deeply embarrassed by their judgments.

This is why it's vitally important as a bride to surround yourself with other nurturing souls who can lend their moral support every step of the way, from oohing over the ring to reviewing the proofs. When you feel safe and secure, you can be free to enjoy all the love and attention that comes along with planning your wedding.

Cancers are initiators. With an action-oriented way of moving through the world, you enjoy coming up with ideas and putting those plans in motion, you just don't want to do it alone. You need loving friends and family with you as you travel around town picking out invites, bridesmaids' dresses, and flower arrangements, or you might feel abandoned at the most important time in your life.

However, sometimes being your friend or fiancé isn't the easiest job in the world. While it's hard for Cancer gals to make decisions, you also don't like being told what to do. When you are feeling bullied, you react in one of two ways. You either get sullen and withdraw or stubborn and completely unreasonable; sometimes you will do both.

If your mother tries to force you to have a big bridal shower when you wanted only your close friends, or your in-laws have a million people they want to add to the guest list, they'd better know exactly how to approach you or your defense mechanisms are going to kick in. And you just can't let go and move on, because once you're moody, you are moody. The only way you can work it through is to take some time to process your feelings. When you're ready, you'll come out of your shell knowing exactly how you wish to handle them.

Cancer brides think with their heart; you want an intimate affair that you can share with everyone who is special to you. With a large bridal party and as many little ringbearers and flower girls as you can find, love rules the day.

The tender touches and sentimental moments are what you will remember most; cultural traditions such as lighting a unity candle, jumping the broom, or breaking the glass. The groom wiping away a tear. The smiles of the guests as you walk back down the aisle a married woman. Cancer bride, you will create a wedding you can look back on with a smiling heart for the rest of your life.

❑ ❑ Scorpio

Passionate, romantic, and deeply loving, Scorpio is the most intense sign of the zodiac. With a strong will and focused drive, you do nothing halfway. Being a bride is no different, you will tackle this job as if you are taking on the biggest project of your life. Using all of the powers at your disposal you will create a wedding unlike anyone has ever seen. (The exception being those Scorpios who want to have nothing to do with all the marital hooplah to begin with and choose to elope, but I'm sure none of those Scorpios are reading this book anyway, so we'll just pass them over.)

Scorpios can't stand "business as usual." The sign of transformation likes to focus their energy on things big and small and change the ways of the world for the better. Investigating motivations, asking penetrating questions, and using your enormous inner strength to improve the status quo. You are the first to admit, planning a wedding isn't like preparing to win the Nobel Peace Prize, but you simply do not get involved in anything unless it holds a special meaning to you.

You will design all the aspects of this affair with passion, diving into color schemes, fabrics, and styles, learning everything there is to learn to make this wedding completely your own. No automatic pilot for you, from the processional music to the presentation of the food you have a keen awareness that every choice and every decision is a reflection of who you are.

A nonconformist, you will eagerly reject everything traditional about weddings. Then you will reinvent it, piece by piece, leading your guests through a transformation of the heart and soul, leaving them changed in a small way forever. It's important for you to find an officiant and create a ceremony that reflects your unique spirituality; you'll choose a reception site that has sentimental value, and add many special touches, from the place cards to the handmade favors.

Creativity is a strong part of that Scorpio passion and will. You need to see your energy at work, doing everything newer, greater, and better than before. A perfectionist at heart, you'll have a hard time giving up control of even the tiniest projects. The truth is, possessiveness is one of your character flaws, but do you really need to make every single welcome basket for the out-of-town guests?

Scorpios have a big need to hide. While other brides love to be the center of attention, you'd rather have the freedom to move about your business largely unnoticed. Exploring, investigating, and reinventing; making decisions on your own after consulting your most precious ally—your fiancé, of course. You have no desire to bring your best friend along dress shopping or your mother along to the florist, nor are you breathlessly waiting to call them with all the latest news—you're way too secretive for that. You'll do things your way and let them in on it when you are ready. (Or maybe they'll just see for themselves on the day of the wedding!)

Scorpios aren't great diplomats; you take great pains to have honest dealings with everyone you come in contact with. When someone asks for your opinion you'll gladly give them the whole truth as you see it; now, whether they like it or not is another thing. Make sure you have a few close confidants around on the day of the wedding who can run interference for you with some of your more vexing guests. You'll need to be able to move about as you wish without needy people demanding more than you can give or you might end up with a situation on your hands.

Generous, romantic Scorpio, when you start something, you see it through to completion like no other sign in the zodiac. This is your most powerful transformation to date; tapping into all of the forces of nature to create a wedding that has special meaning for you and your beloved. Scorpio bride, starting your life together in this most spiritual, mystical of ways is a dream that only you can fulfill.

❏❏ Pisces

Intuitive, compassionate, and ultrafeminine, Pisces women are the po-ets and artists of the zodiac. Being in love is the ultimate journey for the Fish, who need romance as much as they need air to breathe or nour-ishing water to drink. There is not a more perfect time in your life than being a bride.

More than anything, Pisces believe in the fairy tale and your wed-ding absolutely must reflect that ideal. The princess dress, the flowing veil, the beautiful bouquet, the elegant first dance. For a Pisces in love, your wedding represents the best coming-out party the world has ever seen. It's the chance to play the role of a lifetime, making real the dream of forever after, even if it's only for a day.

The Fish live in their imagination. The life of the Fish is a constant search for the highest vision of self, swimming in ever deeper waters of the psyche, exploring the world of feeling, inspiration, and illusion. The ceremony, the vows, and the spiritual or religious rituals are vital to your vision of a wedding. You need opportunities to express your feel-ings, to declare to your groom and the world your highest ideals of love, to create a mystical experience for all to share.

Pisces are extremely impressionable. Totally absorbing the thoughts and feelings of others, you make the most simpatico friend and fiancée; being able to read their minds and understand their problems. But the downside to all this sensitivity is that you can get easily overwhelmed by the sights and sounds of life, needing to withdraw into your own world to rest, unwind, and heal.

This is especially true now that you are designing your big day. Appointments, phone calls, budgets—all this reality is enough to disturb Pisces' delicate sensibilities. It's a good thing you've got a supportive fiancé nearby to give you reassuring hugs when you get upset or all that activity might drive you nuts!

It's true you dislike the harshness of reality. Yet even more than that you dislike being put in a box. You need the freedom to go with the flow, to follow your intuition, to feel and create—to dance to the beat of your own drummer. (Or string quartet if that's what you wish!)

Planning a wedding can be a wonderful and distressing experience for a Pisces. Envisioning all the possibilities is a joy, but having to constantly make firm decisions is not something you do very well. You really want to invite everyone, but have to cut the guest list *somewhere*. You want to choose friends to be in the bridal party but you're afraid of hurting family members' feelings. You don't know whether to go with a mauve or pale pink border on the invitations—it never ends!

Fish shy away from conflict, you'd rather take an unfair share of the burden than start a scene; harsh words are painful for you. When your feelings are hurt, your first response is to cry and cry (and cry). Although every once in a while you can get absolutely unhinged and there's no way anyone can calm you down until you've emotionally exhausted yourself.

If your heart is set on that castle in the mountains and it's out of your price range or the park you've always envisioned doesn't allow weddings, you might not be able to deal with the letdown. You naturally want to ensure that everyone is happy and compromising with your family or fiancé is easy, but there is absolutely no way you can compromise your heart and soul.

Loving, devoted Pisces, you are willing to sacrifice everything for your mate. With a poetic grace you'll create an event where everyone will feel the presence of something otherworldly. Your ceremony will reflect the deep spiritual love that Pisces live for; your reception, every little girl's dream come true. And in the center of all this energy, you and your fiancé, reaching into the unknown together as bride and groom, and entering the most mystical journey, the one as husband and wife.

Just What Am I Getting Myself Into?

A bride can't get married without a groom! Now that you've got your own sign squared away, let's take a look at his. Here's your Mr. Right—the good, the bad, and the ugly—all in one sweet paragraph! Since we're all a combination of our Sun and Moon signs at our weddings, read both his Sun and Moon to get the full story.

ARIES   The Ram is in love with love. Passionate, independent, and spicy, he's up for creating a unique wedding from start to finish, just don't ask him to do any of the boring busywork—and never tell him what to do. Suggest good ideas, work together, let him have an occasional outburst, and you're good to go.

TAURUS   The Bull is a loving traditional groom. Tender, affectionate, and stubborn, this guy will support your plans as long as he's comfortable with them. His biggest need is to feel secure, make sure you don't drop anything in his lap or make last-minute quickie decisions—he needs time to process changes and emotions.

GEMINI   The Twin groom is a fun, easygoing guy. He won't go for the standard stuff, so add some eclectic readings, write your own vows, choose the music together. Other than that, do what you want, just chat with him about everything along the way. He might be a bit spacey the day of the wedding, so don't give him anything to remember!

CANCER   The Crab is emotionally supportive. He loves to be there, holding your hand through the ups and downs and making decisions together. The key to his heart? Always make it safe for him to share his feelings. If he's feeling insecure, he may run and hide. He doesn't like to take risks, so stick with tradition where possible.

LEO The lordly Lion is a generous, outgoing, and obstinate groom. He's up for every party, loves being the center of attention, and treats you like his queen every time. With dramatic displays of affection, he just oozes romance. He can become quite offended when he feels slighted, so make sure everyone recognizes his importance as groom.

VIRGO The sign named for the Virgin Harvest loves to work for you. He feels like it's his job to make sure you have the most perfect wedding of your dreams—he might actually do more work than you! His big issue is that he can get overly critical and see imperfections where there are none. Get him to relax and it'll all be wonderful!

LIBRA The Scales make a gracious and elegant groom. For him, the most important aspect of the wedding is how it looks. He'll only be happy with a classic, beautiful affair; with all the elements aesthetically pleasing. Now, getting him emotionally present might take a miracle, he'll be too busy focusing on what everything looks like.

SCORPIO The Scorpion is a protective and private groom. The idea of having a big wedding may freak him out, especially because his job is making sure you're feeling safe all the time. He'll need his alone time when you're off with your mom visiting florists—give him his space, if he's feeling squeezed he may bite.

SAGITTARIUS The Archer is an easygoing, social, and outdoorsy guy. He needs the wedding to be fun and exciting, so as long as you add lots of spectacular ingredients, he'll be up for just about anything you plan. Don't make him wear anything too restrictive and don't make the ceremony too long, he gets antsy very quickly.

CAPRICORN The Goat is an ambitious, hardworking groom. Now, how much work he'll do for the wedding depends upon how much he's got on his plate. He may just be happy having you do all the work and then having veto power in the end. If he feels like it's not going as planned, he may get too controlling about every little thing.

AQUARIUS   The Water Bearer is a groom that loves his community. He doesn't care about most of the details, what your guy wants is every chance to include his friends and family in this big tribal wedding. He's difficult to handle only when he feels misunderstood, because he might just want to prove his point at all costs!

PISCES   The Fish is a sensitive, expressive, and romantic groom. He will share in the planning as much as you want, doting on his bride-to-be with hugs and kisses when things get tough. He needs his thoughts and feelings to be validated in return. If he feels unheard, he'll either go off and sulk or lash out in pain—or both.

Now that you understand your bridal side better, you are one step closer to planning an extraordinary wedding to remember. Before I let you personal loose to start writing your ceremony and arranging your reception, there's a little more to discuss about your astrology—how you organize, plan, and tackle projects.

Staying true to your natural business sense is just as important as your personal style in order to be an effective wedding planner and make it through your day in one piece. Learn how to use your energy wisely, organize your time efficiently, and bring out the best in your abilities. Don't make another phone call without reading chapter 3!

Chapter

Now that you are aware of how important your astrology sign is to being a bride, you are ready to get down to business. I'm sure you and your fiancé have already begun to share your thoughts and wishes with each other. You might have ripped magazine pages strewn on the floor and a list of dates jotted in a notebook.

Before you can run off to see reception sites and make creative decisions, you have to set a solid foundation, get organized, and have some key discussions with your significant other. Every bride wants to get through her wedding in the smoothest way possible without discovering any surprises along the way—or worse, losing her cool and turning into bridezilla!

Let's first shed some light on your unique operating system, then talk about getting your groom involved, setting your priorities, creating a budget, even tackling the legalities. All this groundwork will ultimately set you up to make perfect choices for a ceremony and reception that reflect your true nature.

One more note: How you organize yourself and your projects is often a reflection of your Rising sign. If you have had your chart done, by a professional or online, and you know your Rising sign, read both your Sun and Rising signs to get the whole picture.

■ Organize Yourself

Every bride has to make phone calls, choose vendors, and sign contracts, no surprise there, but each of the four elements do this with a completely different style. Use your astrology sign to start off right. Organize your wedding material in a way that serves you best; use your time, energy, and money wisely.

❑ ❑ Fire: Aries, Leo, Sagittarius

A Fire sign gal isn't known for her grounded, methodical approach to things—it's as if the minute you got engaged you were off to the races. So many ideas; so little time. You might have even started taking detours on your way home from work to check out venues without creating a space to file all the paperwork. It's really important to take a step back and set up a system before you have messy piles of magazines by your bedside table, something to keep all of your pictures and phone numbers organized without having to do too much to keep it in order.

I suggest a notebook with three-hole-punched pages and a binder with separators that have folders attached. That way you can write everything down, and instead of having to type information into the computer or transpose it by hand, you can rip the scribbles out of your notebook and put it right into the binder—no hassle. When you see something in a magazine, you can rip out the page and put it right into the appropriate folder. You like to go, go, go. Knowing where everything is in an instant will keep you moving and on the run!

Aries will want the notebook and binder to look snazzy; decorate it in your spare time with sparkly wedding photos. Leo wants a high-class notebook and binder; splurge on leather and you'll have a keepsake for the rest of your life. Sag doesn't care about either; just make it small and light so it's easy to carry around and fits into your everyday tote bag.

❑❑ Earth: Taurus, Virgo, Capricorn

An Earth sign girl might have ideas, but you're not going to do a thing without first setting up a system you can live with. I suggest a trip to the bookstore to research all the wedding planners on the market. Pick one with the most useful worksheets—and while you're there grab one of those nifty books listing the million detailed questions to ask vendors so you can easily compare their value and experience.

Next up, spreadsheet software. You're going to want to record guest info, addresses, and budgets on something that you can read easily. Plus, there's nothing an Earth bride loves more than doing a thorough job updating lists and inputting data. Of course you'll need a binder and a notepad to log in the details of every phone call. Save your money for the wedding and recycle one you already have in the house.

Taurus girls can be a bit haphazard; create a folder to throw the odds and ends into until you're in the mood to organize. Virgo will want to rewrite or type notes to keep them neat before entering them into the planner, and Capricorn will set up a system that's automatically cross-referenced in the computer for the most efficient use of your time and energy. Knowing at the press of a button who you've sent invites to, who has responded, and what they've chosen as their main course makes you feel secure and accomplished.

❑❑ Air: Gemini, Libra, Aquarius

We already know that an Air sign bride loves to observe, analyze, and communicate, and that you tend to juggle many things with short bursts of attention. I characterize this interesting set of personality traits as an organized-disorganized. Here's how to work with your strengths and weaknesses.

First, you need notebooks, several of them. Carry one in your bag with a pen (you never know when an idea is going to hit you!) and keep one by the phone. You love to jot down notes and scribble doodles when you're having a conversation.

Keeping an accordion file handy will rein in some of the hand-scrawled notes and torn-out pages from magazines and newspapers. Libra may want to buy one specially created for brides for its beauty; Aquarius, being somewhat of an anti-bride, might like it in a slick black; Gemini doesn't care either way—go for pink.

The Air sign loves to use technology, I'm sure you already have a cell phone; you'll need it for chatting and coordinating all those appointments. Go online and research the latest wedding planner software to keep guest lists, budgets, and to log gifts as they come in. Download checklists and worksheets from wedding sites to get focused on each step of the process, and don't forget to file them or your desk might become overrun with papers.

❑❑ Water: Cancer, Scorpio, Pisces

Cancer, Scorpio, and Pisces women are pretty well organized when they feel safe and secure. First up, create a special wedding binder and accordion file; make it as pretty as you like. Taking on little creative projects in the comfort of your home will not only help you stay calm and focused, but will be wonderful keepsakes that you can look back at on a rainy day.

Everything has sentimental value to a Water sign. Decorate a simple paper file storage box to keep all the wedding folders, photos, price lists, and menus provided to you by potential venues and vendors. Review them for ideas and inspiration.

I'm sure you will use the spreadsheet software already on your computer to keep track of the budget and guest list. Print everything out as you update it and keep them in your binder. Cozy up on the couch with your fiancé and make decisions together, materials in hand. Pisces is more apt to fall for the expensive, romantic wedding organizers they sell online, while Cancer, a better budgeter, might skip those. Scorpio wouldn't waste her time and money on anything frivolous, and likes to keep things hidden anyway, so a regular binder from an office supply store is best.

■ Getting Your Groom Involved

Some grooms take their equal partnership very seriously when planning a wedding; others, not knowing their roles exactly, leave most of the work to their brides. What type of help you get depends a lot upon who you are, what kind of support you need, how you delegate, and how much control you can give up.

Use this opportunity to share in the decision making as a couple and you will develop skills for the rest of your life. Here's a quick look at how to make this process a team effort, bringing you closer as you step down the aisle toward matrimony.

❑❑ Fire: Aries, Leo, Sagittarius

Fire sign girls love their mates. You love sharing your ideas, going on adventures together, and wrestling over all the details. None of you have any desire to roll over and make it easy on your groom (or your parents, for that matter), and life just wouldn't be fun doing all this planning alone.

That said, Aries and Leo wield some serious power. You want your groom's help when you want it, but you don't want to give in either. Sags, being the Mutable of the group, are a bit different. It's easier for you to compromise because so many of these details are unimportant to you. You are a strong-willed woman; learn to ask for his opinions and really listen when he shares them with you. Get him involved by giving him some work to do, then encourage him to do it and appreciate the efforts—and whatever you do, don't take the job back!

One Leo bride told of the difficulties in getting her Capricorn husband involved. "He says, 'Okay I'll do something, but you're going to end up doing it anyway because you think I won't do it well enough or the way you want it to be done.'" Leos (and Aries) are known to be a bit controlling, but unless you want to take the responsibilities for *everything* for the rest of your life, now's the time to practice giving a little of it up!

On the other hand, the Sag bride needs all the support she can get. You'll get anxious if you find yourself controlling too many aspects of the planning. Reach out in clear ways, communicate your wishes and fears, and don't let your need for freedom cloud your vision of the perfect day.

□□ Earth: Taurus, Virgo, Capricorn

Taurus, Virgo, and Capricorn women love to get things done. You are more than happy to sit down at the computer and make lists all night while your fiancé watches the latest episode of *The Amazing Race*. You can easily go around on your lunch hour visiting stationery stores without feeling frustrated that your groom isn't putting in his 50 percent. That's just part of your Earth sign nature.

Where you do need his support is in the appreciation and comfort departments. "Oh, honey, thank you so much for making all those phone calls." "Darling, those lists are awesome, I am so lucky to be marrying you!" "Can I get you a cold drink while you're doing all that work?" If he hasn't figured this out yet, read this to him for a lifetime of happiness.

As you get further into the planning, bring him into all the details. Just because you are so good at accomplishing the legwork doesn't mean he should be an outsider. This is especially true for Capricorn, who, as the most controlling of the bunch, might have her *own* plans. Taurus can get stubborn on a bad day and need to be coaxed out of fixed ideas, and Virgo just loves to plan so much, that if you don't make an effort to stop and ask questions, the whole thing may be done before he's had a say.

One Capricorn bride had a very interesting way of compromising on plans—they just split it down the middle. "The things that were important to me weren't important to him, and vice versa. The one who felt most strongly pulled the other one into it and said, 'This is the way it's going to be.'" And whatever works for focused, driven Earth signs is a good thing!

□ □ Air: Gemini, Libra, Aquarius

The Air sign bride is made for compromise and companionship, so planning a wedding with your fiancé is a relatively easy task for you. You naturally like to exchange ideas, chat about details, and have a great time. In fact, you need the team effort in order to feel whole throughout what can be a long and stressful process.

It's true that women generally take the lead, but in this case, be sure to do only small amounts of legwork on your own before presenting the ideas and looking further into things together. If your guy is one of those leave-it-to-the-bride types, train him early and train him fast! Okay, images of orchids can scare the daylights out of any groom, but coax thoughts out of his head and let him know how much his ideas and opinions mean to you. Bring him to as many venues and vendors as he has the time and patience for, letting him see that this equal partnership starts now.

Laugh, play, and have fun together. "It's nice if your fiancé backs you up," one Aquarius bride told me. "You have to go through this with him and make sure that you are together through the whole experience."

Gemini, the Mutable Air sign, needs the most help, since it can be almost impossible for you to make a decision sometimes. Libra, with its ruling planet of Venus, has cornered the market on beauty, so you have very definite ideas of what you want on your big day, and Aquarius is just happy that everyone is getting along. Or as another Aquarius puts it, "I just don't care enough to want to argue."

□ □ Water: Cancer, Scorpio, Pisces

Having a strong emotional connection is key for Cancer, Scorpio, and Pisces girls. Working together, discussing your feelings, and being understood is an absolute must-have for the Water sign bride. Especially for Cancer and Pisces, who can sometimes have a tough time making decisions on their own. Scorpio is more comfortable moving about more independently, but still, your biggest need is to feel heard throughout this process.

Dreamy and romantic, a Water sign is the best at creating moving ceremonies and fantasy parties, but you can be free to express yourself only when you feel safe—and that job falls to your fiancé as you enter this new phase in your relationship. "How do you feel about this?" is the catchall question he can ask you in order to fulfill his mission. It's vital that he go with you to see reception sites, florists, bands, and wedding coordinators; your sweet sensibilities need to be protected, something you cannot do very well on your own.

Compromise is pretty easy for Cancer and easier still for Pisces, who just wants to make everyone happy. Your biggest issue is not standing up for what you want loud enough. Your fiancé can be instrumental in helping you find your voice. Scorpio can be a bit controlling, but getting married means so much to you that you now have a lot of motivation to learn balance and communication; put in the effort.

One Cancer told me it wasn't just the happiest day of her life, the whole process was inspiring to their relationship. "I really got to see the true colors of the people I love. It brought us much closer together."

Advice That Will Change Your Life

At this stage of the game, your head is probably swimming with ideas, weddings you've remembered, things you've read in bridal magazines, but how do you sift through all the raw information and decide what's truly important to you? Maybe getting to know Leila and Andrew will help!

Thought and originality went into everything about their celebration in their adopted hometown of New York, from the nontraditional ceremony to the carpeted aisle runner strewn with Black Magic rose petals, but what were clearly the most important aspects to Leila, a Cancer with a Sag Rising, and Andrew, a Virgo with a Cancer Rising, were the many sentimental moments.

"I had the most incredible moment right before I walked down the aisle. My best man and my dad were right behind me, and he was just giving me that last hug, just looking at his son about to get married, and we all just started laughing and crying," remembers Andrew.

Leila echoes the sentiment, "When everyone surrounded us and welcomed us with the traditional Middle Eastern music, and everyone just started dancing, I had never felt so deeply affected. I kept looking at my mom and Andrew and saying, 'I am so incredibly happy.'"

Leila's advice for brides- and grooms-to-be: "It can be one of the most amazing days if you make it about who you are. When you realize that this is the one time in your life that you will have all the people you love and that love you the most in the same room, your favorite uncles, your nieces, your best friends, it's really about enjoying that, not worrying about the little details. Nobody really remembers those things anyway."

Andrew, the practical Virgo, adds that if you want quality on a budget, "Find talented people who are just making it into the business and hire them before they increase their prices." Then, get your most creative friends and family involved. A professional lighting designer pal arranged the lights as a wedding present and Leila's friend made the invitations. People gave presents for the reception as well. The cake, the wine, and the wedding favors all have more meaning to the Cancer because they came from close friends.

"Let your emotions rule the day," is Andrew's advice to fellow grooms. "You feel so much if you allow it to happen." He adds, "You think it's all about her. I spent the whole planning process making sure she got everything she could ever want and at the end of the day I realized that it was absolutely the best day of my life as well."

Leila cautions brides with old wise words, "Make sure you eat. I lost track of time and by the end of the night I was so light-headed." And, she chimes in, "Never try a new hairstylist the day of the wedding." That's one thing that they always notice when they look at Andrew's hair in all those fabulous photos from Times Square!

■ Bringing Up the Budget

Oh, yes, it's time to bring up that nasty little *B* word—budget! If you're like most brides, you have big ideas yet you have some financial restrictions to work within. Certain signs handle the bottom line better than others. Here are some tips on how to discuss the money issue, prepare a budget that you can live with, and make it a completely enjoyable experience. This is your reality check.

❏ ❏ Fire: Aries, Leo, Sagittarius

This is a tough topic for Fire signs who have big plans and dislike limitation. When dealing with numbers, the first rule for Fire signs is: Don't make any assumptions. Don't guess what he's got in the bank, don't try to fumble with numbers on your own, and don't move ahead with plans assuming he's on the same page. Aries, Leo, and Sag gals like action, but in this case some thoughtful discussion is in order.

Tossing around numbers doesn't have to be stressful; once you've got some idea of what you can spend, start thinking of it as a creative challenge. One Aries bride told me, "I had all these great ideas, but I knew how much money we had to spend from the start." Although, she confesses, they did go over a little in the end.

The best way for a Fire sign not to get too carried away is to limit your choices to a certain price range, set some money aside early on for upgrades you may have your heart set on along the way, and keep a stash of cash for last-minute splurges. Most of all, set these numbers in stone right now and whatever you do—don't cross the bottom line!

❏ ❏ Earth: Taurus, Virgo, Capricorn

This is an easy issue for an Earth girl who just wouldn't feel secure without having very detailed discussions about money early and often. With one eye on the bottom line, your search for venues and vendors will be grounded in reality.

When it comes to the budget, Taurus is the most able to compromise your ideals without getting upset that you are giving up the wedding of your dreams. When faced with the same situation, Virgo and Capricorn are likely to splurge on (and micromanage) a few very important details while making compromises on the rest.

Earth girl, if you want to stay on budget with your extreme attention to detail and love of beauty, make a list of the two or three most important items to you and the least two or three; only spend real money on those things you feel will make your wedding most special to you. Save money by making the invitations on your computer and creating lovely, low-cost favors—just make sure you skip the expensive paper and high-end ribbon or it won't be economical after all.

❑ ❑ Air: Aquarius, Gemini, Libra

Air signs have mixed thoughts about budgeting. You're not spendthrifts, but you know that a unique wedding is going to cost *something* and you dislike cutting corners. Aquarius and Gemini are more easygoing about the wedding budget than Libra, who knows all the beauty they require comes with a potentially hefty price tag.

The Air sign bride has an ace in the hole. You think with your head and not with your heart. Use your ability to weigh all the options for service and value and you won't make any spontaneous decisions that can end up costing you a bundle. When you get stuck on a high-priced choice, remember that it's not the look of the wedding that's most important, it's the gathering of friends and family.

A destination wedding is a great way for the nonconformist Air signs to have their good time without constantly feeling tied down by the bottom line. One Aquarius bride chose to have her event in Mexico to avoid an ordinary wedding, but the choice had the added bonus of keeping spending down; everything across the border costs a fraction of what it does in the United States. A wise decision by the intelligent Air sign who wanted a week's worth of parties!

❑❑ Water: Cancer, Scorpio, Pisces

Out of all the elements, the Water sign girl has the hardest time talking and thinking budget because you are so emotionally involved with everything. Water sign brides say things like, "I didn't really have a budget, I just spent what I wanted because I knew that I would save with less important stuff," and, "I couldn't imagine not having the wedding of my dreams." When Cancer, Scorpio, and Pisces women feel strongly about something, it's almost heartbreaking for them to let it go.

Combat this by talking about your wishes and feelings with your fiancé, decide on the most important aspects of your wedding, and put your money where your heart is. Along the way, give yourself time to process big ideas before having to compromise, then look for the positive outcome when faced with making a tough choice. Maybe you get a more exotic honeymoon by going with less expensive flowers. Once you know it's for the greater good, you'll be able to embrace the change.

Lastly, you are the creative lifeblood of the zodiac, use your vision to find inexpensive solutions to high-priced problems. When Water signs use their powerful intuition, sometimes things just have a miraculous way of working out.

▪ Setting Your Priorities

To use their resources wisely, every bride and groom must decide what the most important aspects of their wedding are going to be. What one sign may want to spend gobs of time and money on is another sign's afterthought. Making all of this harder is the excitement of close friends and family—you can't let someone else's desires eclipse yours—something that some signs are better at than others. Use your astrology sign to determine your most essential details.

☐ ☐ Fire: Aries, Leo, Sagittarius

The Fire sign girl likes to create a great party, make a grand entrance, and have a bit of an adventure. The things that are most important to Aries and Leo are the splashy extra touches, the stuff that makes people go "Ooh" and "Ahhh." Your priorities are your dress, hair, and makeup to begin with, and then invest in a great first dance, flowing champagne, and a big cake.

Sags like a more natural vibe. Spend your time and money on the perfect location—start by looking for a big expansive outdoor space or a great garden. All Fire signs need fun music, whether you choose a DJ or a band, people must be able to dance all night.

Depending upon how big your budget is, cut corners on the food and flowers. As long as you feed people, they're not going to notice how many entrées are on your buffet table and they're not there for the decorations either, they are there for the great celebration.

☐ ☐ Earth: Taurus, Virgo, Capricorn

Earth signs want a traditional ceremony and a gracious party. Your focus is finding a lovely location that can accommodate all your close friends and family, and feeding them some good food on your budget. Your dress and hair come in a close second.

Beauty is important to each of you and looking good is a must. Taurus wants to see pretty flowers, while Capricorn and Virgo want all the little details to complement one another in a perfect way. You want all the trappings of a nice wedding, but keeping the spending in check is a priority in its own right with an Earth sign.

What's *not* important to you? Besides over-the-top anything (there's nothing you can't stand more than *flashy*), you can skip the big expensive cake, flowing flowers, and top-of-the-line photographer and videographer. Choosing a simple, small cake, understated table arrangements with in-season blooms, and moderately priced photos will make your money go farther.

❏❏ Air: Aquarius, Gemini, Libra

Individuality sprinkled with a little creativity and adventure is the Air
sign's signature. Because of that, the ceremony is a big priority to you.
Aquarius and Gemini want to say "I do" by making a bold statement—
the location, the words, the music, everything. Libra just wants to make
sure it's elegant and beautiful, from the officiant to the stained glass
windows.

The reception site is also vital, find a place that has the exact vibe
you are looking for, then factor in the costs before budgeting the rest.
Another expense worth paying for: a great photographer and videographer. You want the whole affair well documented.

Since Aquarius and Gemini are nonconformists, it's easy for you to
skip just about any tradition: the flowers, the cake, even the DJ. Decorate with your favorite fruit, plants, or pictures; choose a tower of cupcakes, and fill your Ipod with an eclectic mix of tunes. On the other
hand, there is nothing unimportant to Libra, so save on an elegant but
simple honeymoon.

❏❏ Water: Cancer, Scorpio, Pisces

Making everything meaningful is the key to a wonderful ceremony and
reception for the Water sign. Your priorities are the items that most
ooze love and romance; your dress and hair, your flowers, toasts, vows,
and photos. Some of those things cost more than others—heartfelt
speeches are free—but none of you are big spenders, you just need
enough magic to feel special.

Pisces are the most attached to their dream and most susceptible to
the influence of others; to figure out what's truly most important to you,
envision what *you've* always dreamed of and write your list from there.

Cancer needs the sentimental memories just as much as the event it-
self, so hire a great videographer and preserve your dress or flowers.
Scorpio likes the space to research and plan; make sure you budget in a
DSL line or some subscriptions to your favorite bridal magazines.

Least important on the Water sign's list are the loud, splashy social conventions; skip the high-priced reception site, an overly decorated cake, and expensive gifts.

A Completely Do-It-Yourself, Beautiful Gourmet Wedding (On a Budget!)

Aviva always envisioned getting married outdoors. A down-to-earth Taurus, this bride wanted a comfortable wedding that was both well planned and elegant.

When Aviva and her fiancé, Mark, broke the news of the engagement to her mom, she immediately went into action, offering her home and lush backyard for the big event. "I wanted it to be absolutely beautiful," says Sheryl, the mother of the bride, "I didn't want anything to be regular, everyday."

So what did this detailed Virgo decide to do? Cater a gourmet lunch herself, cooking everything from four types of crackers to three main courses. After clearing the menu with the bride, she worked for months cooking and tasting different dishes.

Budget was just as important as beauty for this affair. Both Taurus and Virgo are good at balancing their creativity with the tough choices. They splurged on Aviva's hair and a good photographer and saved money on almost everything else. Her artistic older sister decorated the courtyard and a family friend decorated the drive and walkways. Besides two professional flower arrangements, they ordered six dozen lavender roses and placed them in their own vases around the house, they even borrowed champagne flutes from friends in the neighborhood.

And how did all this planning bode for the mother-daughter relationship? They battled a bit over the music, the color scheme, and oddly enough, the beef. "I talked to my mother more than I'd ever spoken to her in my entire life," says Aviva. "We're much closer now." Although she confesses, "In some ways it was like my mom's wedding. There were a lot of things I felt I had no control over"—something every bride should keep in mind when working so closely with parents or in-laws. "I wish I would've communicated better, but I really did have a beautiful wedding.

"And I love being married"—the most important thing to Aviva. "I hope other brides getting married truly feel like they've found the right guy."

▪ Number of Guests

Before you pick a ceremony and reception site, you've got to decide how many people you want to witness your big event. There are many things that affect how many people you will have at your wedding. Your budget may have a lot to do with the number of invites going out, and choosing to get married in your hometown, three hundred miles away will definitely impact the RSVPs coming back. Logistics aside, let's get your astrological sign's take on attendees.

❑❑ Fire: Aries, Leo, Sagittarius

The Fire sign lady not only loves to party, but you love big displays of affection. Aries and Leo delight in a large amount of admirers, you can't have too many people fawning over you and treating you like a queen. Sag loves a good social occasion, too, but can sometimes find a more formal affair cumbersome, look to your Moon sign to determine how many people you can handle. Wishing to include everyone you know, you may have a hard time limiting the list to just good friends and family—you don't have to invite your entire yoga class just because you all get along!

❑❑ Earth: Taurus, Virgo, Capricorn

Traditional, yet somewhat private, the Earth girl leans toward a wedding that includes just good friends and family. It's easy to avoid the ballooning guest list with a constant eye on the budget, but that's not the whole picture. You want to be surrounded by your loyal clan, but can easily become uncomfortable around too many unfamiliar faces. Earth girls need tender moments of affection that can get lost in a crowd. Capricorn might be the exception: If you're working so hard to have an unforgettable affair, you're going to make sure everyone's there to experience it, so you just may skip gushy displays of affection.

❑❑ Air: Gemini, Libra, Aquarius

Air signs are an interesting breed. On the one hand, you love being so-cial, going to parties, and hanging out with your friends. On the other hand, you live life with a natural detachment. If a large wedding doesn't fit into your plans, it becomes very easy for you to pass over certain people; you can easily choose an exciting destination wedding, rather than have everyone you know in attendance; and you're not one to hold on to old friendships when they're over. Just make sure your fa-vorite people are there and you'll have a blast.

❑❑ Water: Cancer, Scorpio, Pisces

The Water bride is sensitive and sentimental. You can't imagine getting married without the people you love around to share your joy. That's not to say you want the world at your wedding, only the people who mean the most to you. Many Water signs are a bit on the shy side, so you may not fully be able to express your emotions in a room full of people. If a big ceremony seems too scary or impersonal, invite a small number of guests to a cozy, heartfelt ritual and then a larger amount to celebrate at the reception.

▪ Making Early Decisions

Once you have a budget, a list of priorities, and an idea of how many guests you'll be inviting, you can start exploring the world of weddings, checking out churches, synagogues, and reception sites; meeting with officiants and vendors. You don't have to decide on the flowers, band, or DJ until much later in the process, your big priority now is settling on the perfect place to celebrate your marriage. Find the ultimate ceremony and reception site for your sign.

❏ ❏ Fire: Aries, Leo, Sagittarius

While Leo might choose to have a more traditional religious ceremony, none of you have a strong need to say your vows in a church, synagogue, temple, or mosque. Knowing that, focus your search on reception sites first. Many of them have a beautiful garden, lake, or gallery that can be transformed into the perfect place for a ceremony.

You can find everything you are looking for in one location but remember, it doesn't have to be nearby; fiery gals have the perfect makeup for a destination wedding. Where ever you end up tying the knot, it must be dramatic. Look for high ceilings, big windows, and sweeping views. Once you see *the* place, you'll know it immediately, so bring your list of dates with you to check for availability.

Signing on the dotted line isn't tough for the Fire sign, you're a pretty decisive bride. On the other hand, once you've got your heart set on a location, it can be nearly impossible to talk you out of it, so make sure you move quickly to secure the deal.

❏ ❏ Earth: Taurus, Virgo, Capricorn

The first decision for an Earth bride is to choose whether you want to get married outdoors or in a more customary location, such as your church or a venue's on-site chapel. Earth signs can go either way, but the key to making the right decision is finding a ceremony site that has a dignified, traditional feel.

You want your reception site to have a conventional flavor as well, so search for a lovely location (again, possibly close to nature) that has comfortable seating, a nice dance floor, and a classic decor. A good question to ask yourself is, "Will I be proud to hold my wedding here?"

Whether you search for ceremony or reception sites first, you're not going to commit to anything until you have the whole plan figured out, so don't fall for any pressure tactics. Compare everything for quality and price, run the numbers, and mull over these big decisions for a little while. Make sure you are comfortable with your choices before you hand in your deposit. Once you sign up, you can't take it back.

❏❏ Air: Aquarius, Gemini, Libra

Air signs are very independent, forward-thinking people who rarely consider following the norm just because. When searching for the perfect place to get married, seek out unique and interesting sites, something with a hip, gracious vibe. A wine cellar, art gallery, botanical garden, or a penthouse restaurant in the sky, where you can say your "I dos" in front of panoramic views.

Look carefully at a location's flexibility. You might want to have your ceremony outdoors, a cocktail hour on the balcony, dinner and dancing in a great hall, and cake back out on the balcony.

Libra may take a more traditional approach to the ceremony, choosing a church or synagogue service, while nonconformist Aquarius and Gemini are comfortable making their commitment in a place that has no specific religious connotations.

Make sure you look at *every site* before finalizing your decisions. You'd rather find that perfect location and change your date a few times than plunk down cash too early. If something comes up in a few months that you like better, you'll wish you waited. And whatever you do, don't choose something because it's *sensible* or you'll be taking the wind out of your sails.

❏❏ Water: Cancer, Scorpio, Pisces

Water signs need to feel an emotional connection to the space they get married in. You simply cannot tie the knot in any pretty place. Visit your family's house of worship or similar locations that hold sentimental value to you and see if you can make them work; your best friend's beach house, the restaurant you got engaged in, even the city where you went on your first romantic trip together.

Cancer, the most traditional of the bunch, may choose a religious ceremony, while Pisces and Scorpio are more likely to want to craft their own inspiring event. It's key that you find a unique location that can accommodate your emotional creativity. Ask the right questions. Can you hang your favorite flowers over the altar? Can you erect a huppah with backlighting? Can you do a candle-lighting ritual?

Water sign, once you have your heart set on the perfect site, there is no talking you out of it, but you can't simply sign up with the first place you fall in love with. In reality, it's important that you make this decision with your head as much as your heart. I suggest holding the date for a few days while you weigh your feelings with your priorities and your budget.

■ The Gift Registry

Okay, you're engaged. (Yippee!) The very first question people ask you when they first hear the news is, *When's the date?* After they look at the sparkling new jewel on your finger, they're going to want to know the answer to question number two: *Where are you registered?* It's that quick! Use your astrological personality to find the perfect place to shop and learn exactly what you should be putting on your wish list.

❏❏ Fire: Aries, Leo, Sagittarius

Fire signs love to get gifts and picking them out is even better! Aries and Leos enjoy nice things, so choose a store that covers a more highbrow taste. Since you like to entertain, make sure you add a variety of platters, serving pieces, and wineglasses to the standard set of dishes and flatware. Then add some picture frames and crystal vases; things that will add flair and beauty to your new home.

Whatever you do, keep the practical things to a minimum—it's nice to have new towels and sheets, but to be honest, you'd rather have more bling-bling in your life.

Sags on the other hand are a bit more eclectic. Having too many useless gifts around can weigh you down. You'd rather have things that bring you freedom and adventure. Make sure to add items that will make your life easier; a convection oven, food processor, even a dishwasher will get you excited. Consider starting a registry for your honeymoon as well. You could end up with new luggage, a massage for two, or a guided Jeep tour courtesy of Aunt May and Uncle Jack instead of those shrimp forks!

❑❑ Earth: Taurus, Virgo, Capricorn

Earth brides take the job of choosing their gifts very seriously. This is your opportunity to get some lovely things and you're not going to blow it. Be sure to visit several stores before deciding on the best one for your registry. Check their inventory and compare their prices—you want the best value, not only for yourself, but for your friends and family who purchase the gifts as well.

Go for practical, well-made things that you can use every day and keep for a lifetime. A beautiful set of dishes, flatware, and glasses; maybe even some sheets, pillows, and towels. Don't let your fiancé throw too many spontaneous extras on the list—how often is he really going to use those sterling silver ice tongs?

You love to cook and eat a good meal, so register for high-quality kitchen appliances and the latest gadgets that you will use often. Taurus loves *everything,* so be careful not to register haphazardly. On the other hand, Capricorn and Virgo are detail-oriented perfectionists, don't drive yourself nuts trying to replicate that list you saw in that bridal magazine.

❑❑ Air: Aquarius, Gemini, Libra

Before you register, surf the Net for the latest trends in wedding registries, cooking, entertaining, and setting up a home. Start formulating your perfect gift list by picking key items that are not only stylish, but functional as well. While you're at it, locate the nearest hip and cool home store with an online registry, that way you can see your choices up close and personal and your out-of-town guests can have easy access to the list.

You'll need the basics, a good set of china dishes, flatware, and glasses, but you'll want the latest styles and patterns. Libra goes for a more traditional look, while Gemini and Aquarius embrace the new so openly, make sure you know the difference between *trend* and *fad,* or you might be sorry in a few years when the stuff starts looking dated.

In addition, add some highbrow entertaining accessories like bar tools and martini glasses, funky chargers that can function as platters, and a big cutting board for serving cheese or appetizers. As a new wife, socializing with other newlyweds will be on top of your to-do list!

❑ ❑ Water: Cancer, Scorpio, Pisces

Water sign brides need to be surrounded by things that make them comfortable and inspired. Make your home a respite from the world by choosing plush towels, bedding, and pillows. You want the traditional china, flatware, and glasses, but you also need beautiful items that hold sentimental value, so make sure you add some lovely vases, candlesticks, and picture frames to the list.

You might even choose a pattern with happy memories from childhood, serving pieces that remind you of your favorite aunt's Thanksgiving dinner, or a gravy boat like mom's. Making sure your fiancé feels safe and secure is also a priority with you, so turn the scanner over to him to add some electronics or a luggage set. (One Pisces bride's fiancé scanned five Godiva chocolate bars when she was off looking at silver!)

Cancers like to cook, so make sure you add chef's supplies to your registry. Pisces and Scorpio won't put anything on the list you're not moved by, no matter what the experts say, which can create a problem if you don't see any china patterns you like. Your solution: Two stores!

Planning the Longest Wedding in History

So if you're like most brides, you're focused on a rehearsal dinner and one ceremony and reception—and that's stressful enough. Imagine trying to create your perfect day while mixing two different cultures and religions. That's exactly what Simi and Franz, a Sagittarius and a Leo, were facing when they began planning their weeklong nuptials in Northern California.

"German weddings and Indian weddings are extremely different, I was really worried how they would all get along," says Simi of her elaborate wedding. "It's very overwhelming at first, because you have so many things to think about. But we just broke it into steps and we put a lot of work into it." Good advice for any bride.

They had tons of help from her parents and enlisted all of her cousins to act as ushers-cum-ambassadors, creating detailed instruction sheets for each of them.

She does confess that the budget got a little out of control toward the end (okay, they *are* Fire signs), but they were very organized (she set up a binder right away), and made sure their guests knew exactly what was going on at all times. Since about fifty of them were traveling from Germany, Franz designed an intricate Web site, in both German and English, with cultural details, family photos, maps, RSVP lists, and hotel bookings.

Simi began to relax only when the German guests started arriving early in the week in traditional Indian saris: "They were so interested in talking and sharing the culture, I was amazed at how well everything worked out."

Here's how it all went down: Their big day began at nine thirty in the morning with a Sikh greeting and welcoming breakfast. The traditional Indian ceremony started at ten thirty, followed by a huge Indian luncheon for the entire community of three hundred-plus people. They changed into traditional western wedding garb just in time for a German-style evening reception of appetizers, cocktails, dinner, and dancing (the waltz!), held for a more manageable number of one hundred. The evening reception ended at midnight, when they moved the celebration to a friend's place nearby. Whew.

"We were up for about twenty-four hours," Simi adds. It's a good thing both Sag and Leo like to party!

▪ The Invitations and the Printing

After you've settled on a date, time, and place, you have to start thinking about exactly how you're going to tell the world of the big event. In addition to the invitations, you might have save-the-date cards, thank-you stationery, announcement cards, programs, and place cards. Are you the do-it-yourself kind of sign or are you making a trip to the print shop?

❑❑ Fire: Aries, Leo, Sagittarius

Since Aries and Leo are most likely to have a grand affair, start off by creating a save-the-date card six months early. You'll be letting everyone know you're engaged and clearing their schedule at the same time. Even though Sag is more down-to-earth, you might consider doing the same thing if you're having a destination wedding and want your guests to have extra planning time.

Fire sign brides are very creative, but don't love tiny details. Choose your invites from a print shop only if they reflect who you are. If you choose to design your own, keep the busywork to a minimum. Leos like top-of-the-line quality, so go for the high-end announcements if you can afford them. Order your thank-you cards at the same time to ensure they complement the announcements.

Aries and Sagittarius are independent thinkers. You may skip the traditional RSVP cards to save on printing costs and postage, find lovely stationery online, or make the place cards yourself. If they're not exactly uniform, who cares: You'll have a great time with this do-it-yourself project.

❏ ❏ Earth: Taurus, Virgo, Capricorn

Invitations, programs, and place cards are perfect projects for Earth brides, because you are detail-oriented, efficient, and love to save money. The key is to find dignified, beautiful paper, and elegant wording so that they look store-bought even if you are making them on your PC.

Earth brides' tastes run on the traditional side (unless you have an Air sign Rising), so you might want to take a trip to the local print shop to see and feel their samples up close before scouring the Internet for the perfect stationery. And don't forget to buy an embosser for your return address; a quality look without the price.

Earth girls love to be proud of their hard work. Taurus are the easiest because you find beauty in almost everything. There's a potential problem with Capricorn and Virgo's perfectionistic tendencies, the more you understand about the printing business, the more you'll be able to spot a homemade invite. That, and you just might drive yourself crazy trying to perfect the ribbon. Maybe you want to go to the print shop after all!

❏ ❏ Air: Aquarius, Gemini, Libra

Air sign brides love tackling all the printing jobs for their wedding. You love researching different options, writing and rewriting the words, and sifting through countless fonts and stationery styles. It takes time and energy to create invitations that perfectly reflect you and the wedding you are planning.

Instead of a trip to your local printers, research new software and wedding invite trends on the Internet. You'll get far more updated ideas online than you would anywhere else. Once you have your ideas, don't order the invites too early. Not only may your tastes change, but you'll want the theme of your wedding to carry over into all the printing. Nailing down those special details first will help make the invites, place cards, and thank-yous just perfect.

Air signs love finding new ways of expressing the same old thing. Trendsetting Aquarius and Gemini want to add a touch of humor (think comic strip invites or rhyming poetry programs), while Libra needs a completely high-end traditional look to their printing. This is something worth spending the money on.

❑❑ Water: Cancer, Scorpio, Pisces

Being in love is the most wonderful thing for Water sign brides and you want to make sure your invitations, programs, and thank-you cards express that. Search high and low for the perfect printed materials. From the color to the texture of the paper, everything must make your heart smile.

In fact, you're probably feeling compelled to create them yourself as no pre-fab invite will truly reflect who you are. It's in your nature to envision elaborate designs that transform the simple task of inviting or seating people into an inspiration for all to share. Setting the place cards among rose petals and fairy dust or placing the programs in rusty watering cans, they become props in the Water sign's dream.

As far as the wording goes, Cancer and Pisces tend to use more traditional language, understanding the sentimental value of including your parents' names as they give you away on your special day. Scorpio, on the other hand, must make sure the words completely reflect your feelings about making such an important commitment.

To Hire a Wedding Planner or Not to Hire a Wedding Planner: That Is the Question!

Brides of certain signs enjoy making all the arrangements while others can't decide what to eat for breakfast without the help of someone close. Should you hire a coordinator or do it yourself? Let's take a look at the signs.

Cancer, Libra, Sagittarius, and Pisces Sun and Rising signs find big projects involving too many decisions totally nerve-racking. A wedding coordinator that can hold your hand through each step is worth her weight in gold. Choosing the right coordinator is very important to you because her biggest job is making you feel safe and understood.

"It's good to have a wedding planner," were the words of one Libra; her bustle came down as they were beginning their first dance and their coordinator was right there with a safety pin before she could even utter a word.

Of course these signs also have an easier time giving up control than some others. Take Taurus, Scorpio, Leo, Virgo, and Capricorn, the signs who like to do things themselves, make the decisions, and generally run the show. For you, working with a wedding planner might be more hassle than it's worth.

One Scorpio worked with an equally headstrong coordinator friend who clearly had her own vision for their affair. She tried to dissuade them from choosing their location, compelled them to work with specific vendors, and kept them in the dark about some details. "I trusted that she wasn't going to ruin my day," this bride said, "but there were so many frustrations."

If you are one of these signs, the questions to be asking are "Is this worth it?" and "What am I getting out of this relationship?" It paid off for that patient Scorpio, who had a wedding out of a magazine for half the price.

The perfectionists should be careful as well. Virgo, Capricorn, and even some Leo brides are going to be able to relax and enjoy their day only if their coordinator has everything under control. One Gemini-Virgo couple who planned every ounce of their wedding spent too much time being hosts when, as he puts it, "We should've been the guests of honor," because their onsite coordinator didn't do her job well enough.

Lastly, there are the signs who want nothing to distract them from their joy and their party—Aries, Gemini, Leo, Libra, Sag, and Aquarius. Take advantage of any site coordinators or give the reins to a trusted friend so that on your special day you can simply be the bride.

■ Tackling the Legalities

Before we move on to the fun stuff, we've got one more short dose of reality to focus on, and that is taking care of the legal issues. For some couples, this can range from getting a simple marriage license (a piece of cake!) to signing a prenup (a touchy subject). Here's how to use the strengths of your astrology sign to execute the things you can't avoid.

☐☐ Fire: Aries, Leo, Sagittarius

Truthfully, legal stuff is just not that important to Fire signs. You've already made the commitment and that's what matters most to the Aries, Leo, and Sagittarius bride. During the planning, your officiant will go over everything with you and it's fine by you to wait until then for the details. Fire sign girls are smart, but you may not care to ask enough penetrating questions.

Every state has a different waiting period from the day of your application and each state's marriage license is valid for different lengths of time. Just to be certain, research the current laws in your state and get those details early enough to ensure making it legal won't interfere with your party plans. Same thing goes for name changes, joint tax returns, wills—do your homework.

Fire signs are very trusting people, the thought of a prenuptial agreement goes against your grain. The flexible Sagittarians can handle this more easily, while Aries might get hot under the collar, and Leo will find the whole thing undignified. You are marrying for life, hedging your bets is something you just don't do. That said, if you are planning a prenup, approaching it *in theory* might help you get through this process. You can sign anything as long as you think it's just a formality.

☐☐ Earth: Taurus, Virgo, Capricorn

Researching current laws, discovering how to get a marriage license, and gathering up the paperwork is all in a day's work for the Earth bride.

Knowing exactly what your responsibilities are early on makes you feel comfortable. In fact, you'll probably end up with this information way before you really need it. Creating a good structure helps you feel grounded. You might have already added a trip to City Hall in your planning calendar while you were mapping out other key dates, times, and events.

Name changes, joint bank accounts, health coverage—go a step further and research everything while you're at it, that way you'll know exactly what to do the day after the honeymoon. Taurus, Virgo, and Capricorn girls like to have time to think things over and decide on the best course of action.

Securing your future is very important to Earth signs of all ages. You understand the need for detailed financial discussions and potential prenuptial agreements before sailing off into marital bliss. While other signs may find this a tough blow to happily ever after, being in love and protecting yourself aren't mutually exclusive in your book.

On the other hand, your engagement is a wonderful opportunity for spontaneity and affection. Do your research, then forget about it. You don't have to have the answers to *everything* before taking the plunge.

❑❑ **Air: Aquarius, Gemini, Libra**

Addressing the laws and legal paperwork is actually fun for the Air sign brides. One Google search will reveal the marriage regulations in your state, details about the license, paperwork, and any extras you may need to prepare for—such as a blood test or physical exam. Aquarius, Gemini, and Libra, you love learning new facts and tidbits so much that after you're done jotting down what you need to know for your own wedding, you may spend a whole evening reading about the quirky laws in the other forty-nine states.

Although with Air signs, learning about these things and actually setting out to accomplish them are two different things. You are much more of a thinker than a doer. Once you have the info, you'll put it into the schedule eventually, even if it is a bit delayed.

It's not difficult for Air signs to tackle the rest of the dirty work as well, even the tough stuff like a prenuptial agreement or a joint bank account. Your intellectual approach to facts and numbers allows you to mix it up without getting emotionally involved. That said, if this is your fiancé's idea, he better bring it up right or Aquarius may get indignant and Gemini, insecure. On the other hand, all Libra asks is to feel heard and respected and that any legal agreements be fair and balanced. Easy enough.

❑ ❑ Water: Cancer, Scorpio, Pisces

As a Water sign bride, you get so involved in your emotional commitment that you forget there's legal work to do. You'll spend so many hours perfecting your exchange of the rings that the signature and paperwork is more of an afterthought. Water signs do their homework though. You may not be that interested in these details, but you'll know exactly what's expected of you when the time comes.

Marriage license aside, it can be tough for Water brides to talk legalities, especially anything having to do with money—prenups, joint bank accounts, even household expenses. Every word is full of emotional meaning, chatting about monthly minimums can be like walking through a minefield—you just never know when something will upset you. Particularly the sensitive Pisces and the intense Scorpio. At least if Cancer gets unsettled—you are more likely to brood quietly than weep or wail—ingredients that can make for quite an altercation!

Add to this the potential need for a prenuptial agreement and you've got some seriously hazardous conditions. If this is something important to you or your fiancé, the best thing to do is create a safe place to have this discussion (or go to a safe place, like a marriage counselor—no kidding, it'll be the best decision you ever made!). Understand that the need to protect yourself doesn't have to put a black cloud over the wonderful love you share with each other—now or in the future.

■ ■

Now that you've got the business out of the way, you are free to create the the wedding of your dreams. Let's start at the beginning: your ceremony.

But first, here's a little secret about your groom that'll make your job a whole lot easier. Shhhhh . . . don't kiss and tell.

How to Talk Your Groom Into Just About Anything!

Want to add another twenty guests to an already busted budget, but can't figure out a way to ask your other half? Wish you could avoid asking his sister to be maid of honor, but don't want to insult him? Long for his tie and cummerbund to match your eggplant-colored calla lilies, but know he'll call it all off if he has to wear anything resembling the color purple? Just look up his Sun or Moon sign to uncover the secret to these two words, "Yes, dear."

ARIES   Give him a choice. Never tell him point-blank: "This is the way it's going to be." Take the two or three options that best suit your needs and then present them with a cheery, "Which one would you prefer?" Voilà, you get your way without him ever knowing it!

TAURUS   Don't surprise him with anything. With plenty of time to spare, give him the suggestion, "I'd like to do *this,* think about it." Then drop it. Give him time to mull it over and come around. Once he thinks it's his idea, he'll love it.

GEMINI   Let him have a say. Give him all the potential options, discuss all the pros and cons, and then simply say, "This one works best because . . ." Once he understands your reasoning, he'll give his nod of approval.

CANCER   Present your ideas in private. Give him the space and time to process his feelings. Being comfortable is a big thing for him. Beware, he may ask for a compromise if something is really off the wall, but he'll rarely say no. If that doesn't work, cry.

LEO   Flatter him. First remind him that he is such a wonderful, generous person and you are *so* lucky to be marrying him. Then throw in your idea followed by a few hugs and kisses. He'll melt like butter once he feels like he's the best fiancé in the world.

VIRGO   Get him involved. Start with, "I need something and it's very important to me." Then let him know how he can *help make you happy* (key words to use!). Remind him how much you appreciate him. Avoid the "my ideas are better than yours" contest, or all bets are off.

LIBRA   Do your homework. First come up with an elegant description; once he hears how beautiful your idea is, he'll graciously agree, unless it's unfair to him. Find a way to give in on something else, after all things are in balance he'll get on board with whatever you ask.

SCORPIO   Crack the hard shell softly. Start with "I love you . . ." then tenderly add what you want to do and why you want to do it— and give it to him with passion. If he responds with silence, cheerfully say, "Why don't we talk about this later?" Give him some time to process his feelings.

SAGITTARIUS   Act like the planning is a big adventure. With the most excitement you can muster, exclaim, "I've got a great idea!" Then go on to tell him how much freedom he'll continue to have under your wonderful plan. If he feels like something is about to close in on him, he may run.

CAPRICORN   Let him know he's the boss. Remind him that all his hard work at the office is making the whole shindig possible, then keep planning the wedding! Give him a job or two along the way that's all his and he'll stay out of your hair.

AQUARIUS   Present a win-win solution. He's not going to let go of something that's *really* important to him. Your creative mission is to figure out a way to incorporate both of your wishes. He'll be fine with it as long as he feels heard and respected.

PISCES   Share your ideas in a safe, loving way. Stress your *needs* and *feelings* (he's doesn't care if something is sensible or logical). He'll go along with most anything, just make sure your ideas don't compromise his gentle heart or you'll hurt his feelings.

Chapter *Four*

Now that the chapel is booked and the deposit set on your reception hall, you're ready to focus on creating your perfect look, equipping your groom, and dressing other key members of the wedding party. In addition to choosing outfits that perfectly reflect the location, theme, and season of your big day, you want a dress to express your inner essence.

You might already have images from magazines that you were just compelled to tear out; pictures of ball gowns, tuxes, bridesmaids' frocks, even accessories such as veils or headpieces. Look to your astrology sign for guidance on your own gown, on how to bring out the best in your mate, and in selecting outfits for the supporting cast that complement everyone's style.

Don't make a trip to your neighborhood bridal salon without first getting a glimpse into your star's style.

■ The Wedding Dress

Some brides dream of their perfect gown from the time they are little girls, others don't know what they're looking for until they begin shopping. While some brides spend days searching every bridal boutique within a thirty-mile radius, some just go to one store and there it is. The one thing brides of all signs say: Once they saw their dress and put it on, they immediately knew that was *the* dress.

Before you head to the store, peek into the crystal ball and let your astrology sign reveal the perfect look.

❑❑ Fire: Aries, Leo, Sagittarius

The Aries and Leo bride want to stun the crowd. You are the queen of the ball and you want your whole look to reflect that honor. Aries go for a grand gown that makes a bold, beautiful statement, so choose something with pretty detailing around the neckline or bodice, some pearls, sequins, or lace.

The Ram girl definitely wants to turn heads, but can compromise on the expense as long as the look is there. "I picked out the cut I wanted, I spent very little on the dress, and I loved it," Summer, an Aries bride, recalls. "As whimsical as I am about things, I also knew I was only going to wear it once."

The Leo loves a grand, if slightly more traditional look. Wendy, a recently engaged bride, calls her style "classic with a twist." As a modern Jackie O, this Leo is having problems deciding on a gown. "I have an idea of what I want, but a lot of my friends have been married in similar dresses and I don't want to wear the same dress as someone else." Oh, so Leo.

Something Leo brides should remember, the quality of the fabric and the manufacturing is just as important as the style. Pay attention to the craftsmanship when shopping, the last thing you want is to feel second-rate on your big day.

Sagittarians are a slightly different breed. Just as bold as your Fire sign sisters, you want to look good, but you must be unencumbered as well. Pick a dress that allows you to move around freely without having to worry about *it* wearing *you*. A tight lace-up bodice or too many undergarments will drive you crazy all day.

Another thing that cramps Sag's style: The dramatic pursuit for the perfect outfit. Too much shopping can be stressful. Kawana, an easygoing

Sagittarius bride happily picked up an off-white cocktail dress with lovely beading and a chiffon shawl for her beach wedding off the rack at JCPenney. "And it was on sale," she says confidently. "Sold!"

☐ ☐ Earth: Taurus, Virgo, Capricorn

The Earth bride wants a classic look. When shopping for a dress, think understated elegance; rich, unadorned satin; an A-line cut; and a short simple sweep train. The Earth girl is dignified in everything she does—even though it's her big day, she's not about to show up looking like Cinderella.

With Earth signs' sophisticated taste, the dress needs to look clean, neat, and decidedly bridal. No chic, cutting-edge designs, no splash of color, and definitely no overabundance of tulle. The detailing must be absolutely perfect because you are going to notice every last stitch. Whether you choose an embroidered bodice, pearl accents, or beaded trim, you want the finishing to add just a touch of class and nothing more.

This is especially true for Virgo and Capricorn brides, who are fastidious about their appearance. Both Virgo and Capricorn brides have exacting specifications, where other brides may see similar dresses, you know that every nuance counts in a big way. One small variation can make the difference between loving one dress and being almost offended by another.

The Taurus bride has a slightly different take. Taurean girls' love of beauty trumps her Earth sisters' pretentious need for perfection. You delight in nice things. The Bull's fixed nature makes you very decisive, but visit a bridal boutique and you will just like more styles than Virgo and Capricorn. Sometimes the Taurus bride needs some frilly lace or a pretty bustle to feel like a princess. Now is not the time to be modest or you won't feel beautiful on your special day.

One thing is true for all Earth sign brides, you will do just about anything to find your perfect dress. You aren't just about to get this over with in one day or buy the first dress you fall in love with (that is, unless you have a Gemini, Aries, or Sag Rising!). Visit competing Web sites and boutiques, read many bridal mags, compare different styles, and analyze dresses for quality and price. Once your search is over, you'll rest easy knowing that you've got the most beautiful, flattering dress ever made.

▫▫ Air: Gemini, Libra, Aquarius

Air brides have a great sense of style—elegant, sophisticated, and perfectly put together. Clothes are an important way in which you express who you are and stand out from the pack. Other brides may have different priorities, but shopping for a perfect wedding gown, one that looks and feels *just so,* is definitely one of yours.

This is especially true for the Libra bride—a graceful gown is almost as important as your groom! Libra has some of the most refined (and expensive!) tastes in all the zodiac. Start your search by visiting hot designer and couture Web sites. Print out examples of chic, highbrow looks and carry them with you as you shop local bridal boutiques. Consider a strapless silhouette that highlights your great bod, beautiful brocade trim, an illusion fabric, even an elegant Watteau train.

Sari, a Libra bride, found the perfect dress, but refused to pay the premium price and instead shopped around to find the only other boutique carrying it, which charged one third the price. The strapless, beaded gown of her dreams was still pricey, but well within the budget.

Nonconformist Gemini and original Aquarius reject the more traditional gown in favor of exploring the latest trends. You are way more comfortable in something hip and happening than a big pouffy ball gown. From a wispy off-the-shoulder sheath to a sleek A-line with a halter neck, you want a dress that is sophisticated, yet bold and whimsical. Look to hot wedding Web sites for the latest articles and photos.

Gemini, along with her Mutable sign sisters Sag and Pisces, have the most flexible approach to dress shopping. One busy Twin bride went to a sample sale with her soon-to-be sister-in-law and fought off other brides to grab seven dresses between them. She was thrilled to find one she really liked—and for $207! Good for her, but not being able to pick a specific style or designer, waiting in a long line for the dressing room, and choosing from what's available isn't something most brides can handle.

❏ ❏ Water: Cancer, Scorpio, Pisces

To a Water sign, a wedding dress is no simple garment. It's a magical gown that transforms her into a princess bride; a reflection of her ever-flowing love. It's the dress she's always dreamed of; a peek inside her heart and soul. Water signs take their choice of dress very seriously.

Make the most of this sentimental element by choosing a modern gown with a period flavor; nothing evokes romance like a Victorian corset, an Empire waist, or bell sleeves that sweep toward the floor.

For Pisces, it's the stuff of dreams and fairy tales; a beautiful ball gown with a cathedral train and poetic bustle, a sweetheart neckline, and a full skirt of taffeta, chiffon, or silk organza. One rather angelic Pisces bride described her A-line frock as reminiscent of peace and doves. "Actually," says Kristye, "the back looks like it has wings."

Cancer brides fall on the more traditional side, choosing the same romantic ball gown with a more classic look and simple embellishments. One Cancer bride chose a very understated 1950s Grace Kelly–inspired gown with romantic cap sleeves, then paired it with a dramatic cathedral-length scalloped veil for the church ceremony.

The bolder Scorpio bride may choose something a bit sexier. A tight embroidered bodice with a little push-up padding and a dramatic two-toned skirt or a mermaid dress with a halter neck and a short sweep train. Emily, a Scorpio, knew *exactly* what she wanted. After trying on every dress in two cities, she came across the perfect dress, fell in love with it, then had it massively transformed to fit her vision.

On the other hand there's always an occasional Scorpion that finds the entire wedding dress phenomena unappealing. Lois, a down-to-earth Scorpio, spotted an off-white cocktail dress in the window of a boutique, only to find out that this dress just happened to be designed by Vera Wang. It fit like a glove. "I thought, okay, this is the one trite thing that I'm doing for my wedding, that I'm wearing Vera Wang."

The Courageous Bride Who Made Her Own Dress

Lisa Shepard Stewart, author of *African Accents,* first learned to sew at age twelve. Now, as an adult, she loves to sew her own clothes whenever she can. Once she got engaged, it was just a given that she'd make her own gown. "The clothes I make for myself are the ones that I get compliments on, the ones that flatter me the most; I just feel better in them."

A bride sewing her own dress is unusual enough, but Lisa is a Sagittarius, an outdoorsy sign that wouldn't naturally gravitate to such a homey, detail-oriented hobby. The secret to her sewing success is astrologically clear: her Virgo Rising. Her Virgo side loves to dive into details and spend long hours focusing on her goals.

Lisa is a great example of how your Sun and Rising signs work together, as her wedding reflected both the adventurous, easygoing Sag and hardworking, budget conscious Virgo. "We thought we'd do something different, a little dramatic and fun," says this bride, "But we're both busy people so we wanted to keep it manageable. A lot of things that people usually obsess over, we just decided weren't important to us."

She and Glen chose to celebrate on a boat that cruised up to the Statue of Liberty—a real Sag adventure for the couple and their guests. She also chose to forgo expensive flowers, making candle centerpieces wrapped in African ribbon and creating the bridal party's bouquets from loose silk flowers she purchased wholesale; practical Virgo decisions she is very proud of.

They decided to go with the cake that came with the boat's wedding package and spiced it up with a custom topper that looked exactly like them, down to his goatee. Glen, an accomplished musician, composed the processional music and her mom baked the favors: three hundred cookies packaged in glossy white boxes, customized with gold monogram stickers.

Lisa and Glen did a great job avoiding the typical wedding stress, creating a wonderful day of laughter and fun. Incorporating their own unique talents made it an unforgettable day. "All of our guests were like, 'Oh, I've never been to a wedding like this,' " Lisa reminisces. "It was really cool."

■ Completing the Look: Shoes, Accessories, Hair, and Makeup

Once you know what type of dress you are going to wear, you can begin to round out the look. An updo or a blow-out? Rhinestones or pearls? Flats, pumps, or slingbacks? There are more choices than ever for a bride to create that special vibe. Classic, modern, funky—some brides stick with one style, while others mix and match with great results. Read this before you accessorize to make a one-of-a-kind look that's all your own.

❏❏ Fire: Aries, Leo, Sagittarius

Fire signs are very expressive brides. There is nothing more fun than sorting through all the wonderful jewelry, shoes, and veils out there to choose accessories that reflect your unique personal style.

When it comes to the finishing touches, "larger than life" yet "well put together" is Aries' goal. A longer cathedral veil to go with the already long train, a beautiful tiara to show off your elegant updo, pretty pumps with pearl accents to match your one-of-a-kind jewelry.

Contrary to how indulgent this sounds, most Aries can prioritize. One chose a simple dress and went crazy with her hair and jewels. "I probably spent more money on my hair and jewelry than I did on the dress because I can wear the jewelry for the rest of my life," says Summer. The tendrils of fiery red hair falling around her distinctive tiara and her bold makeup made for some unforgettable photos.

The royal Leo loves dramatic accents as well. A rhinestone bunwrap for your traditional updo, a stately fingertip veil, hanging earrings, smokey gray eyes, and rich red lips. You want just enough flash to feel like a queen—and nothing more—so choose which accessories mean the most to you instead of getting them all. Looking good in pictures is also a priority, so make sure you experiment ahead of time with makeup that not only flatters your skin tone but looks good to the camera, too.

Sagittarians love being brides, but pass on the bling-bling for a more natural look. A delicate headband of satin and rhinestone flowers, an elegant gemstone bracelet, and low-heeled mules to complete the look. Sag may even choose to skip the veil, although don't pass on the hair and makeup. You can get a natural look that's more polished by a talented professional.

If Sag's don't watch out, you can be easily influenced. Don't let anyone else's idea of the perfect outfit sway you. Sag Kawana, who got married on a beach says, "I didn't want to wear shoes. My mom insisted that I get a pair of shoes, still to this day I haven't worn them."

❑❑ Earth: Taurus, Virgo, Capricorn

Earth brides are very particular about what accents they choose to wear. You love being a bride, but most of the accessories you run across in the bridal boutiques and wedding Web sites you would not even let touch your body. Let's face it, too much bling-bling, bad design, poor quality, these are things you notice from a mile away. It's a good thing you are a perfectionist with great understated taste, because when you finally do settle on your shoes, veil, hair, and makeup, it'll be the epitome of beauty and elegance.

Virgo and Capricorn brides already have a classic dignified gown, so pair it with a simple elbow or fingertip-length veil, a single strand of pearls, and some beautiful slingback shoes. Instead of the more classic headpiece, consider a backpiece, an elegant pearl and rhinestone clip or comb set in the back of your hair right below the classic bun.

Taurus can use the bling of a traditional tiara and the sparkle of tasteful rhinestones or diamonds around your neck and wrists. Above all else, Taurus wants to look beautiful, so forget the budget this one time to buy an exquisitely embroidered veil or to-die-for pair of designer shoes. For her outdoor wedding, one Taurus bride bought two pairs of shoes—flats for the grass ceremony and heels for the indoor reception. Whatever you do, just make sure they're comfortable, something very important to the Bull nature.

All Earth brides like a face that's natural with a tiny touch of drama. Splurge on a makeup artist and a hairstylist. Make sure they know exactly what they are doing before they begin and leave plenty of time for redos. You're such a perfectionist that when it doesn't come out exactly as you expect it to, you will want them to do it again!

☐☐ Air: Gemini, Libra, Aquarius

Independent thinkers, Air signs have a distinctively modern taste that runs from delicate to bold. Mixing and matching styles with ease, Gemini, Libra, and Aquarius brides have a great instinct when it comes to accessorizing their dress—you know exactly how to put things together to create that flawless look. Add makeup that's elegant and beautiful, and a sleek updo, and you're a bride in a class all your own.

As the most traditional, Libra will be attracted to an unadorned fingertip veil, a finely crafted bunwrap or tiara, a simple satin clutch, and an embroidered pair of high-end pumps. The accessories are perfect little accents to the Venus-ruled Libra—the hair, the veil, the shoes—everything working together in beautiful harmonious balance.

The chic Gemini and Aquarius, on the other hand, like to turn heads and make a statement. You can effortlessly mix an ultramodern headband and sleek ankle-strapped sandals with your grandmother's chunky faux-pearl bracelet as long as it looks cool and fits in with the total look of the day.

Air sign brides, whether you are going for vintage or modern, take your friends shopping with you for all these goodies. Besides enjoying a good social occasion, Libra and Gemini find it hard making a decision without having someone around to discuss all the options.

Gemini and Aquarius are the anti-brides of the zodiac. One Gemini I spoke with toyed around with wearing high-top Converses under her dress instead of dress shoes. An Aquarius bride responded to a passing rain shower by taking off her white satin shoes and donning a pair of clogs before going on with the party. Even a classic Libra got into the mix by changing into white platform thong flip-flops after her first dance (and no one knew!).

You might not want to go that far, but you'll be happiest adding just a touch of an "I might be the bride but I'm not quite buying the hype" attitude. Whether you do that with your handbag, shoes, or even your garter is up to you!

❑❑ Water: Cancer, Scorpio, Pisces

Shopping for shoes and accessories are highly emotional events for Water sign brides who perpetually think with their heart. To make this a memorable and pleasant experience, review the huge selection of photos online and collect your favorite pages from every brides magazine you can get your hands on! Have some idea of what moves you *before* you venture to the bridal boutiques.

For a Pisces that means romantic lace-up pumps, a delicately accented veil, and a traditional rhinestone tiara. Cancers prefer the more classic ballet slipper, an unadorned veil, and pearl drop earrings. The dramatic Scorpio, on the other hand, will be attracted to a jewel-toned headpiece, hanging earrings, a chapel-length train, and a lacy garter. That Scorpio private side loves the hidden lingerie as much as the outer accent pieces!

And talk about sentimental—the expression "Something borrowed, something blue" was definitely created for the Water sign bride. Create great memories by adding family heirlooms where you can. As a Pisces bride, I carried my mother's handkerchief inside my grandmother's beaded purse, wore my cousin's blue garter, and tied the knot in a ring that many of my relatives wore before changing into my own band for the reception.

Water signs have a great need to be creative, make a small wristlet pouch bag out of vintage lace and ribbon for your lipstick, powder, and tissues—with your emotions on high there will lots of teary moments and you'll want to touch up for the many cameras that will be pointed in your direction.

One more note for Cancer and Pisces, don't go shopping for these items alone. For one thing, you need constant emotional support, but besides that too many choices can make you dizzy! A good Earth sign buddy can help you make decisions you won't regret later. Scorpios are a different breed entirely, you'd much rather shop for the extras alone. If you're in the mood for company, bring along one simpatico Pisces or Cancer friend to share the love.

Wedding Dress Disasters and What You Can Learn From Them

According to my completely informal, unscientific poll, approximately 30 percent of brides have some sort of dress mishap. Different signs, different disasters—read up and avoid them all.

ARIES This Fire bride carefully purchased her dream gown at a sample sale years before her wedding. Stress eating and working around the clock before the wedding made for quite a surprise when the dress didn't fit. A budding designer, Troy Artis, made her a new frock, completing it literally hours before the start of the ceremony. Brides of all signs: Watch what you eat once the dress is in the closet.

TAURUS This Earth sign bride promised her family she would cover up the tattoos on her arm and back. When she fell in love with a dress, the store didn't have her size. Holding the sample up to her body, it certainly looked like it would hide the offending images. Her true size did not. Oops. A lesson for all the zodiac: Make sure your dress covers sensitive areas before you order it.

CANCER This Water sign did everything right, bought her dress, had her fittings on time, kept it pressed. The last few weeks before the wedding she was so busy that she lost some weight. She kept having to adjust her strapless gown all night. Something she says was "stupid and embarrassing." Brides listen up: You're going to be busy before the wedding, make sure you eat.

LIBRA When this bride arrived for her fitting, she discovered her dress was altered so poorly that she had a meltdown. The owner of the boutique took charge and redid the job. The bride had the right idea, she brought a friend with her for support the second time around.

Two lessons learned: One, don't freak-out when something can be fixed, and two, never accept mediocre work.

SCORPIO   After her fittings, this bride left her beautiful dress in its garment bag without a second thought. When her maid of honor took it out of the bag the morning of the affair, it was a wrinkled mess. The bride was blissfully unaware that the family had rushed over to the nearest mall and borrowed a steamer from an understanding dress boutique. Brides beware: Make sure you examine your gown a few days before the wedding.

AQUARIUS   This Air bride bought a very sophisticated dress in New York City for what ended up to be a beautiful outdoor wedding in Mexico. After realizing that it just didn't jive with the location, she returned it, choosing a simple gown in a local shop across the border. The seamstress made her a bolero jacket with leftover fabric; it was perfect. Brides of the zodiac: Don't buy your dress without choosing your location first.

PISCES   This Pisces author (that'd be me!) carefully carried her gown through two plane rides and three countries only to find a small tear in the plastic garment bag upon arriving at her destination wedding—and some grease from a trunk or overhead luggage compartment on the dress. The wedding coordinator covered the spot with white chalk. Word to the wise bride: Make sure your dress is well protected.

■ The Groom's Attire

With your look out of the way it's time to turn your eyes to the groom. You are juggling a new set of issues getting him dressed. Not only must his suit fit into the theme, location, and time of the wedding, it's got to complement your gown, look good on him, appeal to both of you—and most important, be something he is actually going to want to wear.

Since it's not only you that has to be pleased with this decision, there's both a his and hers section in each element. Make sure to read his sign, too, and combine them both to make everybody happy.

☐ ☐ Fire: Aries, Leo, Sagittarius

The Fire sign bride wants her groom to look absolutely smashing. Aries is up for a bold look, noble Leo leans toward a grand and stately appeal, and Sagittarius, as the most forgiving of the three, likes a casual yet put-together feel. To please an Aries or a Leo, go for the latest tux, paisley vest, and ascot tie, for Aries a splash of color is nice, Leo prefers gray, and Sag will most likely be happy with whatever her groom chooses.

On his side, the Aries groom wants to look just as majestic as his bride, it's easy for him to don a tailcoat with a colored tie and vest. As long as the general look is there, the Aries man can skip the details such as fine stitching and French cuffs.

As the ultimate escort to his lovely queen, Leo wants a gracious-looking tux and a vest with a little edge to it (try silver herringbone). Skip the very traditional bow tie for a wide collar shirt and a hip Euro tie. The details like French cuffs and cuff links are also important to the Leo groom. Watch him turn a jacket or shirt inside out for inspection.

One highbrow Leo groom wore an ivory dinner jacket, black pants, white shirt, and a blue-and-red polka-dot bow tie to his island wedding. Despite the expected Hawaiian heat he was quick to say no to the casual island style his mother-in-law had envisioned.

Sagittarius guys are usually repelled by classic dress and have a great flair for fashion. This combination makes for a bold, edgier look on the big day. Pass on the tux for a white dinner jacket and trousers or skip the traditional lapel for a mandarin collar and you can get away with not wearing a tie—a thought that makes the freedom-loving Sag very happy.

☐ ☐ Earth: Taurus, Virgo, Capricorn

Dignified is how the Earth bride envisions her groom; formal minus the bling-bling, bold patterns, and bright colors. Virgo and Capricorn like a tux (no tails, please) with meticulously chosen accessories to finish off but not distract. Taurus brides are more apt to choose a little color for the tie, vest, or cummerbund, and patent leather loafers rather than the dress shoes already in his closet.

As for his taste, Earth guys like a well-groomed, traditional look and care enough to do their own formal wear research. They make no spontaneous decisions. They want to understand the terminology, know what's out there, and make sure they choose a look that best suits their style. If you are the kind of bride that has a hard time letting go, then do this work together, but in order to have a happy groom, you must let him have his say.

Virgo and Capricorn grooms examine every last buttonhole, cross-stitch, and pleat before choosing their perfect tux, finishing it off with high-end cuff links and formal lace-up oxfords bought special for the occasion. These details may escape some Taurus grooms, who love to look good, yet might not care to go through every jacket in the warehouse to find the one with that perfect lapel.

Earth sign grooms love to dress. My Taurus husband delighted in wearing a traditional kilt to our wedding in Scotland, "I have a casual style but I like clothes with an edge," Ed says, "I was totally up for wearing such a manly garb to get married in a castle. It was a once-in-a-lifetime experience."

As another Earth sign puts it, "I knew what I wanted [to wear] since childhood. I had probably thought about my tux longer than you thought about your dress," this exacting Virgo groom admitted to his bride. She agrees wholeheartedly, "He was clearly the bride."

❏❏ Air: Gemini, Libra, Aquarius

The Air sign bride wants her groom to look handsome and elegant; a perfectly chosen outfit with a modern style. Libra prefers a classic, graceful look, one that balances out her delicately detailed dress. Gemini and Aquarius take a more nonconformist approach to dressing their groom, choosing an Armani suit instead of a traditional tux, a paisley vest, or a tasteful pin-striped traditional tie rather than a bow tie.

As for the Air sign groom, he has a sophisticated style that is both daring and understated. The Libra guy has very highbrow taste and is used to spending a lot of money on his clothes; he may even skip the rental to purchase a beautiful tux that he will own for the rest of his life. He'll also choose an elegant shirt with French cuffs, a three-button vest, and modern Euro tie. The perfect surprise for your Libra groom: a fabulous pair of cuff links to match his grand new suit.

Gemini and Aquarius grooms are a bit bolder in their approach to their formal wear. Yes, they want to look graceful and sophisticated, but can easily go for a tux with a mandarin collar, a dinner jacket with coordinating trousers, or a shirt with a band collar instead of the standard wing collar and buttons.

Libra Sari says of her Aquarius groom, Victor, "He has good taste in clothes, he picked out a tux I really liked a lot." She adds, "I really wanted him to wear a silver tie." An idea he was into. For his part, he says, "At first I didn't want to wear a vest. After seeing a few weddings I changed my mind." The result was fantastic: A modern, elegant look that complemented her carefully chosen gown perfectly. On their wedding day they looked great together.

❑❑ Water: Cancer, Scorpio, Pisces

A Water sign bride wants nothing less than the fairy-tale knight in shining armor to ride in on a white horse and sweep her off her feet on her wedding day. As far as his digs go, your groom better know what he's getting himself into! For a Pisces it means a romantic tux with tails; for Cancer, a classic morning coat with a beautiful bow tie; and for a Scorpio, rich-colored accents like a ruby red pin-striped vest or handkerchief.

For Kristye, a Pisces bride in Texas, this modern-day fantasy translated into a formal Western style. Her Leo groom Jeff wore denim Wranglers, black boots, and a black tuxedo jacket with tails. At the reception he added his silverbelly, a gray felt cowboy hat, while all the groomsmen wore black cowboy hats. She relates, "His attire looked great with my dress as it accentuated the whole 'country' theme."

As for the Water sign groom, he wants an outfit he can feel

comfortable in; one that totally plays up his role as host and bride-groom. Pisces likes the drama of a pink vest on a gray jacket, Cancer will chose a sedate but formal tux, while Scorpio wants to make a state-ment by wearing a designer suit, bold colored socks, or even passing up shoes altogether for a pair of Birkenstocks.

One Pisces groom marrying his Scorpio sweetheart skipped the tux for their summer wedding and instead purchased a navy blue Hugo Boss suit, blue shirt, and green-and-blue striped tie. "It was clearly the most expensive article of clothing he ever bought," says Lois. Some-thing brides understand well. "I had to convince him a little that good clothes cost more, but in the end he saw how worth the money it was," this Scorpio says. "He looked sharp!"

▪ Dressing the Bridal Party

A chapter on dress wouldn't be complete without discussing outfits for your band of attendants. A loaded topic for any bride who has ever per-formed the task herself. The time, date, and place can dictate the dresses you choose for them, but the style of your own gown, your taste, color, and theme will have a lot to do with it as well. Here are some tips to pick a dress that you love and that they will feel comfortable in.

Do you want to know how your bridal party feels about the style and accessories you've chosen for them? Each element includes a bit about bridesmaids of those signs. Read their sections as well for a peek inside their minds. Need help dressing your mom or mother-in-law? Read your Sun sign section and hers, choosing key words to pass on that will help her find something you both can live with.

❑❑ Fire: Aries, Leo, Sagittarius

Fire sign brides like to put their unique stamp on everything and that includes the look of the bridesmaids. Aries and Leo are definitely the more controlling Fire signs—since it's your day, you'd like everyone to look a certain way. Sag doesn't have that same desire. The Aries chooses a bold color and dramatic cut, Leo goes for a more regal look, while Sagittarians are attracted to something a little spicy, think muted tones, halter bodice, and flowing shawl.

Independent Aries bride Summer was very kind to her maids, choosing two shades of the same color and then having each of them design their dress from thirty varying patterns. "They all wore different style dresses, so everybody felt very comfortable and unique." Something that was important to her after being a bridesmaid *nine times.*

Instead of dictating your dress wishes to a Fire sign attendant, work with her to choose a rich jewel-toned color and a flattering, dramatic dress. Allow her to pick out her own accessories. Aries chooses something sparkly, Sag, something more minimalist, and the Leo wants pieces of the highest quality. Fire sign bridesmaids love to look good and get pampered so make hair and makeup appointments for one and all.

❑❑ Earth: Taurus, Virgo, Capricorn

Earth brides make traditional choices for the bridesmaids dresses; beauty and elegance is of utmost importance to you. Virgo and Capricorn choose a muted dusty color, one that is both understated yet still presents a classic bridesmaid look. Taurus likes her bridesmaids to look like attendants as well, but is more apt to choose richer colors, lavender, violet, even midnight blue.

The Earth sign bride can get a tad controlling when it comes to creating the look they want, so plan on being extra nice to your attendants. Andee, a Goat bride, totally agreed, "I'm very picky about the bridesmaid's dresses, but not in a conventional way. I took them [shopping] with me and basically said, 'This is the color I want, pick something,' but I took them to Vera Wang so it was easy, 'cause there's a lot of ugly stuff out there." Amen to that!

Earth sign bridesmaids are very loyal and will basically wear anything you ask them to, although they're not going to feel comfortable in anything too bold or eye-catching. If you've chosen a rich color for the dress, then skip the gloves and oversized earrings, and let them choose their own hairstyle. If you hire a makeup artist, make sure she is very talented or your Earth sign maids will be very unhappy.

❑❑ Air: Gemini, Libra, Aquarius

Air sign brides are always on the cutting edge and like their brides-maids to reflect a totally current, yet elegant look. Libra goes for a classic biased cut in a beautiful rich satin. Gemini and Aquarius are more likely to experiment with color, fabric, and accessories, creating a more happening vibe.

Patty, an Aquarius bride-to-be, took her friends to a reasonably priced bridal chain, picked out the color, a dusty Victorian lilac, and then had them each choose different styles. "Everyone always says, 'You can wear it again,' but nobody ever does," she admits frankly. "If they are only going to wear it for one day, it might as well be a style that looks good on them." Not only that, but a chain store has great flexibility for out-of-town bridesmaids, once you've got the color, they can choose a dress that fits them best.

Air sign bridesmaids like to look modern, sleek, and sophisticated. The fastest way to tick off one of these ladies is to pick out a flowery Laura Ashley number. For happy bridesmaids, choose dignified black, silver-gray, or even ruby red, and an elegant cut straight from the runway. They can individualize with their jewelry, hair, and makeup—something they love. The Libra will want more classic accents, Gemini and Aquarius may be a bit funkier in their tastes.

❑❑ Water: Cancer, Scorpio, Pisces

Out of all the signs, Water element brides are the most emotionally connected to their bridesmaids; choosing their gowns is something very close to your heart. Cancer and Pisces lean toward a romantic dress, maybe with a sheer illusion overlay, while Scorpio is into something more dramatic—a drop neckline or slit up the back. Pisces are attracted to soft pastels, while Scorpios like rich jewel tones. The Cancer bride can go either way as long as the color moves you.

The sensitive Cancer bride Leila got together with her five maids, had them choose a color, lipstick red, then went to a special salon that lets you to pick out fabric and design each dress individually. "I had the girls decide since I didn't want to be like bridezilla," she jokes, " 'you must wear sea foam green.' " Now we know why they say Cancers make the best friends.

The Cancer and Pisces bridesmaids are natural people-pleasers, so they'll like most anything you pick out for them and even if they don't, they intuitively understand how important this is to you and will happily follow your wishes. On the other hand, it's hard for a Scorpio to go along with anything they disagree with, so make sure you get her input before shopping if you want her to be your friend for life.

How to Respond to Inappropriate Guests, Useless Bridesmaids, and a Controlling Mother-in-Law

Why does planning a wedding go down in history as one of the most stressful times in a young woman's life? Yes, it's often hard to coordinate all the different aspects of a wedding and make tough choices but we all know the truth. The biggest obstacle for any bride is a steady stream of overbearing people who clearly have no manners and no boundaries! Most brides have the horror stories to prove it.

Here's how to protect yourself from the mother who tries to dictate all the details, an old friend who pressures you to bring a date when the guest list is tight, or the disappearing bridesmaid who complains about *everything*.

ARIES Think before you act. When people behave badly, it's hard for you not to just let them have it. Preserve your relationships—don't say the first thing that pops into your head. Memorize this: "Let me get back to you on that!" and walk away. Formulate a diplomatic response that still gets your point across. Calm down first and then share your feelings.

TAURUS Be open to compromise. You like things the way you like them, dislike change, and hate when people try to tell you what to do.

Learn the difference between a suggestion worth incorporating and an outrageous one, but until you do, practice saying, "That's a great idea, let me see if that will work." Then, think about it before you make up your mind.

GEMINI Keep your mouth shut. A Gemini girl's solution to everything is to talk about it. You talk to work through a problem, you talk when you get nervous, you talk to please people. Everyone listens to a bride. *Never* say anything you don't mean and never say a word until you have a well-thought-out decision or you might end up having a wedding you don't want.

CANCER Figure out how you feel before compromising. Cancer brides can feel very alone when the people they count on for support become difficult. Don't just clam up or agree to make it easy on them. Take the time to process your feelings. Get a hug from your groom or best friend—then have the guts to stick up for your desires. It's your day.

LEO Don't take things personally. Leo gives respect and in return expects to be treated with that same dignity. Except, you can't control other people's behavior. If someone acts up, use your charm to put them in their place, but don't hold it against them for the rest of the wedding. Forgive them for being inappropriate.

VIRGO Remember you don't have to fix everything. We already know the famous Virgo work habits. You love diving into all things bridal, but when faced with a seemingly insurmountable problem, don't just suck it up and keep on going—and whatever you do, don't take on everyone's job! Speak up, tenderly tell the truth, and unburden yourself.

LIBRA Don't hold it in until you're ready to blow. It's pretty easy for you to compromise unless someone asks something that's unfair or completely unattractive. Analyze the situation, find the right words, and clear the air immediately. If you continue to feel pressure, at some point your scales are going to tip and then all bets are off.

SCORPIO Whatever it is, let it go. When faced with difficult or manipulative people, the Scorpio will brood until she gets home, have quite the temper tantrum—and then plot revenge! No matter how badly people behave, let go of your anger, it's the only way you'll truly enjoy being a bride. Remember you have to live with some of these people.

SAGITTARIUS Be honest *and* diplomatic. Nothing really bothers the easygoing Sag bride, but if people ask too much of you, you might just let them know exactly how their inappropriate request makes you feel. No matter how ridiculous it seems, there are tactful ways to say things that don't compromise your idealistic nature.

CAPRICORN Pick your battles wisely. You drive yourself hard and can hold others to your exacting standards. If a guest has the nerve to overstep your boundaries or a vendor does subpar work, you might just get *very* indignant. Choose your words (and attitude) carefully, know when to give in, and most of all, forgive and forget.

AQUARIUS Recognize people's limitations. You are an openminded bride. In your planning, you'll likely come across people who just don't get it. Instead of finding their ignorance contemptible and potentially starting an argument (which Aquarians sometimes find enjoyable), offer a creative compromise—or at least *yes* them with a smile as you go about your plans.

PISCES Don't try to please everyone. It's painful for you to be confronted with a pushy person or to have to say no. Use your strong, supportive fiancé as a buffer so you don't have to do the tough stuff alone. When dealing with anybody difficult, remember these magic words, "Let me run that by my groom first." Then process your feelings together.

Chapter *Five*

Before we get to the most important part of the planning, let's bring our attention to the other fun parties that lead up to getting married. Although you can have countless celebrations before your big day—engagement parties, bridal party brunches, even novelty parties—we're going to focus on the big three: The bridal shower, bachelorette party, and rehearsal dinner.

Way back when brides used to follow rules (what's that?), a bridal shower was a women-only luncheon where the bride was showered with gifts to fill the kitchen in her new home. Of course, the bachelorette party came along, because why should the guys have all the fun?! Now there are lingerie bridal showers, coed bachelor-bachelorette parties, and all sorts of hybrids of the two. Anything goes means that the distinction between events becomes a little blurred. The cool thing is that it's entirely up to you how many of the customs you wish to follow in the events leading up to your big day.

You might not be completely in charge of planning these events, but you still want these parties to reflect your signature style. Whether they're organized by your mom or your best friend, share the ideas within these pages. A few preplanning chats will guarantee wonderful parties that you can really enjoy! Relax, here's what you need to convey to those running the show.

■ The Bridal Shower

Bridal showers are usually the realm of close family and key members of the bridal party. Luncheons, gifts, games, and girlie things are standard fare, but you can get as creative as you want!

. Getting the bridal shower of your dreams depends upon a few things: how well those in charge know you, how well you communicate your desires, and how well they work together (and we already know that some signs are easier to work with than others!). You can't control other people but you can make sure they know where you're coming from. Here's a guide to your perfect bridal shower.

❏ ❏ Fire: Aries, Leo, Sagittarius

Aries and Leo brides want something big, lively, and impressive. This is the one time in your life that you get to celebrate your marriage and you want an event fit for a queen! Skip the standard luncheon at your aunt's house and ask that the event be held in a restaurant's private room or outdoor terrace. Have members of your bridal party decorate the place so it looks festive and beautiful. Aries wants eye-popping and colorful, something that screams bridal shower! Leo generally goes for something a little more subdued and monochromatic, like large bouquets of the same colored flowers.

Summer's Aries celebration sums it up perfectly: "My bridesmaids hosted a big tea party, with lots of sangria and flowers, hats and summer dresses—it was fantastic!" (Only at an Aries or Leo's tea party would the featured drink be sangria—you definitely know how to have a good time!)

Spontaneous Fire signs are good sports when it comes to surprises, but both Aries and Leo need to feel like you're dressed appropriately, so remind the powers that be who may be planning a surprise to keep that in mind. You don't much care about the food as long as people are having a good time.

Aries and Leo are outgoing and sentimental. You love receiving gifts and you love your friends and family even more. Make sure who-ever is hosting your party knows you are looking forward to warm moments and cherished memories. Summer's bridesmaids designed a wonderful memory book that was, in her words, "The most special thing ever." Everyone got a large page from a photo album and wrote down memories, drew pictures, or made photo collages. Guests who couldn't attend the party mailed their pages back in advance. As Summer says warmly, "My mom's page still makes me cry."

The Sag bridal shower is a lot more mellow, you love hanging out with your friends but can pass on the glitz and glam. You are much more at ease with a small backyard gathering. Sag Lisa had a lovely shower at the home of a member of her bridal party, "I was fine until gift time when everyone was saying all these nice things about me and the emotions kicked in—I was laughing and crying at the same time."

If you are uncomfortable with having a bridal shower, plan to skip this and have one combined bridal shower–bachelorette party, as Sagittarius Kawana did, "My mother tried to have a surprise party but couldn't pry enough telephone numbers from me." Another option for caring Archers: do something meaningful. Instead of presents for you, have everyone buy gifts for the local animal sanctuary and spend the day walking the dogs.

❏❏ Earth: Taurus, Virgo, Capricorn

Earth brides love their bridal showers. Gathering together old pals, college buddies, work colleagues, relatives, and those kin soon to be; enjoying their company, opening presents—you wouldn't miss it for the world!

Even though you're not planning your shower, it's important to you that those invited have a delicious meal, a welcoming place to sit, and a good time. Unless you have a wild Rising sign like Aries, Leo, Aquarius, or Gemini, that means no surprises, no offbeat locations, and no unusual food and drink your guests have never tasted before.

Earth brides enjoy following tradition. In different parts of the country that means different things. For Shannon, a Taurus in North Carolina, that meant having several showers—five to be exact. She had a lingerie shower thrown by her bridal party, one hosted by her mom's church friends at a local café, a work shower, one for relatives given by an aunt, and one from all her old neighborhood friends at a country club.

If the powers that be are planning to play games, make sure they know to keep them on the clean, lighthearted side. Earth girls are private, mindful, and a bit stubborn, you're not about to be tricked into revealing something you might regret later. At Shannon's second shower they added a creative twist to the classic bridal shower game that is perfect for the reserved Earth girl. Instead of focusing on the bride, they had all the women tell embarrassing stories from their own weddings. "Boy, did I hear some funny stories," Shannon says.

You can't stand surprises, and I'm sure your friends are aware of this already. Knowing the date for your shower and being able to prepare is the way to make an Earth girl feel most comfortable.

Having your friends and family go the extra mile and decorate the room with fresh flowers and tasteful crepe paper means a lot to you as well. "The two women hosting the shower made beautiful Gerber daisy centerpieces and napkin holders," recalls Shannon of her second shower. "And I was so happy they did because they inspired my bridesmaids' bouquets!"

Taurus loves getting just about any gift, Virgo and Capricorn like something useful and well made, but Earth girl's modest nature may make it hard for you to receive all that good stuff. As one Earth bride reveals, "it was great to see all my friends, but I did not enjoy sitting in the middle of the room and opening presents in front of everyone."

Some Taurus, Virgo, and Capricorns don't drop their practical, hardworking nature just for their bridal showers. If you are really busy or live far from home, you may choose not to have a shower at all. Combine it with the bachelorette or rehearsal dinner and you'll never feel like you've missed a thing!

An Unforgettable Unbachelorette Party

When her friends approached her about having a traditional bachelorette party, Dennie Hughes, an independent Aries and author of the book *Dateworthy,* balked—no way was she going to have a party with strippers, a lewd cake, and a list of what she considers demeaning tasks to perform.

Her best friend Gina, a Capricorn, found the perfect solution. "She came up with the idea of a Meet My Friends party," explains Dennie. "She said, 'You have so many great girlfriends you've talked about over the years that I've never met.' "

This is where a best friend who knows you well and has great taste comes in handy, no matter what her sign. Gina had about a dozen of Dennie's friends meet at the fountain in front of the famed Plaza Hotel in New York before loading into a limo for a night they'll talk about forever. Their first stop was a restaurant in Little Italy followed by dancing at a nightclub that spins music from the '70s, '80s, and '90s.

Fun, quality friendships are vital to warm Fire signs. "I realized when I looked around the room that this was about twenty-five years' worth of solid people in my life," says Dennie, "I got to tell all the girls about who was the oldest friend right down to the one that was my newest." The greatest thing about the night is that they all exchanged numbers and kept in touch. "They're all amazing, strong, interesting, smart women," she says proudly of her pack. "I definitely didn't want a bachelorette thing, but this was cool."

❏❏ Air: Gemini, Libra, Aquarius

As you already know, Air sign brides love a good opportunity to party. You're definitely not passing on your bridal shower like some others in the zodiac! Graceful and girlie, you want a lighthearted, fun event where friends and family can taste interesting snacks, drink unusual drinks, and maybe even play a few games.

The traditional luncheon is a great choice for Libra, sipping punch and nibbling on light, elegant fare in between lovely conversation is your idea of perfection. An afternoon high tea would be perfect for Gemini and Aquarius brides, who are always up for something new. Find an out-of-the-way teahouse that serves an assortment of teas with different courses that blend interesting flavors for your guests to try. You might even be up for a coed shower, if you can imagine your guyfriends with tea and mini-scones with raspberry-laced butter.

Air brides even like to play games as long as they are fast-moving, creative, and keep the group's attention. At Aquarius Louise's brunch, the hosts split up the group into little teams and gave them riddles to solve for little prizes. The fun games continued as winners got a chance to steal the little prizes from one another. "It really helped to set the mood among all the women who didn't know one another or even speak the same language," she says.

Like your Fire sign sisters, you are also up for a surprise party. (Are you ever *not* in the mood to socialize?) The thing you don't necessarily like about bridal showers: cheap, awkward gifts, things for your kitchen that you will never use, and ugly lingerie you will never wear. This is especially true for Gemini and Libras, who have exacting tastes; Aquarius brides might be more into the sisterhood of the affair to notice.

Of course you can't tell anyone what to get you and you certainly appreciate every gift, but you can make sure the host tells everyone where you are registered, and if asked, can produce a list of stores you like and items you need.

This is how one Gemini put it: "I really appreciated that [my mother and stepmother] organized the gift process. My major message to them was—please help me avoid receiving crap that I don't need and can't return!" Recent brides who have a pile of boxes in their basement say amen to that!

Air sign brides love reading and learning new things. A great gift for any Air bride is a box filled with index cards of recipes, well-wishes, and personal stories that they can thumb through forever. One Libra bride who had a very small shower received a recipe book and was thrilled to see recipes from many of her friends who couldn't make it that day. In a crafty twist perfect for the multitasking, creative Air sign, all the girls decorated the book during the luncheon.

□ □ Water: Cancer, Scorpio, Pisces

To a Water bride, a bridal shower is a momentous occasion. It's a once-in-a-lifetime opportunity to share your love and joy with those closest to you. For Pisces, Cancer, and many Scorpios, a ladies luncheon filled with your family and friends is all you've ever dreamed about. (The exception is the Scorpio, who finds this tradition superfluous. With a strong will and a mind of your own, it'll be downright impossible to convince that Water bride to have one at all!)

It would mean so much to have your best friend, sister, and mom work together to plan and decorate, just knowing that they're all playing such an important role warms your heart. It doesn't matter whether this shower is held in your aunt's house, your maid of honor's backyard, or an elegant restaurant, as long as everyone you adore is there. You'd love nothing more than to walk into a room filled with lovely bouquets of fresh flowers, be greeted with warm hugs and kisses, eat delicious food, and open gifts.

Pisces can handle the largest party, while the more private Cancer and Scorpio likes to keep it on the small side. Pisces Samantha had a whopping seventy-five people at her beautiful luncheon overlooking the water. Her sister, whom she affectionately calls Martha, created place cards out of little straw hats with ribbons and flowers—wonderful memories for such a sentimental sign.

Because water signs are supersensitive, your bridal party should be cautious when preparing games. Pisces is more apt to go along with some lighthearted fun; Cancer and Scorpio are a bit hesitant of what those games might reveal. There's nothing worse than being the guest of honor *and* being mortally embarrassed right before your own wedding.

Jenn, a Scorpio who chose to elope, even got in on the fun. "I am not a big fan of bridal showers. Even though I eloped, my friends decided that I was not robbing them of an opportunity to party, and so they planned a surprise bridal shower. Fortunately, I have wonderful, insightful friends who decided to forgo the whole women only, sit on chairs, and ooh and ah over the gifts party in exchange for a wild Hawaiian-themed party at a hip bar where all the guests wore leis and grass skirts and drank copious amounts of alcohol." Whoo-hoo—you go, girls!

Instead of gifts, her friends passed around a journal and had everyone write down memories and wishes for the happy couple. A Water sign bridal shower wouldn't be complete without one of these sentimental keepsakes. Make sure whoever is in charge understands how important this is to you. Whether it's a book of memories and photos from all of your guests or a stack of recipe cards, it's the gift you will cherish most from this special day.

When Customs Collide: Two Different Bridal Showers, One Very Confused Bride!

After reading stories from a diverse group of brides, it's clear that wedding customs vary from place to place. When one suburban New York Leo bride (who shall remain nameless!) got engaged to her Southern sweetheart, both her New York bridesmaids and her soon-to-be Southern in-laws threw her bridal showers—little did she know what she was getting herself into.

Her Southern shower was a casual open house, where, quite frankly, she was lost. "I'm welcoming guests, and then half-sitting and opening gifts, and then people are leaving, so I'm getting up to shake their hand, and then other people are arriving and I need to be introduced to them, then half-sit and open a gift—it was exhausting."

It's always uncomfortable when you don't know what to expect, but even more so for a Leo, who prides herself on her social grace and ease with her pack. How can you be the elegant guest of honor if you're unsure of what you're supposed to do?

"My New York shower was really fun, sexy, funky, and cosmopolitan," she says next. "It was a brunch held in a nightclub, and it was also cool because it was coed," this bride reveals. "As a Lioness, I never really mixed well with other women, most of my friends are guys, it would've been weird not to have them there." This fun-loving Leo enjoyed watching her friends and family mix and mingle. "And my fiancé had to wear that awful bow hat." She laughs. "Now *that's* love!"

The gifts also threw her. "The presents were not what I was expecting. I don't want to sound ungrateful because I know the customs are different." In her fiancé's part of the South, typical shower and wedding gifts consist of small kitchen items like a knife set or a spice rack. "No checks at the wedding, no overflowing table of china and crystal," she laments.

On the other hand, she did get a cookbook and a book on how to make love seven nights a week from two male college buddies. "It was nicely inscribed 'So you can cook and cook,' which I thought was really funny." There are definitely some benefits to having a coed shower.

▪ The Bachelorette Party

Once the sweet bridal shower is over and your family has had their turn, your best friends take over—now you're talking *fun!* Bachelorette parties run the gamut from a quiet dinner with your pals, to a visit to Chippendales, to barhopping while wearing a headpiece of pink tulle covered with tiny plastic body parts!

What exactly are you up for? Let's take a peek at your absolute perfect bachelorette party!

❑❑ Fire: Aries, Leo, Sagittarius

The term *bachelorette party* was invented for Fire sign brides—you love to laugh, dance, drink, and have a good time! Whether you're into wild and crazy or sophisticated and social, this is one party you are not going to pass up.

Because this night is so important to you, make sure people who know you best plan it—you have definite ideas of what you consider fun and what you consider beneath you. Having to sit through something you can't stand is the worst thing for a Fire sign, you'll go home feeling very upset that your last night of fun as a single woman was a complete waste of time. On the other hand, if this party is designed well, you'll love to get all dolled up and have an unforgettable evening that you can laugh about for the rest of your life.

Aries and Leos like a long night of partying with your friends, cool drinks, and great dancing. Choose a hip, edgy restaurant or bar to start the night off. Leo Mary Ellen's only request, "I wanted to go out dancing with my friends because I love to dance," but first her crew took her to see *Birdie's Bachelorette Party,* a show where she got on stage, sang karaoke, and drank a shot without using her hands, then they went to a club and danced all night.

On the flip side, Summer's B.P. was decidedly more mellow (for an Aries!). "I was not into going too crazy. A bunch of us girls got all dressed up and went to a funky restaurant downtown, drank, ate, and just had fun," she explains. "Lingerie was given, then I went home and had a slumber party with a few of the girls. We watched movies and stayed up late. It was perfect."

Sag can skip the pomp and circumstance for a down-to-earth dinner with your buds. If you want it to be festive, find an offbeat, cool place to gather. Not that you need the in crowd, you just need good music and the perfect vibe. That's exactly what Sag Kawana did, "A couple of my closest girlfriends and I had dinner, it was really nice."

Fire signs are risk-takers, it's not hard for you to grab the spotlight. Some Fire signs, especially Aries and Leos, see a fun list of tasks, like Mary Ellen's, as a rite of passage. You've probably put those friends who came before you up to some crazy antics as well and I'm sure you weren't easy on them. Although your pals should definitely know where you stand on this ahead of time so they don't show up with a pink feather boa decorated with condoms that one of them may ultimately end up wearing if you're just not that into it.

☐☐ Earth: Taurus, Virgo, Capricorn

Some Earth brides look forward to having a classic bachelorette party, some do quiet dinners with their friends, and some choose to skip this event altogether. Getting together with your loving pals is one of the things you value most about all the events leading up to getting married. Although that doesn't mean you like to go crazy. Earth personalities are on the laid-back side, you prefer to hang out with a few of your closest pals rather than gather up every female you've ever known for a wild night on the town.

Your perfect night involves sitting for a three-course dinner at a restaurant that serves really good food, sharing several bottles of wine or champagne, seeing good friends, and reminiscing about old times. That's exactly what Virgo Heather went for. "We did have a great, what the English call a hen, party. Two nights before the wedding, I met with my closest ten female friends for a raucous dinner and drinks at the Cowgirl Hall of Fame, in Santa Fe."

Taurus Shannon had the perfect Earth bachelorette shindig that was both relaxing and fun. Ten girls gathered at her parents' beach house for the weekend. They went for a jog in the morning, played bocce ball, then lay in the sun all day. "The goal was to get a good tan for the wedding!" explains Shannon. (Warning: Do not try this at home without sunscreen and a strapless bikini.)

Her matrons of honor cooked up a scrumptious brunch, followed by her lingerie shower, "Which I have to admit was fun, but a little embarrassing," this bride declares. That night they went out for dinner and dancing. "It was a nice, relaxing weekend—unlike most bachelorette parties," says Shannon. Spoken like a true Earth bride.

Bridesmaids beware: Earth signs don't like to be blindsided or flustered. Lists of humorous and humiliating tasks, eye-catching bachelorette headgear, suggestive accessories—this can be the stuff of nightmares for such a reserved element. Although, Earth girls do enjoy following classic traditions, so your friends might just be able to get away with this if you are prepared for the occasion!

This is especially true for those with an Aries, Leo, Aquarius, or Gemini Rising, such as the irreverent Capricorn Andee, who is a little edgier than most. "We had a very hilarious evening at New York City's finest all-male strip club, Hunkamania, which I must admit, turned out to be far classier a joint than I had expected," exclaims the sophisticated city girl. "Of course I was all dolled up in the typical bachelorette paraphernalia and everyone enjoyed quite a bit of champagne." If I didn't get this straight from the horse's mouth, I might never have believed it!

❏❏ Air: Gemini, Libra, Aquarius

Fun, social, and sophisticated Air brides enjoy any occasion to get together with the girls and your bachelorette party is no exception. You love hanging out, looking good, sipping cool drinks, tasting sophisticated food, and dancing the night away.

Take Louise's exotic-destination bachelorette evening of dinner and dancing. Held near her sister's home near a resort town, it drew the girls not only for the party but for a vacation, as well. "I had fun seeing women I hadn't been with in a long time—we are now spread out across the United States," says this Aquarius to whom sisterhood is everything.

Air signs love to talk fast, move quickly, and get bored at the drop of a hat. Since you love hip bars and restaurants and enjoy a whirlwind of activity, tell your friends to rent a limo so you can hop all over town. Your perfect evening starts at the bar of the hottest hotel. After all the girls have gathered, move on to dinner at a happening restaurant, then follow it by dancing and more drinks at yet another cool joint.

The edgier Gemini and Aquarius might be up for the typical bachelorette fun along the way—a list of crazy things to do, a tiara of pink tulle,
and tasteful body shots off a convenient male bar patron. Libra, on the
other hand, would never be caught dead doing something uncouth. The
Scales stay balanced with socially graceful activities such as dinner and
dancing. You might be up for a little something racy after a few drinks,
but taking a lemon from some guy's mouth or asking him for his under-
wear is out of the question!

Typical Air signs love to hang out in large packs—unless you have a
Taurus, Virgo, Capricorn, Cancer, or Scorpio Rising, then you might
enjoy a lively but more low-key evening. One Gemini with a Scorpio
Rising had a few friends sleep over for a bachelorette weekend that was
at times both mellow and energizing. "Friday night was a sushi feast
with tons of champagne. Saturday was spent getting manicures, pedi-
cures, and lunch," says this Gemini.

This is where it gets wild. "My bridesmaid organized a sex toy party
and a sales representative came to provide a workshop about all the
items. It was silly, educational, chatty, and fun," she recalls. Oh, how
Air signs love to learn new things! Afterwards they headed to a cool
dinner, then a dance club. "The night ended at two A.M. with egg and
cheese sandwiches and silly games." Specially created fill-in-the-blank
bridal Mad-Libs—the perfect game for an inebriated Air sign bride
and her pals!

❏❏ Water: Cancer, Scorpio, Pisces

Most Water signs are totally into having a bachelorette party—the exception being the occasional Scorpio to whom this tradition means
nothing—although each Water sign has their own taste when it comes
to this shindig. The flexible Pisces is more apt to go along with some
racy fun and games; Fish just have an easy time expressing feelings in
front of people, whether we're talking about joy or embarrassment!

Although Cancer likes to follow established customs, you are a private soul and can be concerned about what your friends might try to pull. You can get mortally embarrassed at the drop of a hat, so if your friends are set on playing some raunchy games, keep the party to a small group you are truly comfortable with.

Scorpios enjoy gathering with their girls, but are so independent and private that wearing the typical accessories and playing games is absolutely out of the question! Make sure your friends tread lightly around this subject. A night hanging out at a hip dark bar tucked away behind an unmarked door is all you'll ever want in a B.P.

Knowing who you are and what you can handle is definitely a good thing. For Pisces, a traditional Texas bachelorette party like Kristye's is perfect. "My matron of honor showed up with the veil with the little remarks on the tulle and she made me a list of things I had to do."

One thing on the list was to go out on a balcony overlooking the San Antonio River Walk and scream out at the top of her lungs, *"I'm getting married!"* Kristye recalls, "When I did that a guy at the very bottom yelled back, 'I'm sorry!' " That is a wonderful fun memory! It helps that her friends and bridal party are all tender, loyal Taurus girls who make her feel safe and instinctively know how far they can push all this fun.

For a Cancer bride, a lively but intimate dinner works best, at a down-to-earth place where you can sit for hours and eat nourishing food, drink festive drinks, and hang out with the girls. "We went to this Mexican place on the Lower East Side, hit some bars, then ended up at this grungy dance club," says Nina, a Cancer.

Cancer girls can handle some good-natured ribbing, but your friends should know where you stand on all the bachelorette accoutrements. "My maid of honor made me penis-shaped cupcakes, which was pretty funny," and she did wear a red veil and boa throughout the evening. "It wasn't a particularly wild night out," recalls Nina, "but there was the usual assortment of sex gifts." It's a good thing she opened them sitting down with a trusted group of pals—after a few margaritas!

When Bridesmaids Go Wild!

Traditional bachelorette parties are an opportunity to do some memorable and wacky things we may not get to (or want to) do ever again. Take Samantha, a delicate, sophisticated Pisces, who was put in some very well-planned compromising positions by her best friends, all in the name of fun.

"I got an invitation via e-mail to be ready, but I didn't know who it came from," this fashionista recalls. Her three best friends surprised her at her apartment for a scavenger hunt. "They gave me clues and I had to guess where we were going."

They went around the neighborhood, first to her favorite doughnut shop (pretty innocuous), then to her groom's favorite bar (to do a blow job shot!), then to Blockbuster (to rent a movie on sex!). "It was all about embarrassing me," a state that's downright scary for the sensitive Fish. "I felt like I was in a sorority getting hazed," says Samantha in jest.

Along the way they stopped at a friend's place where they gave her two posterboards to wear. "On the front it was a picture of my husband with a drink in his hand and on the back it said BRIDEZILLA." The last stop of the scavenger hunt was a bowling alley where the rest of her bridal party was waiting. "I had to bowl with the sign on, it was hysterical."

The games were followed by a serious night of fun. "I'm really into new and trendy places," this city girl relates. After a champagne toast at her place, her friends took her to dinner at a cool restaurant, then to a hot new lounge for drinks and dancing—a reward for being such a good sport.

"I have a really good group of friends; we are superclose," Samantha says fondly. "It was a really fun bachelorette party."

■ The Rehearsal Dinner

For some, the rehearsal dinner is an intimate gathering, for others, it's a reception that includes the bridal party, extended family, and out-of-town guests as well. There's no standard rule on who should plan this event, on some occasions it's the parents of the groom, for others it's the parents of the bride—and once in a while the bride and groom plan and host their own rehearsal dinner.

Of course, who is in charge of planning this party will create the style of the event, but if you have a say, here's a guide for what to include in the plans.

◻◻ Fire: Aries, Leo, Sagittarius

It is almost as exciting for a Fire sign to think about the rehearsal dinner as it is to think about the wedding. The fun-loving Fire signs know that the minute you hit that rehearsal your wedding festivities begin.

Aries and Leo want a special party that is both unusual yet inviting, something that will wow your guests and make them feel welcomed at the same time. You love to share your happiness with others, so make this a large, casual celebration, one where you can let your hair down a bit and have some fun.

Take your time shopping for the perfect outfit, too! If you've got the funds, splurge a little. After all, this is the start of your wedding weekend and you want to make a great first impression on your friends and family.

With tons of great ideas, it's hard for Aries and Leo to give up control of this dinner no matter how much other planning you have to do. It's very generous of your parents or in-laws to want to give this dinner to you as a gift, but make sure they know that you're looking forward to some input when it comes to the decisions. They should at least know to run key elements by you before setting them in stone.

Skip the classic restaurant for one with a sophisticated theme or interesting location that will entertain your guests. Spend some time thinking about how to decorate the room to make it yours for the evening—without adding personal touches, it's just going to look like an ordinary restaurant and not *your* rehearsal dinner!

"Being the Aries that I am," says Summer, "we hosted this event, too." No surprise there! "We hosted it at a lovely little French restaurant around the corner from where we were married. Since our wedding was totally old-world romantic, we went more modern with our decor—Red Envelope boxes for everyone and bamboo centerpieces—and had a really rich dinner."

Sagittarius, as usual, is another story. Since you're more apt to have an unusual wedding, you might not require the standard rehearsal and rehearsal dinner. That's exactly what Sag Kawana and her groom Joe did—running off for a destination wedding in Jamaica to skip the stress. "We did a lot of partying at the resort before the wedding," she says, but none of it was an official rehearsal dinner, which was just the way they wanted it.

Sagittarius bride, if you are having a classic wedding with a rehearsal, make your dinner a casual, outdoorsy gathering, like a barbecue at a local lake or a buffet out on a terrace with great views; add an acoustic guitar or steel band as background music.

Earth: Taurus, Virgo, Capricorn

Earth brides cherish their rehearsal dinner. Sharing a gentle hug with your best friends, showering warm words on your parents, eating a good meal—these are the things that mean the most to the tender and loving Earth sign.

Other elements want to make this a big kickoff celebration, but Earth girls are more inclined to have an intimate, relaxed gathering, where you can sit down and have an actual conversation with the family members and out-of-town guests you might not have seen for a while. As excited as you are about your quickly coming nuptials, you'd rather save the bulk of your energy for the big day.

The garden of a quiet restaurant, the backroom of a century-old inn, the home of a close family friend—these are perfect locations to sit down and chill after what might be an exciting and potentially distressing rehearsal. A location where you don't have to feel out of place or all dolled up in uncomfortable clothes (you'll get enough of those in the morning).

Now it's time to think about decoration. Being surrounded by loads of plants, flowers, and well-executed sentimental photo collages is a must for the nature-loving element. Especially for the hardworking ambitious Earth brides who choose to have a more formal rehearsal dinner, you'd never consider leaving a room bare.

You love diving into the details and corralling your loyal group of friends to help in the creations. That's exactly what Taurus Shannon did for her Carolina-themed rehearsal dinner, engaging her soon-to-be mother-in-law's photographer friend to shoot artistic photos of the happy couple around historic Chapel Hill for picture centerpieces and table names. Shannon adds, "We plan to have a slide show of pictures from our youth—including old pictures of friends, too." That is sure to be a crowd-pleaser!

Food is very important to the Earth bride as well. You want a delicious and satisfying meal that people can sink their teeth into. Take Taurus Aviva's warm and cozy dinner. "We had a wonderful rehearsal dinner, where we went over the details of the ceremony and then had an amazing home-cooked meal at the house of my mother's boyfriend," says Aviva. "Very elegant but laid-back." A perfect evening for the mellow Earth bride.

And the rehearsal dinner just wouldn't be a rehearsal dinner without some heartfelt speeches. Why not invite some close family and friends to share a few words at this informal celebration who ordinarily wouldn't speak during the wedding? They'll feel honored to have a voice and you'll always remember the wonderful things they say.

The Greatest Bachelor Party in the History of Weddings——Hint: No Strippers!

The phrase *bachelor party* sends a shiver down the spine of brides everywhere, but it doesn't have to be that way. Let's take a look at one modern, wholesome, and totally guy's-guy party at which the gambling, cigar smoking, and stripping were conspicuously absent!

"I had a bachelor day," says Andrew, the tender Virgo you first read about in chapter 3. It started with his best man and groomsmen at a sports facility where they got to know each other by rock climbing and playing basketball. "We had some cocktails, hung out in the pool and Jacuzzi, just the guys," Andrew recalls. "Then I had my bachelor party with the rest of my hooligans."

Both brides and grooms shouldn't feel pressured to do the traditional bachelor-bachelorette thing; it's an opportunity to gather all your friends and do what's memorable to you. "As a musician," Andrew said, "I thought, 'what would I like to do?' I wanted to go jam." So after dinner at his favorite steak house with all his pals, his musician friends rented a studio. "We all got together with instruments and just jammed all night."

"At least that's what they say," his Cancer bride, Leila, jokes.

❑❑ Air: Gemini, Libra, Aquarius

After the wild, spontaneous fun of the bridal shower and bachelorette parties, Air brides now get to be the social sophisticates they were born to be. While some brides may be nervous by now, this is the beginning of your wedding celebration, you are truly looking forward to your rehearsal and rehearsal dinner.

This is where I usually say something about how elegant Libra likes things one way and edgy Gemini and Aquarius like things another, but not when it comes to the rehearsal dinner. All Air signs are in complete agreement on this one: This dinner party must be a refined, lively social event.

If you have any say, pick a lovely restaurant near to your church or reception site. One with beautiful decor and a light and airy feel that has an interesting menu and really good food. This isn't the quiet before the storm, it's the beginning of your wedding weekend. Some signs may want to hide, but for you, gracefully entertaining your guests, chatting the night away with a drink in hand is both relaxing and energizing—medicine for your Air sign soul!

After all the months of stressful planning, this rehearsal dinner should be a nice release. Make sure there is enough room in the restaurant and the budget for extra heads so you can invite not only your immediate family and bridal party, but anyone who you feel very close to.

That includes any friends who've been with you through this process that might not be members of the bridal party, extended family, and of course, out-of-town guests. Two close friends sang Aquarius Patty and her groom Todd a heartfelt duet at their rehearsal dinner. "It was amazing," says Patty, "Aquarians are blessed with the best of friends!"

This a chance to really appreciate all the people who mean the most in your life, so plan some informal toasts or speeches that might not fit into the wedding day. That's exactly what Gemini Elizabeth and her groom Eric did when they hosted their rehearsal dinner. "Both our fathers planned very heartfelt speeches and delivered them with emotion," she says, "this was one of my favorite moments during the whole wedding weekend."

Air signs are creative thinkers and problem solvers; to include the rest of the out-of-town guests without feeling the burden of paying for dinner, or for those who wish to have a more intimate meal yet still experience a satisfying party, consider Elizabeth and Eric's solution. "We invited the rest of the wedding guests who were staying in town on Friday night to stop by for coffee and dessert on the veranda, while the bar remained open in the restaurant." Good thinking, Air sister!

❑ ❑ Water: Cancer, Scorpio, Pisces

For a Water sign the rehearsal dinner borders on a spiritual experience! Nothing is completely smooth sailing with the sensitive, emotional Water element. Along with all the joy this stage of your life has brought, you've had your ups and downs with your bridal party, emotional moments with your groom, and run-ins with the folks.

Now that you've finally made it, it's time to breathe easy. After the nervous excitement of the rehearsal, you just can't wait to spend quality time with your family and close friends; this dinner is truly a celebration.

Water signs don't really care where this party is held or who hosts it as long as it's a warm and loving evening. This is especially true for the more flexible Cancer and Pisces who just want everyone to get along. Scorpio, on the other hand, likes to have some nod of approval; you just like to know what's going on and you don't like surprises.

All Water signs prefer an intimate gathering over some huge festivity. Scorpio wants to feel safe to concentrate on the things that mean the most to you (like the wedding!). Cancer's love of all things nurturing makes the food a priority; it doesn't have to be lavish and expensive as long as it's a good quality meal. Pisces can be more into creating an illusion (and having a good drink after climbing this hurdle!).

Take Pisces Kristye's well-planned rehearsal dinner held at a perfectly chosen cowboy-themed steak house that kicked off her country-themed weekend. The bridal party all wore denim, she wore a shirt that said BRIDE, all the bridesmaids wore a shirt that said BRIDESMAID, and the matron of honor wore a shirt with her title as well. Pisces can really get into the role as did the rest of the guests. "Everyone else dressed in Western attire," says Kristye, "kind of cowboy giddy-up."

Another vital aspect to the rehearsal dinner of a Water sign: the heartfelt speeches. It doesn't matter if people get up and make long prepared toasts or let their emotions lead to spontaneous gestures of affection, these are the memories you will most cherish. Make sure you walk around and exchange warm words with everyone there, telling them how much their presence in your life has meant to you throughout the years.

Take Cancer Leila and her groom Andrew's rehearsal dinner at a family-style Italian restaurant on Manhattan's Upper West Side. In addition to lots of loving toasts, "Andrew's family surprised him by singing a rehearsed song they had been working on—very fun!" exclaims Leila. What does she remember most about the occasion? "Lots

of family and friends surrounding us with sincere love and support."
Spoken like a true Water sign!

How to Get Along with Your Mother (and Mother-in-Law) Under Any Circumstances

We all know that dealing with our parents and their issues isn't always easy. Let's face it, every family has their stuff! During this stressful time in your life, if you're getting squeezed from all sides, instead of receiving unconditional love, then this is the list for you.

When your mother starts demanding the best tables for her guests or your mother-in-law wants total control of the rehearsal dinner, here is exactly what to do to calm them down. It's the answer to the age-old question, "Can't we all just get along?"

ARIES   This is a mother who wants to play a big role and loves to get attention. Let her know that you're thrilled she wants to be involved, and that you'd like to give her the job of (fill in the blank!). Then set clear boundaries of what's your job and what's hers—and let her run with it. Always be excited to see her and hear about her plans. She might need to be reminded once in a while that compromise is the best solution. For more, read Leo.

TAURUS   Your loving mother definitely has her own opinions on how things should be done. She loves the traditions of weddings and is very budget-conscious. She may try to slow you down, make sure you're making the right decisions, and even try to change your mind. Give her lots of hugs, go over details often, and let her see that you've got a good head on your shoulders. Compromise, if it's her money; that's very important to her.

GEMINI   This chatty mom is pretty easy to get along with. All she wants to do is share her wonderful ideas with you (all the time). If that's wearing on you, make a special date each week that you can sit down and talk. In between just remind her that you're busy and you're looking forward to hearing her great ideas next week. Give her a mother of the bride notebook and pen, and tell her to write it all down!

CANCER This doting mother's only goal is to make sure you're feeling nurtured and loved. She may need to be involved in everything from the dress shopping to the rehearsal dinner. If you like all this mothering, great. If not, then make sure you tell her how much you love her and how much she means to you before and after you tell her that you'd like to make some of these plans on your own. Also read Scorpio.

LEO A Leo mother is loads of fun, but likes to be recognized for her important role in your wedding. Let her choose which party or project she wants to be in charge of and make sure she knows who is in charge of the others. She's a very generous mother when she feels like she's getting the respect she deserves. Whatever you do, don't take a job away or minimize her role. When she feels dissed, she'll get difficult.

VIRGO This mother is the helping queen, she can never do enough for her baby. Let her do all the legwork (so you don't have to), then present her findings for discussion—just appreciate her every effort. Unfortunately Virgo can get nitpicky. Don't take *anything* she says personally. Calm her with words like "Don't worry, no one is going to notice that," "It's all going to work out fine," and "Let's find you something else to do."

LIBRA Your mother just wants everything to be gracious and everyone to get along well. Since she's more of a diplomat than most, she may be trying to calm *you* down. Honor her by making sure her corsage is beautiful, her guests are treated well, and that responsibilities of the mothers are split fairly. If she gets upset about something, offer compromises that rebalance the situation, and it will blow over quickly.

SCORPIO This is one loving and overprotective mother. Remind her often that in getting married you are changing your priorities and that someone else is stepping in to take care of you—and start this early. Once she knows you love and appreciate her, you can begin to tell her when you need help and when you prefer to do something on your own. She's difficult to calm once upset, so ask her what you can do to help her let it go.

SAGITTARIUS This easygoing mom is all about freedom—for you and for her. As long as she believes you are making the right decision, she'll be very happy to show up where and when you tell her. Instead of giving her a whole party to organize, give her a list of guests to welcome and socialize with. If you need more from her, ask, she may just be giving you space because she doesn't want to intrude.

CAPRICORN This mom raised you to be independent, but may still think she knows best—especially if she's paying for the wedding. Work with her by doling out specific items in the budget to different people. If she knows her cash is going to pay for the food and the flowers, she may not wrestle over other details. Set boundaries by using phrases such as "I love you," "I'm an adult capable of making my own decisions," and "This is what I prefer."

AQUARIUS If your mom is an Aquarius, thank your lucky stars. She's generous, fun-loving, and will rarely tell you what to do. Give her a party to plan and she'll be very happy. On the off chance she feels strongly about something, recognize how much she's given you and make a compromise. A simple "We obviously have a difference of opinion here, let's find a solution that works for both of us" will keep everything running smoothly.

PISCES This devoted mother only wants to make sure you're taken care of, which is lovely, but may come across as a bit attached or needy. Gently tell her you love her, that you'd like to take care of some details on your own, and that you'll keep her in the loop. On your own schedule, call her or send her little e-mails letting her know you love her and that everything is okay. (Do this often or she may call you!) Also read Scorpio.

Chapter

From unconventionally spiritual to traditionally religious, understated elegance to drama queen, each sign has her own unique way of saying "I do." Instead of going with the standard customs, this is the perfect time for you to get creative. More and more brides are finding the confidence and individuality to make the ceremony their own.

Start your marriage off in a way that's true to your style. Explore your astrological essence and create a ritual that completely reflects who you are. In this chapter you'll find wonderful suggestions for vows, readings, and processional music to add flair and flavor to this important component of your special day.

■ Officiant and Ritual

Along with figuring out whether you want to get married beside a lake or in a synagogue, you have to decide what type of officiant you want to marry you and what sort of rituals you are both comfortable with. Your religion and culture can have some impact on how you make it legal, but your astrological personality will have a lot to do with it as well. Listen to the wisdom of your sign.

❏❏ Fire: Aries, Leo, Sagittarius

As an independent, passionate woman you enjoy expressing your individuality in dramatic fashion—and your special day is no different. Your ceremony must reflect that fiery nature and make a statement for all to remember.

Aries, instead of the standard "I dos," work with a modern nondenominational officiant to craft a unique rite of passage from start to finish. A slightly more conventional Leo might choose a traditional setting and then add those unique personal touches that set you apart, like an intricate candlelit processional. On the other hand, Sag likes uncomplicated, lighthearted rituals that display the idealistic beliefs you hold so dear. Ask yourself, What about this ceremony is important to me? And go from there.

Aries Summer avoided religious traditions and gender roles by choosing a female interfaith minister and marrying at the reception site. "We met with Lori Sue five or six times to talk about what we wanted to accomplish in the ceremony. It felt very personal."

It was important for religious Leo Mary Ellen to get married in a church, but she made the ceremony her own by having readings for happily married couples to recite together, something she had to petition the deacon to achieve. "It meant a lot to me to have family in it as much as possible," she says.

Sag's easygoing nature is evident whether they marry on the beach or in a house of worship. Lisa married in the church where Glen's childhood friend is the minister. "He told stories of when they were growing up; we laughed and joked; it was so nice."

❏❏ Earth: Taurus, Virgo, Capricorn

Experiencing familiar customs brings the Earth bride comfort on a day when you can be a bit sensitive to uncertainty. Choose a caring officiant and meet with her several times to go over each aspect of your ceremony. Leave nothing to chance or you may have a mini-meltdown when suddenly the idea of not being in control becomes all too real.

The unspoken aspects of the ceremony can be more important than what's said to the sometimes reserved Earth girl, like being close to nature. This was true for both Taurus Aviva, who wanted an outdoor ceremony, and Virgo Heather, whose ceremony was held in a forest.

Aviva chose a justice of the peace, as she and her husband don't practice the religion of her family. "I thought that would be perfect, that way there's no denomination." But Taurus girls like a simple, down-to-earth ritual, no matter who is performing it. As Aviva puts it, "I didn't want a fuss."

The detail-oriented Virgo loves sifting through readings, analyzing words, and creating the perfect rite of passage. "We had a quiet ceremony that allowed us both to have the very private moment that we needed," says Heather. "But I worked on the ritual, because I am who I am, for nine months."

A Capricorn bride, the most conventional Earth sign, likes a traditional service in an awe-inspiring location that reflects your ambitious, perfectionistic tendencies. For Capricorn Andee that translated to a little chapel on the lush island of Kauai. Why go five thousand miles away from home? Because it's halfway between New York and Australia, her groom's native country. A decision both enterprising and practical—how positively Earthy of her!

❏❏ Air: Gemini, Libra, Aquarius

Air sign brides are the thinkers of the zodiac, it's hard for you to commit to something you don't believe in. Before you make a commitment to an officiant or any particular type of ceremony, analyze your options and decide what's important to you. When you interview clergy, discuss these beliefs and find one that will incorporate your ideas into the ritual.

Elizabeth and her groom, Eric, chose a female justice of the peace, something that was important to this Gemini bride. "She was amazing," says Elizabeth. "I really wanted a woman. She's very lovely, very calming, and very sophisticated." Exactly what an Air sign needs to help craft the perfect ceremony.

We already know Air sign brides are untraditional trendsetters, but that's not to say every Air sign bride is automatically going to have an unconventional ceremony. Have a traditional ceremony and add Air touches by choosing unusual readings, swapping gender roles, or reinterpreting old customs. Sari and Victor, a Libra and Aquarius couple did just that with their Jewish ceremony by adding a Tish, a traditional male roast where the groom discusses a lesson from the Bible. To mix things up, Victor included all the guests, both men and women, for his informal chat.

Be warned that you might not be able to have it both ways. An Aquarius bride I spoke to was having problems convincing her rather traditional Presbyterian minister to allow her talented friends to sing a love song, because it wasn't religious. If you butt heads with your officiant, use your cunning charm to outwit him!

❑ ❑ Water: Cancer, Scorpio, Pisces

As with every element, there are some Water sign brides who fall on the traditional side and some who are completely untraditional in their approach to a marriage ceremony, the one thing you all have in common is your emotions; you're all about feeling connected.

Take the unconventional Scorpio who absolutely can't commit to something she doesn't believe. Harness your bold, fearless nature and you are undaunted in your pursuit of the perfect ritual. Scorpio Emily did just that, "I drove my mother insane, we didn't want a religious ceremony, we didn't want a pastor. I kept thinking, 'Why do I want someone to be a part of this incredible personal moment in our lives that doesn't even know us?'" She ended up asking her dramatic actor-writer brother-in-law to get ordained just for their special day.

Think about what rituals reflect your spirituality. Kristye, a Pisces, knew she wanted to be married in a church, but didn't quite feel comfortable with the one she grew up in. "We went church-hopping until we found a church we could raise our kids in." One with a reverend who is both religious and spiritual, something that is very important to her.

Water signs are private people, unless you have a Moon sign that just loves to share, so choosing a religious ceremony is a great way to hide from the emotional hot seat. One Cancer had a beautiful Russian Orthodox ceremony and got away with speaking just once. "I was terrified the whole time," she reveals. They considered other options, but thank goodness she knew herself well enough to make the right decision.

▪ Readings and Vows

After you've got the basics of the ceremony down, you get to pick the readings and vows that best suit you as a couple. Your astrological sign has a lot to do with the flavor of your readings but has the most impact in the vows that you recite.

The more private signs will choose short traditional vows led by your officiant while couples with bolder astrology enjoy writing their own. Still others fall somewhere in between, passing up traditional vows to create a modern common pledge they can recite that reflects their shared values. What kinds of readings and promises are you most comfortable with? Read your element to find out.

❏❏ Fire: Aries, Leo, Sagittarius

Fire sign bride, just because you are independent and outgoing doesn't necessarily mean you like to get all mushy and gushy and express your deepest feelings in front of a crowd. In fact, writing your own vows is one aspect of a wedding many Fire brides can skip. You like the ritual to be meaningful but short and the party long!

If you are creating a modern vow to recite, there are some phrases that express your astrological nature. Aries likes an "Equal partnership to encourage each other's growth and self-expression." Leo speaks in sweeping romantic phrases such as "You are the light of my life and the center of my world," while Sag likes to make a more light-hearted commitment: "My best friend, I want to share the rest of my life with you."

Two great quotes that embody Fire love: "We love because it is the only true adventure," written by Nikki Giovanni, and one by Tagore, "Let my love, like sunshine, surround you, and illuminate your freedom." A great biblical reading that shares many Fire sign ideals are the words from 1 John 3:18, "Let us love in deed and truth and not merely talk about it," and 1 John 4:18, "There is no fear in love, but perfect love casts out fear."

In contrast are the nonreligious words of Shamaan Ochum Climbing Eagle: "Keep your passion alive—it will warm you when the world around you grows cold. It will not allow comfortable familiarity to rob you of that special glow that comes with loving deeply."

❑ ❑ **Earth: Taurus, Virgo, Capricorn**

Earth brides are so private and tender that writing your own vows isn't appealing. Instead, read a book on the many traditional vows available and pick the one that speaks most to you as a couple.

If you have an Aries, Gemini, or Pisces Moon, and you're comfortable expressing yourself, then here are the phrases for you. Taurus wishes to "create a beautiful home together, that we may love and support each other for the rest of our lives." For Virgo and Capricorn it's "nurturing each other's dreams, creating shared goals, and commitment to family."

Sarah Bernhardt's "Your words are my food, your breath my wine. You are everything to me," and Antoine de Saint-Exupéry's "Love does not consist of gazing at each other, but in looking outward together in the same direction," are quotes that perfectly reflect the Earth bride's marriage. Two biblical verses from Ecclesiastes also share that ideal. Excerpts include, "If one falls, the other will lift up his companion. So also, if two lie together, they keep each other warm," taken from 4:10–11, and these words from 9:7–9, "Go, eat your bread with enjoyment, and drink your wine with a merry heart. Enjoy life with the wife whom you love."

The following highlight from *The Art of a Good Marriage II* by Wilferd Arlan Peterson is a wonderful way to express your Earth nature: "Across the years I'll walk with you, in deep green forest, on shores of sand, and when our time on Earth is through, in heaven, too, you will have my hand."

❑❑ Air: Gemini, Libra, Aquarius

Air sign brides differ on their views of vows and readings. Gemini thoroughly enjoys finding the perfect words. The Aquarius bride is more into the party, yet still needs to express her unconventional nature through speech, and Libras just want whatever is said to sound beautiful.

For vows, Gemini honors her love with phrases such as "I love your kind and generous spirit and the way you make me laugh." A simple "You complete me" or "I love you more every day" works well for the gracious Libra, and Aquarius likes to talk companionship: "Through friendship, through love, through good times and bad—we are greater together than we ever can be apart."

These words by Rumi perfectly reflect the Air sign's essence, "Love is the energizing elixir of the universe, the cause and effect of all harmonies," as does this candid quote by Paul Valery, "Love is being stupid together." One Bible verse that speaks to your philosophy is 1 Corinthians 13:1–8 of which verses 4–7 are most popular: "Love is patient; love is kind; Love is not envious or boastful or arrogant or rude. It does not insist on its own way; it is not irritable or resentful; it does not rejoice in wrongdoings but rejoices in the truth. It bears all things, believes all things, hopes all things, endures all things."

Finally, this excerpt from Kahlil Gibran's *The Prophet* is a perfect nonreligious choice.

You shall be together when the wings of death scatter your days.

Ay, you shall be together even in your silent memory.

But let there be spaces in your togetherness,

and let the winds of the heaven dance between you.

◻◻ Water: Cancer, Scorpio, Pisces

Vows and readings are where romantic Water signs shine, especially Pisces who, like her Cancer and Scorpio sisters, feels everything deeply, yet has the easiest time expressing those feelings in words.

Depending upon your Moon sign, you might choose to create a short vow that is meaningful yet not too revealing. Here are the phrases important to your astrological nature. Pisces likes sweet and sentimental: "Your love makes my heart sing" and "With you in my life, all things are possible." Cancer wants to remind her groom: "Your love supports me and nurtures me; you are a safe haven for my soul." Scorpio expresses it this way: "I love you with all my heart and all my being."

Two quotes that are perfect reflections of the Water essence: "Where there is love there is life," spoken by Mahatma Gandhi and this one by Antoine de Saint-Exupéry, "It is only with the heart that one can see rightly: What is essential is invisible to the eye." The perfect Bible verses for a traditional Water sign are the many great excerpts from the Song of Solomon: "Set me as a seal upon your heart, as a seal upon your arm," or "Many waters cannot quench love, neither can floods drown it," and "I have found whom my soul loves."

Lastly, Rumi, one of the most poetic writers, is a great choice for a reading. Here is just one of his many works: "Apart from Love, everything passes away. The way to Heaven is in your heart. Open and lift the wings of Love! When Love's wings are strong, you need no ladder."

The Most Powerful Twelve-Minute Ceremony
Ever Created

Elizabeth and Eric have been together since college. A Gemini and a Virgo, they are both independent thinkers, who love to learn, write, talk, and analyze—well—everything.

When it came time to tying the knot, these voracious readers and writers didn't take the ceremony lightly. Once they found their officiant, they started reading—books on vows, poetry, wedding poems, traditional wedding prayers, and not so traditional wedding prayers. As Eric, the Virgo micromanager says, "I must've tabbed twenty-five books." Then they created their ceremony piecemeal.

"We wanted all of the attendees to say something," affirms Elizabeth, the word-loving Gemini. So they printed out a favorite poem for all to read. "We wanted them to be clear that they had a responsibility to be our community and be a supportive network for us in the future, because we know that that's a huge piece of being a family."

They lovingly parceled out the lines of another poem to each of their parents and grandparents. "Eric and I have been in each other's lives for so long, we've been around for the births of nieces and nephews and the deaths of family members," Elizabeth relates. "It was really nice that our families were able to say, 'You've always been this to us, but now we are proud to officially have you be this to us as well.'"

And how did all their hard work pay off? "I think we were both surprised," says Eric. "We had put a lot of thought into it, but we didn't know exactly how we were going to feel when our parents and grandparents were saying the things that we had written. Watching people's reaction to it, that was pretty powerful."

There was a heavy rain shower the day of their outdoor wedding that miraculously cleared a few minutes before the ceremony. The months of writing worked out better than they could've expected. In addition to one hundred guests, they had butterflies and rainbows to mark the occasion. "The sun actually came out while we were saying our vows," Eric recalls.

John Milton couldn't have written a better beginning.

■ Creating the Perfect Ambience

You've booked your location and you are busy writing your vows, but there's so much more to the ceremony than just words, rings, and a celebrant in black robes. Before we take a look at each of the different design elements involved in a ceremony, let's first envision how they work together to form a wedding unique to you.

Creating a special mood for your guests involves putting together the color of the bridemaids' dresses, the flowers, the lighting, and the music. Setting the perfect tone so that they gasp upon entering your mystical sanctuary—this is what wedding planning is all about.

This is where knowing yourself and your unique astrological makeup comes into play, so give yourself permission to follow your heart. Before you visit vendors, sit down and envision what you want the ceremony to look and feel like, then work each ingredient together to create that special mood you sense in your heart and soul.

❏❏ **Fire: Aries, Leo, Sagittarius**

As the actors, dancers, and singers of the zodiac, Fire sign girls instinctively know how to set a scene. Your job is to use your location and your theme and get as creative as you can. You love coming up with great ideas, making inventive decisions, and shopping at craft stores. Now's the time to purchase craft-making books and incorporate any interesting ideas into the design.

Aries delights in adding every touch that the budget will allow, while Leo chooses several accent projects and sets about creating them in a way never seen before on the planet. Imagine your guests as they enter the chapel to an abundance of pedestal candles decorated with tiers of bold-colored flowers, cascading ivy, and ribbon. Under the mood-setting lights they read the beautiful handmade programs, anticipating the start of the ceremony as the string quartet plays in the background.

On the other hand, Sag is likely to pick an expansive location that needs few accents to begin with. Enhance the decor with simple, beautiful adornment. Use shades of green, lots of ivy, and moss to create a garden sanctuary in which to wed. Now that is Fire sign magic!

❑❑ Earth: Taurus, Virgo, Capricorn

Earth girls are very tender. Create a nurturing environment for your ceremony filled with beautiful flowers and lots of greenery that will envelop you and your guests in tranquility and delight the senses. You are very tactile, so make special use of rich fabrics, a satin aisle runner, thick satin bows or tulle to wrap the chairs or flower arrangements. Earth girls love family; enhance the mood by inviting children to hand out programs or flowers to guests, or even to walk with you in the processional.

Taurus brides like a lot of everything. To ensure that you actually create what you envision, make a mission statement and stick to it. If you aren't careful, you might end up with a hodgepodge of beautiful things that don't exactly work in a cohesive way. Virgo and Capricorn, on the other hand, are so focused on each element down to the tiniest detail, that you are going to set the most perfect stage anyone has ever seen for your nuptials even if that means you have to work 24/7 to make everything yourself.

❑❑ Air: Gemini, Libra, Aquarius

The social and sophisticated Air bride likes to create a mood for her "I dos" that is both joyful and elegant. You want to give people something to talk about, to make them think rather than feel. Design a short ceremony that celebrates your love, your unique personality and style, and leads perfectly into a delightful and engaging reception.

Imagine a light and open space, with pale flowers set in modern arrangements on the altar, an arch or huppah decorated with elegant ivy, stephanotis blossoms, and tiny glowing lights that look starry and angelic. Each chair decorated with white satin ribbon and ivy accents; the faint sounds of a harp invite your guests inside, where they marvel at the beauty and harmony all around them.

Sounds positively enchanting, and for an Air sign, absolutely doable. Not only are you are a master at creating that special vibe, you also have a ingenious way of creating things on a budget. Whatever mood you are going for, you are sure to find unique ways to create it without putting a big hole in your pocket.

❏❏ Water: Cancer, Scorpio, Pisces

Creating the perfect mood is the lifeblood of a Water sign, how you feel is just as important as the sacred vows you make on your big day. Born with a profound ability to visualize, it's easy for you to imagine dramatic, romantic details that perfectly enhance the ceremony without overpowering its spiritual elements.

Black Magic rose petals strewn throughout the walkways greet your guests, a candlelit satin aisle runner for the bridal processional. Petals or birdseed wrapped in beautiful tulle and ribbon sit with the parchment programs on each carefully decorated seat, waiting to be thrown at the happy couple.

Creating a special, mystical world all your own is a Water sign's dream come true! Pisces is the most sweetly romantic; you'd release doves or butterflies as long as you knew for sure they'd be safe. Cancer needs to plan the details carefully, you must feel comfortable and safe in order to enjoy the ceremony. Scorpio, use the power of your sign, make sure every element is beautiful *and* has a special meaning, hidden to all but you and your closest confidants.

A Traditional Ceremony for a Very Untraditional Bride

Dennie Hughes, the Aries you read about earlier, and her fiancé, Peter, a Capricorn, had been together for ten years before making it official, experiencing everything together from her bout with cancer to his job loss to the passing of loved ones along the way. When it came to tying the knot, they chose to marry in a Catholic church, because it was important to her that their union be a spiritual one.

Aries feel everything passionately yet with a Libra moon, Dennie likes to stay emotionally balanced and graceful under pressure. She was so overwhelmed by the intensity of the ceremony that she passed on the typical Aries' expressiveness and let the priest lead them in the vows. "We had gone through so much together. I had written down something really wonderful, I literally couldn't get through it without bawling. I could not do it."

The independent Aries pick and choose the wedding traditions they wish to observe, as do many Sagittarius, Gemini, and Aquarius brides. Dennie and Peter followed their classic ceremony with a very untraditional act—they hopped on the subway to their favorite Greek restaurant for a wonderful dinner with their sixty guests.

They skipped just about every other reception tradition as well. They had no flowers besides her handmade bouquet (put together from flower arrangements sent by colleagues); they made tapes of their favorite music; and had a tower of baklava in lieu of a cake. Her one splurge was the photographer. "I just don't buy into the wedding industry stuff," says Dennie. "I just wanted to get married and have a great party."

This bride says that, most of all, focus on the commitment. "Before you walk down the aisle and you say those vows about for better, for worse, in sickness and in health, richer or poorer, be sure that you've experienced each one of them with this person and know those are promises you can keep."

And what did this adventurous Aries and her tender groom do as an encore? They hopped on a plane to Greece for a second ceremony and an amazing honeymoon. How cool!

■ Flowers

From the bouquet to the altar arrangements, perfectly chosen flowers add an aura of bridal beauty to your ceremony. The smell of fragrant roses, the accents of delicate garlands; you will forever remember the sights and smells of the moment you make that lifelong commitment. Read all about your ceremonial blooms and be in *your* element.

❑ ❑ Fire: Aries, Leo, Sagittarius

Fire signs aren't afraid to choose bold tones, oversized blooms, and unusual accents. Whether you are doing simple altar arrangements or filling your sanctuary with flowers, they will have a striking, regal appearance, adding beauty and life to your ceremony.

Fire signs love big splashes of color—shades of red, orange, and gold. Take Summer's very Aries fall wedding. "Our colors were the turning leaves of the season; very earthy, fiery colors." For her bouquet she chose antique roses with a cascade of snapdragons interwoven with burnt orange and brown gerbera daisies, "The spiral of flowers went down to about the middle of my leg," says Summer. A very dramatic walk down the aisle.

Leo goes for the same noble look with a more classic appeal. Try a trio of different-size flowers with the same hues, like royal velvet amaryllis, spray roses, and russet calla lilies. These same flowers can line your chapel on pillar or pew stands, accented with hypericum berries or strands of angel vine.

Sag likes a more down-to-earth look. Carry a petite hand-tied posy instead of a more elaborate bouquet, wear a wreath of flowers in your hair, and forgo the typical altar arrangements; adding garlands of green with tiny floral accents around columns or arches is much more your style.

❑ ❑ Earth: Taurus, Virgo, Capricorn

Whether you are surrounded by flowers or choose them as understated accents, indoor or outdoor, they are a vital part of an Earth bride's vows.

Taurus girls have a special connection to buds and blossoms. As an extension of your soul, you need an abundance of overflowing arrangements on hand. Whether you are creating a bouquet or entrance pillars, choose soothing colors like lavender, violet, and blue, with lots of green leafy accents bursting through. Always budget-conscious, it's easy for you to go for an overall look and color scheme while avoiding expensive, out-of-season blooms.

As perfectionists, the Virgo and Capricorn brides obsess over flower design, choosing just the right amount of buds to enhance their sacred space without overpowering it. Virgo enjoys studying the meaning behind each bloom to ensure the bouquet you are carrying bears the ideal message. You are flexible with color as long as the look is clean and neat.

Capricorn brides love traditional white flowers and an elegant design—calla lilies or roses. Most important, choose an impeccable florist who can make something unique that still has a traditional appeal. Your efforts are well worth it, Earth bride; there is nothing you love more than your guests gushing over all this beauty for years to come.

❏❏ Air: Gemini, Libra, Aquarius

For the lofty Air sign, flowers have a special aesthetic purpose. With a natural understanding of space, harmony, and design, your ceremony flowers will be minimalist, clean, hip, and totally modern. Since some florists are stuck in the Middle Ages, make sure you get that look by researching the latest trends and collecting lots of photos.

Libra chooses a bouquet of pale colors, whites and pinks, with an elegant design; consider flowers like peonies, tulips, lilacs, and lady's mantle. A nosegay tied with white satin ribbon is the perfect size for your graceful walk down the aisle. The accents of flowers on your aisle runner, arch, or huppah absolutely must be flawless and beautiful for you to feel inspired on your big day.

Flowers aren't the most important thing to Aquarius and Gemini unless you have a Libra or Taurus Moon or Rising. Aquarius and Gemini brides are visionaries willing to take a risk; look at your ceremonial space first before choosing color and design. Try simple, structured pew ends and small bold altar arrangements that show off architectural details such as windows or arches. You want to make a bold statement with your bouquet as well. Try a small round bundle of calla lilies, antique roses, or tulips wrapped in unusual greenery such as geranium leaves or galyx leaves.

❏❏ Water: Cancer, Scorpio, Pisces

Flowers are as essential to a Water bride's ceremony as a groom—you just can't imagine getting married without this most romantic of scene-setters. That's not to say you need a huge amount of blossoms, just that they perfectly reflect who you are as you bind your heart and soul to another.

Black Magic roses are a great color for all Water brides. In addition, Pisces likes whites and soft pastels, Scorpio goes for more jewel-toned hues, and Cancer's palette falls somewhere in between.

When decorating a chapel, Pisces likes beautiful arrangements on ornamental roman pillars, garlands of greens, and cascading ivy. If your budget was no concern, you surely would design flowers fit for a princess. Look into a hand-tied bouquet of romantic roses with accents of Queen Anne's lace or lady's mantle.

Scorpio likes dramatic and unconventional blooms. Go for a modern mix of red amaryllis and russet calla lilies or incorporate the alluring cymbidium orchid or gloriosa lily into your bouquet. Scorpios love adding meaning and mystery; have the florist include your grandmother's scarf or a piece of your mother's veil in the design.

The more minimalist Cancer bride likes her accents on the traditional side. Small rose and hydrangea for pew end or chair decorations, uncomplicated altar arrangements, and a clean, round classic bouquet. You can have romance and simplicity—just the way the tender Crab likes it.

▪ Music

One of the classic ways you can separate yourself from the pack is with your choice of ceremonial music. Your choices start with a prelude, then move through the processional, featured musical pieces, recessional, even a potential postlude, but here we're going to focus on the most important pieces—the processional and recessional.

A string quartet serenading guests as they are seated has a completely different feel from an organ piping "Here Comes the Bride." Take a peek at your astrological tastes before committing to the instrument and song choices, you never know what you might discover!

▢▢ **Fire: Aries, Leo, Sagittarius**

Fire signs make very creative choices when it comes to ceremonial music, not just with the type of instruments that are played, but the song styles as well. The tunes at Aries and Leo weddings are original and dramatic. You want pieces that perfectly complement the ceremony you've designed, the dresses, the flowers, and the sacred space—but they have to be pieces not often heard during wedding ceremonies. A tall order for any bride.

Leo tends toward classical pieces that have a regal, majestic feel. Start with an organ or string quartet (you might want to ask if they can add a trumpet to the string quartet for a small fee, which will make the quartet sound more regal). For your processional consider Handel's "March" from *Scipio* or Bach's "Sinfonia" to Wedding Cantata BWV 196 for a long formal walk down the aisle.

Aries may go for something a little less formal, for example, twentieth-century composer Rachmaninoff's *Rhapsody on a Theme of Paganini*. For Leo and Aries the upbeat recessional "Rejouissance" by Telemann from *Musique Heroique* and the "Trumpet Tune" from Purcell's *Indian Queen* are great choices.

Sagittarius is a completely different breed; one I spoke with had no music, "just the ocean waves." Consider Spanish classical guitar or a simple violin and cello duet. Have your musicians create unique down-to-earth arrangements of your favorite songs, like "If" by Bread or "When a Man Loves a Woman" by Percy Sledge, for your way up the aisle, and the Eurythmics' "There Must Be an Angel (Playing with My Heart)" for the way back.

⊓⊓ Earth: Taurus, Virgo, Capricorn

Earth brides like their music to sound like wedding music and since many Earth signs choose to get married in a traditional church, that often means an organ. You like familiar sounds, but instead of walking up the aisle to the typical "Wedding March" by Mendelssohn, consider an instrumental arrangement of Puccini's "Musetta's Waltz" from *La Bohème* or the love theme from Tchaikovsky's "Romeo and Juliet Overture."

For Earth brides marrying outdoors, think informal contemporary music played on easy-to-transport instruments. An acoustic guitar playing "One Hand, One Heart" from Bernstein's *West Side Story* or a flutist's rendition of "All I Ask of You" from Andrew Lloyd Webber's *Phantom of the Opera* will create an aura of tenderness for your walk toward matrimony.

Capricorn might want a classic formal sound for a long church processional; composers Purcell and Stanley each have a regal "Trumpet Tune" just for the occasion; Vivaldi's Violin Concerto in E Major for your recessional. Taurus goes for gentle beauty. Look to Pachelbel for the walk up, skip the common "Canon in D" in favor of the similar-sounding yet often overlooked "Allemande" from the G Major Suite; consider Tchaikovsky's "Waltz of the Flowers" from *The Nutcracker Suite* for the walk back down.

As Virgo likes music that has both beauty and meaning, consider the instrumental of an old standard like "Unforgettable" written by Irving Gordon for the processional and "Love Changes Everything" from Lloyd Webber's relatively unknown musical *Aspects of Love* as a recessional piece.

❏ ❏ Air: Gemini, Libra, Aquarius

Air brides know exactly how to use music to create the perfect mood. Independent thinkers, it's not in your nature to choose tunes without first doing research. Use the Internet to hear many different pieces before making your distinctive choices.

Libra wants music that is light and elegant. Choose flute, harp, or string instruments that evoke delicate grace. And remember to get creative—any piece you find compelling can be performed on any instrument. For your processional look to Handel's "Alla Hornpipe" from Water Music Suite, no. 2 in D Major, HWV 349, or Liszt's "Liebestraum" for Piano S 541 played on an airy flute instead. For your recessional go for the romantic "Salut d'Amour" by Elgar.

A Gemini and Aquarius bride's music has that same elegance with whimsical overtones. Since you aren't afraid to make bold choices with the style or the instruments, you might have a keyboardist playing an ethereal arrangement of your favorite Enya tune or a solo pianist playing a jazz rendition of a Rolling Stones song if a piano is available.

For a contemporary processional, consider Granger's light and lilting "Bridal Lullaby." "Humoresques for Piano," op. 101, no. 7, in G-flat Major by Dvořák is a fun choice for a recessional piece, but if you want to go unconventional all the way, consider a lively instrumental arrangement of "We Go Together" from *Grease*.

❏ ❏ Water: Cancer, Scorpio, Pisces

Music underscores your emotions and creates special meaning for the Water sign bride. You aren't going to choose your tunes lightly. First listen to the most commonly recommended pieces to find composers who tug at your heartstrings, then listen to their other compositions to make selections that perfectly reflect who you are.

Cancer likes music with an understated elegance; a string quartet is your perfect sound. Pisces likes to evoke etheric romance with her tunes; explore a flute, harp, even a solo pianist for your ceremonial walk. Classical pieces such as Pachelbel's "Canon in D" and "Allemande" from the G Major Suite or Bach's "Arioso" are wonderful processional pieces for both Cancer and Pisces. Grieg's "Triumphal March," op. 56, has the sweet, soft, yet dramatic energy for the perfect recessional, Elgar's "Salut d'Amour" is a lighter, more celebratory choice.

Scorpio likes to go for something different with her music. First choose an unusual combination of instruments—a flute, oboe, and bassoon trio for example—and consider unconventional songs.

Modern pianists and composers offer the sweeping, romantic yet uncommon sound you are searching for; check out Henry Mancini's "A Time for Us," from the movie *Romeo and Juliet*. For a traditional procession, consider Handel's "March" from *Scipio*, or his "Réjouissance" from *Music for the Royal Fireworks* HWV 351. As for your grand exit, the "Arrival of the Queen of Sheba" from Handel's opera *Solomon* or the "Trumpet Tune" from Purcell's *Indian Queen* will accompany your style perfectly.

Advice from Brides Past

Some books and Web sites will have you think that planning a wedding is a whirlwind of fun activities but what they fail to say is that planning a wedding can also bring up many raw emotions. Without the help of brides who came before you, you may think you're the only one who has ever felt this way. Read some wise words from the four elements to make your journey a little easier.

The first piece of advice is to realize that no matter how hard you are working today, you are going to want to enjoy your wedding and not get stressed over anything. "It's a party as much for you as for everybody else," says Louise, a social Aquarius who had issues with a controlling sister when she wanted to reorganize things on the fly. You can't make family members be on their best behavior, but you can have someone running interference for you. As she recommends, "Get somebody outside the family to be running the show at the last minute, if you have any problems with your family it's going to come up."

Lois, an unconventional Scorpio, reminds brides that there are no rules you must follow, just your own creativity. "Really use your own vision, don't let other people try to influence you away from what you really see for yourself," says Lois. "Things don't have to be like you see on TV or read in books, you can really craft the day exactly as you want it, even if it seems nontraditional."

Aviva the tender Taurus agrees: "If there's something that you want, make sure you get it." On the other hand, she says, be realistic. "Brides planning a wedding need to think about traditions from their families and what will make everyone happy, not just them." It's true, families need to adjust to their new roles as well and it's easier when everyone feels included in the ritual.

Last, remember, every bride that came before had the same budget issues. "Give yourself the time to plan. The reason we were able to stay within budget is because we gave ourselves so much time," says Summer, a bubbly Aries. "People think, 'Wedding, you have to spend a lot of money,' but it's amazing what you can get if you ask." And she adds, "You don't need everything you think you do. Sacrifice a little bit in order to have a really great honeymoon because that's going to start your marriage off right."

From the party girl to the adventurer, a little something for everyone.

▪ Photography and Videography

Wonderful photos are a priority for brides and grooms of all signs. Although most brides and grooms do have a video, too, many just buy the raw footage or even have a friend with a videocamera record the occasion. How should you best document your ceremony and reception? Let's have a look-see!

❑ ❑ Fire: Aries, Leo, Sagittarius

Fire signs are hams who love a good picture. Make sure there is plenty of time for photos by either shooting them before the wedding or having a long cocktail hour. Aries and Leo want a lot of images to choose from, Sagittarius would rather take a few great photos and enjoy the party.

Put someone you trust in charge of the picture list and prepare the bridal party ahead of time so everyone is ready to hop into the photo when they're called. Spontaneity is very important to Fire brides; photojournalistic images and joyful kitschy posed photos are the ones you'll prize the most when this is over, so don't waste much time on the standard (boring) variety.

You'll want to relive your party over and over again so a video is important. If you're trying to save money: Aries, purchase the raw footage and create your own video using your computer; Leo, find a talented student from a film school nearby to make a finished product you can be proud of. Sag is very happy with a home video as long as you can see and hear it.

❑ ❑ Earth: Taurus, Virgo, Capricorn

Earth brides love a good photo as much as anyone else, but are much more concerned with value and perfection than some others. When hiring a photographer, choose one that has good photos and a package that works best for you. Make sure you interview them first to figure out how easy they are to work with; some Earth signs are on the reserved side and can use some lighthearted cajoling for the best photos. You want the popular photojournalistic images, but you also want the classic portrait and elegant posed shots so make sure he or she can do both well.

Some budget-conscious and easygoing Earth brides may feel that video is a splurge but don't skip it without getting creative first. If you're planning to buy a videocamera anyway, hand it off to the most talented friends you have for the day; having two trade off means they both get to be in the video (and can eat and drink!). Earth brides love a good project even when the wedding is over. Learn a simple editing program on your computer, create a five-minute video, burn it onto CDs, and send them to close family and friends.

❑❑ Air: Gemini, Libra, Aquarius

The photos are vital to Air brides who love documenting everything. Hire a creative, multitasking photographer who takes black-and-white, sepia tone, and color photos—preferably high-quality digital. In addition, have many disposable cameras on tables and in dressing rooms— and even slip them to some guests at the ceremony. Let your family know you would love them to bring their own cameras as well.

The artistic, well-composed, spontaneous photos, along with fun creative shots are your favorites. Cut out or download for inspiration any photos that catch your eye. Libra needs romantic, elegant shots of bride and groom; plan to take those ahead of time when your makeup and hair are at their freshest. Aquarius and Gemini love group shots, so make sure to include many family and bridal party photos on your list.

A video is a must. If money is an issue, find out how many friends and family members have videocameras and buy them some videotapes to leave behind after it's over. You might get so caught up in the party that you miss some details and it'll be a pleasure to go back later and watch all the fun!

❑❑ Water: Cancer, Scorpio, Pisces

Romantic, sentimental photos are a must for all Water sign brides. Find a photographer who can use creative techniques to capture fairy-tale photos of the two of you and can take great spontaneous shots of the wedding as well. Make a list of all the photos you'd like to be taken and go over it with your photographer a million times. After the wedding, if you discover that he or she missed a photo of you and your beloved aunt Marilyn, you'll be heartbroken. Do some location scouting to find the scenery that is most evocative to you and put that on the list. It's not just about the guests, you want to capture the magic of the venue, too. Plan to take photos before the ceremony; you can't stand feeling rushed and distracted.

Having a video filled with all the special moments you worked so hard to create is priceless. You don't need the most fancy package— you don't even need a professional if it's not in the budget. Find out which friends and family members own a videocamera and can be pressed into action. Just make sure you listen to the quality of the audio ahead of time, you might want to buy them an inexpensive microphone as a gift for their efforts.

▪ Transportation

Everyone needs to get to the ceremony, reception, and back again, but how you get there is completely up to you. Here's where your astrology comes in—are you going for a classic vintage car, a slick limo, or a horse-drawn carriage? Even if you're on a budget you can use your sign to make creative choices that suit your soul—here's how.

❑❑ Fire: Aries, Leo, Sagittarius

Fire signs are adventurous. What better way to express that side of you than to choose an unusual ride to your nuptials? For Aries these wheels have to scream romance, Leo wants luxury, and the Sag, something fun and down-to-earth. Out of the three of you, Leo is the most likely to like a beautiful limo as long as it's really nice inside and has no funky horn playing "Here Comes the Bride."

Aries and Leo, consider hiring an upscale classic car like a Rolls-Royce or Bentley. Although risk-taking Aries might like a Porsche Boxster a little better! Sagittarius, unless you are having a formal affair, let your sense of adventure be your guide. A rented convertible, Vespa scooter, or a vintage Beetle make the ride a true experience.

Fire signs have expensive taste. Save money by getting your exotic auto from the ceremony to the reception, it'll be great for the photos and you'll feel like a million bucks. Since you like to party like there's no tomorrow, skip the dramatic early exit and switch to a town car for the ride back home.

❑ ❑ Earth: Taurus, Virgo, Capricorn

Earth girls like classic romance and bridal traditions; a beautiful black or white limo is a perfect choice for most Earth brides. Unless you have an Aquarius, Gemini, Aries, or Sag Rising, then you might want to go for something a little more unusual.

Make sure you take a look before you sign the contract, something important to each Earth sign. Taurus brides like comfort and luxury. Virgos are likely to analyze the offers from several companies and Capricorns just want the best. And since Earth brides like a good deal, get them to throw in the champagne gratis.

If you think all of this luxury is a waste of money and resources, cut corners by taking a practical and stately sedan to the ceremony and save the limo for the most important ride of the day. If you're planning to make a grand exit, do something a little romantic and earthy; imagine pulling away from your reception in a horse-drawn carriage.

❑ ❑ Air: Gemini, Libra, Aquarius

The transportation is a great way for an Air bride to express her hip creative side. Although some Libra brides like the elegance of a limo, most of you can skip that ride and still get the classic look by choosing a chauffeur-driven Bentley or Rolls-Royce.

For Aquarius and Gemini, a combination of grace and style is the way to go. A vintage Jaguar or Aston Martin gives you the elegant edgy feel you're looking for. For the hard-core nonconformist, consider a Stretch Hummer or rent a Porsche convertible and drive it yourself. You just might have to fight with your groom for the wheel!

When most brides are happy to take a sedan or drive their own wheels part of the way to cut costs, Libra wants to be surrounded by beauty. Don't skimp on this aspect of your affair unless you're sure no one will see your entrance or exit. Gemini and Aquarius are much more flexible. One honest Aquarius taking a limo said, "I could care less how we get where we're going. Knowing me, I'll let anyone who wants to hitch a ride with us do so."

❑ ❑ **Water: Cancer, Scorpio, Pisces**

A Water sign's wheels are going to be utterly romantic and perfectly complement the mood of the day. To a Cancer, the most traditional among you, that can likely be a beautiful stretched limo, large enough to take your tight bridal party or close-knit family along for the ride.

Since the Scorpio bride won't go for a frivolous expense, your choice of transportation says a lot about who you are. A bit of a nonconformist, go for a classic vintage convertible if you're having a formal wedding, or rent a fun Mini Cooper for a less formal affair. Being able to drive it yourself and come and go as you please suits you.

Pisces, on the other hand, wants to feel like a princess as she rides off into the sunset. Hire a wooden sailboat if you are getting married near water; a horse-drawn carriage dripping with flowers for a garden affair. If you have budget concerns, hire the chauffeured trip for the most picturesque portion of the day and get your best man to drive you the rest of the way in an upscale rental.

■ The Morning Of

No chapter on the ceremony would be complete without discussing what do to with your time once the big day arrives. Prepare your sign's favorite stress relievers and plan for potential problems ahead of time. Everything might just go so smoothly that you actually enjoy your last few hours as a single girl!

❏❏ Fire: Aries, Leo, Sagittarius

Aries and Leo girls are self-confident, enthusiastic brides who love to hang out with their entire (usually large!) bridal party. It's important to make your morning a girlie celebration. Invite everyone over to your hotel suite for a specially prepared breakfast, have an iPod playing your favorite tunes as you have your manicure, pedicure, makeup, and hair appointments.

You want to be a good hostess and be catered to at the same time, so make sure room service is available if anyone wants anything. Have your maid of honor bring over a basket of your favorite snacks and sodas. Avoid caffeine, you don't want to get overstimulated too early.

Sag brides like a more laid-back atmosphere, so before you begin your beauty routine, go for a hike with your fiancé and your dog; having the people you love close by can keep the jitters at bay. Have a TV set tuned to the Discovery or Travel channel as a distraction before your pals arrive. Have your manicure done the day before so that you'll have more free time to explore the hotel and enjoy the morning with your best friend.

❏❏ Earth: Taurus, Virgo, Capricorn

Earth brides want to wake up to a well-planned morning of relaxed activities. Breakfast with your mother and aunt, hair appointment with your longtime stylist, dressing with your maid of honor. Don't overschedule your morning and make sure everyone doesn't arrive at once. You want to look beautiful, but you also need plenty of quiet time with people closest to you in order to feel comfortable.

Good healthy food is also a must; skip the snacks and prepare a tray of finger sandwiches in advance. Make sure there are some sophisticated teas on hand with small chocolate desserts, and you might want to splurge on a cookie along the way.

Taurus, skip the pedicure for a reflexologist to massage your feet. Virgo, save a last-minute project to keep you busy during downtime, such as writing heartfelt notes to your groom, family, or bridal party. Capricorn, bring all your checklists for a last-minute meeting with your coordinator. Once you're at ease, you can thoroughly enjoy your beauty routine.

❏ ❏ Air: Gemini, Libra, Aquarius

Because Air signs thrive on constant fun and excitement, the last thing you want on your wedding day is a dull morning. Have your bridal party show up early with video games, newspapers, and magazines to keep you busy. Plan a full day of facial, manicure, makeup, and hair appointments. Since you don't like to eat heavy meals, have platters of fruit, cheese, and tasty appetizers on hand for everyone to snack on along with a cooler of fizzy fruit drinks. Bring your digital camera to document the activities with your quirky sense of humor.

Since Air signs can get a little caught up in a crowd, keep the prewedding party quiet with five to seven people and make sure there are some Earth signs around to keep you grounded and relaxed. Avoid caffeine, sugar, and carbohydrates—you don't want to get spacey and light-headed.

Libra wants the day to be graceful, so invite your mom to join you for high tea and play elegant piano music to stay balanced. Aquarius and Gemini, make sure there are plenty of things to talk about and laugh over. Have someone bring tapes of celebrity weddings to make fun of while your nails are drying!

❏ ❏ Water: Cancer, Scorpio, Pisces

The morning of a Water sign wedding is filled with sentimental moments. Start off by having breakfast with your family. Prepare heartfelt toasts or handwritten notes on beautiful stationery to let each one know how special they are to you.

As you get together with your closest friends for your beauty routine, remember to keep it low-key and relaxed. Stagger the arrival of each member of your bridal party throughout the day so that you can have a moment with each one and avoid getting overwhelmed by too much noise and excitement.

Pisces can handle more people than Cancer and Scorpio brides on such a sensitive day. Cancer or Scorpio Sun or Moon, make sure to keep a light schedule. If you want to close the door or take a walk with a pal, you can sneak away before putting your dress on.

Pisces and Cancer have sensitive stomachs, so along with whatever snacks you have, make sure there is chamomile tea and sparkling water on hand as well as bland foods like yogurt and crackers. Have a buddy scout out nearby nature for you; sitting by a lake or a garden will help to calm your nerves.

Moon Signs and Last-Minute Freak-Outs

Your Moon sign is what shows itself under pressure. The closer you get to your wedding—and the florist screws up your order or the bridesmaids' shoes come back dyed the wrong color—the more your Moon exerts its influence. Get to know more about this hidden aspect and you'll learn how to handle your worst nightmares without your heart skipping a beat.

Since the Moon changes signs every two and a half days, figure out this sign by visiting one of the free astrology sites on the Web—all you need is your time, place, and date of birth. If you don't know the exact time, an approximate will usually do. If you don't know your Moon, reading your Sun is still reasonably accurate.

ARIES MOON No matter what your Sun sign, you are a bit impulsive. Don't make last-minute decisions alone, especially if they're going to cost you a bundle. If disaster strikes, you get very angry, have a temper tantrum, and quickly let it go. Don't say *anything*—instead of blowing your top, walk away, take a few deep breaths, and let your Sun sign kick in before you take care of business. It'll be over in a heartbeat.

TAURUS MOON You need to feel secure in order to really enjoy your wedding. Last-minute changes can be very unsettling, especially if they're going to take a bite out of your wallet. You've got a lot of common sense, but you can get so stuck on something that you'll need your fiancé or your mom to talk you into changing your mind. Realize that sometimes things happen; whatever it is, let it roll off your back.

GEMINI MOON On a good day, you love analyzing your feelings and talking things through with your best pal. When you become uncomfortable, you get restless, indecisive, and incessantly chatty. When presented with a problem, don't talk before you think. Hold off until you can figure out how you feel with someone you trust. Great solutions just pop into your head as you bounce ideas off people.

CANCER MOON You are extremely sensitive to those you love most and feel everything deeply. All this emotion can make you a bit unstable. When faced with an obstacle, you may want to run away, hide out, and cry. Don't try to take care of anything alone, make sure your mom, groom, or best friend is there to support you. If you need some alone time first before addressing something, take it.

LEO MOON Secretly, you love to be admired. You must have a large, romantic celebration to feel fulfilled as a bride—and what better time than this to be the center of attention? However, you can be stubborn, melodramatic, and even a bit self-involved on a bad day. Remember that issues are bound to occur, so don't take anything too personally and learn to let it go—after you act it out for all your friends, of course.

VIRGO MOON An exacting perfectionist, no doubt you've worked tirelessly to create a warm down-to-earth day. Although watch that your detail-oriented nature doesn't become nitpicky, especially when things aren't quite working out as planned. Don't get so wrapped up in small things that you miss the big picture. There's a way out of every situation; use your wonderful analytical ability to find solutions.

LIBRA MOON In many ways this is the best and worst Moon to have for a wedding. You have such a charming and gracious personality, yet you are so sensitive to others that when they misbehave it can literally make you sick. Make sure everything is harmonious by getting someone you trust to run interference with difficult family members (so you don't have to), and put someone strong in charge of last-minute problems.

SCORPIO MOON You have intense emotions and a deep understanding of humanity. Because you are so sensitive and have a hard time expressing your feelings, you can get very hurt when people act inappropriately—which is bound to happen. Recognize that they don't know any better and let things go. Consider taking the high road. You have a great memory, but you can't hold on to these slights for the rest of your life.

SAGITTARIUS MOON You are optimistic, easygoing, and have strong personal beliefs. The typical wedding stresses don't bother you, you're more likely to get upset if people try to force you into a corner and tell you what to do. When you feel your liberty taken away, you want to run. Express your thoughts and feelings accurately and diplomatically and never agree to anything you don't believe in.

CAPRICORN MOON This Moon adds a driven, ambitious nature to any Sun sign. You enjoy working hard to achieve financial success and social status. You want a wedding that will impress people and make you proud. If you do run into problems after all this effort, you're not about to be very forgiving, although you have to try. Realize that not everyone has your exacting standards and that people only want to share your joy.

AQUARIUS MOON Having this Moon makes it very easy to plan a wedding. You are very open-minded and fairly easygoing, unless something is very important to you, then you'll make sure you get your way no matter how stubborn you have to be. You really understand there's no problem too big to fix and that as long as you have family and friends around, nothing else matters. Spread this accepting attitude to those you love!

PISCES MOON You are a psychic emotional sponge, picking up the moods of those around you and feeling everything as if under a microscope. It's wonderful at weddings to be so expressive, but this can make you very vulnerable to the typical stresses along the way. Take time for yourself, arrange relaxing activities like yoga and massage, and make sure you've always got someone you trust to lean on and distract the offensive party in case of emergency.

Chapter *Seven*

Design a reception that is unique and your guests will remember it for years. When you think about it this way, it's absolutely worth taking the time to make wise, educated decisions. When your goal as a bride is to craft every element to reflect both of your personalities and celebrate your love, you start your marriage off in a style you are accustomed to—yours!

With everyone reading the same wedding Web sites and bridal mags, and potentially tapping into the same wedding trends, here are the personal touches that you can add that make your affair both genuine and memorable.

■ Setting the Tone

The idea that your various choices add up to a creation all your own was well illustrated for you in the last chapter. Now you get to set the tone and create the perfect ambience for your reception as well. As one Sagittarius groom said, "The more you plan, the better [your wedding] is going to be, and the more you personalize it, the more memorable it's going to be."

Let's take a look at how you can design your ideal scene and make it one that is absolutely unforgettable.

❏ ❏ Fire: Aries, Leo, Sagittarius

As we well know, Aries and Leo like drama. Your reception site is already a showplace—now it's time to make it smashing. When people enter the reception hall, they are greeted by a path of lush rose petals; each place card entwined in a garland shows them to their seat where they find rich-colored tablecloths, napkins, and bold-colored blooms, every detail chosen to pop and delight.

Since you both like everything you do to be unique, consider going for unusual mood lighting, beautiful displays of personal photos, a guest sign-in that allows them to express lovely sentiments, and uncommon flower decorations. Use your wellspring of creativity no matter what your budget.

The Sag bride's perfect reception is an indoor-outdoor affair where people are free to dance all night or take a moonlit walk. Continue the lighthearted, natural vibe from the reception by choosing sage-green table linens and accent tables with garlands, plants, and fruit. Imagine a Caribbean steel drum serenading your guests as they enter—you'll be creating a lively mood before they even walk in the door!

❏ ❏ Earth: Taurus, Virgo, Capricorn

The Earth bride's reception is filled with all the classic elements of a wedding. Taurus and Virgo go for an unfussy, down-to-earth elegance while the ambitious Capricorn chooses a more polished aesthetic. Where Taurus and Virgo are happy with a more intimate setting, Capricorn wants to make a bigger statement.

Creating the perfect scene is both an aesthetic and practical exercise for you. Earth girls invite only those they truly love to their affair and want to make sure these guests are well cared for. You'd never sacrifice food and comfort for looks any day.

Envision a lush welcoming environment, with beautiful decor down to the smallest detail. Use your appreciation of nature and artistic abilities to create beautiful twig, evergreen, and silk butterfly accents for the guest book, place cards and cake tables. Hire a harpist to play as people mingle at the cocktail hour.

It's not just about what's added that makes a scene. Make a run-through of the location early so you can have them move unsightly tchotchkes—if you don't, you may just obsess over that weird garbage can or garden gnome for the rest of your life.

❏❏ Air: Gemini, Libra, Aquarius

Air sign receptions are held in big, open, airy spaces with minimal decor and a thoroughly modern appeal. Working with that fresh aesthetic to create the flawless finish will be one of the most fun, creative projects you can imagine!

The traditional Libra bride wants everything dripping in an understated elegance from the moment your guests arrive to the moment they leave. Start with satin aisle and carpet runners, white linens, and just the right amount of white flower accents in the perfect places. Visualize the most elegant ball you can imagine and go from there.

Everything must have a gracious look to the Gemini and Aquarius bride as well, but with a twist; a little something unconventional within all that classic beauty. You want the place to have attitude!

Go for that edgy look by combining old and new decor elements and use them in creative ways for which they aren't originally intended. You will have done your job well if your eclectic mix of guests are constantly saying "cool" after every new surprise, as they snack on unusual hors d'oeuvres, sip unusual cocktails, and bathe in lights from thousands of mismatched glowing candles.

❏❏ Water: Cancer, Scorpio, Pisces

Water sign brides set the scene early with an emotional heartfelt ceremony that les your guests know this is no ordinary wedding. Now you get to create a special world that welcomes all your guests for the reception as well, one infused with utter love and romance.

Some Water signs love the traditional fantasy of the ballroom affair, with its beautiful chandeliers and elegant decor—a scene-setter that needs nothing but music and flowers. For the Water brides who wish to create a different ambience, start off by thinking waterfalls, lush green plants, and flickering candlelight. All of which can be created with a little handiwork and a few trips to the craft store, if they're not in your sacred space already.

For Pisces and Scorpio, who are the emotional risk-takers of the zodiac, it's easy to take this all the way and transform any space into a mystical wonderland. Research different periods in history for inspiration. Cancers, on the other hand, are drawn to a more elegant look. Candelabras instead of lanterns and classic flower arrangements in lieu of lush greens will reveal just the right amount of romance for you.

▪ Seating Your Guests

Something all brides and grooms struggle over is exactly how and where to seat your guests. Once you've taken family dynamics into account—which can be hard when Aunt Diana is feuding with Aunt Sue and Uncle Bart is stuck in the middle—you get to have fun and make some creative table and seating arrangements.

The usual advice still applies: It's a good idea to seat together family and friends who are excited to catch up, but beyond that it's up to you and the elements!

❑ ❑ Fire: Aries, Leo, Sagittarius

You know that making the perfect seating arrangements will ensure your guests have a great time. Although you're not one to follow the rules. If you are not getting married in a standard hall with round tables of eight or ten guests each, it's a great opportunity to get creative. Consider seating people at unusually shaped tables to give your party a different look and feel. Mix and match square and rectangular tables, for instance.

Leo wants comfortable seats and regal-looking arrangements, there should be no mistaking that this is a wedding. Aries and Sag are willing to take more risks. Once you've organized each table, stagger them so that groups of family and friends are mingled together. Sag, if your wedding is intimate and casual, you might even consider open seating, just make sure your guests are up for the challenge. Some people aren't as outgoing as you are.

❏ ❏ Earth: Taurus, Virgo, Capricorn

Earth girls like classic table and seating arrangements, you want to make sure that the families sit together, that the friends have their own space, and that anyone who might not get along is sufficiently separated. Virgo and Capricorn are so detail-oriented that getting this aspect of the wedding right can drive you batty. Practical Taurus is more of a realist, you will just do the best job you can with what's presented.

Earth brides having an informal garden wedding can avoid all these common issues by having open seating, where guests can mix and mingle at their leisure. If you are concerned about potential conflicts, just add a few extra seats so that no one feels boxed into a corner or enlist the help of trusted friends to run interference.

Add beauty and intimacy to more formal affairs by using different-size round tables: some that seat four, some six, and some eight. It's much easier to find the perfect seating arrangements when you have more options.

❏ ❏ Air: Gemini, Libra, Aquarius

Air signs look at seating as a fun puzzle to solve, analyzing personalities and family history, moving people around until it's just right.

With a keen understanding of social dynamics, Libra will agonize over where to seat everyone—you aim to please. Just don't get so worried about creating a harmonious environment that you become a nervous wreck. Your guests are going to have a wonderful time either way.

Of course Aquarius and Gemini want everyone to get along as well, but are not as concerned with the small stuff. You're so socially adept that you assume everyone can get along for a few hours. Just stay away from making the table arrangements one big social experiment, and everything will be fine!

If you've rented raw space for the reception and get to bring in your own party supplies, think about creating a table plan that works aesthetically within the environment. An example: several long rectangular tables; your guests can still be close to the family and meet new people at the same time.

□ □ Water: Cancer, Scorpio, Pisces

From the moment a Water sign gets engaged they daydream about all the little sentimental details of this day. This includes the bridal party, the first dance, and yes, the seating arrangements! You can't wait to go over the final RSVP list and play around with all the different seating possibilities—it's another opportunity to live out your wedding fantasy!

The Scorpio bride likes to make these arrangements on her own before consulting key members of her tribe. The best way for Pisces and Cancer to tackle this sometimes difficult task is to make the seating charts with your mom, groom, or mother-in-law. You are way too aware of the subtle personality issues to try this on your own; besides, too many choices can be stressful for these signs.

Water girls have an intuitive understanding of energy and space; when you are creating the look of your party, make the table placements a part of that design. Highlight large windows or romantic architecture by shuffling the tables and dance floor around until it feels right.

Two Sophisticated Perfectionists Do
a Destination Wedding

Planning a wedding away from home takes a lot of faith and trust. With only photos, phone calls, and e-mails, you have to be ready for anything. What happens if the bride and groom have detail-oriented, potentially demanding astrology signs? Let's take a before-and-after look at one couple and find out.

Andee, a driven Capricorn, and Santiago, a lordly Leo, tied the knot in Hawaii without ever seeing the inside of the chapel or a floor-plan of the reception hall. How did they handle giving up that power? "I took extreme control over everything that I could control," says Andee. In addition to being "superpicky" about her dress and the bridesmaids' frocks, the floral arrangements got a lot of her attention.

With a Gemini Rising, this bride is both conventional and unconventional. An ambitious creative type, she designed seven-page vintage airline ticket save-the-date cards; created and printed the invitations; and taught herself calligraphy, hand inscribing the address and place cards. "Yeah," she admits, "everyone was telling me, 'You're crazy!' "

Santiago's Virgo Rising makes him a hands-on groom and gives his regal Leo even more exacting standards. "I found it very relieving that the party was not here because I knew I would be crazy trying to control everything," he reveals, something that brides and grooms with a Virgo Sun sign or Virgo Rising have to watch out for.

So how did it all work out? Besides a flu going around the island, two brief visits to the hospital with different guests, and a fainting sister-in-law, it was the best five days of their lives. The flowers, the tuxes, everything was awesome. "Nothing we were worried about was even remotely an issue," says Andee.

"I would never do it any other way," says Santiago, who wholeheartedly recommends destination weddings. "You don't get anyone who doesn't absolutely want to be there." Andee agrees: "We got to spend quality time with every person at the wedding."

Between family gatherings, drinks with friends, and a coed
bachelor-bachelorette surfing party, this high-strung New York couple
had plenty of time to chill before saying "I do." As the unusually laid-
back Andee related, "It was very, very relaxed." And who would've
predicted that?

■ Food and Drink

Whether you are going for a sit-down dinner or a lively buffet, hip
cocktails or a champagne toast, the creative choices that go into
selecting the menu say a lot about who you are. Whatever your budget, you can design the edibles to reflect your astrological style.
Here's how.

❏❏ Fire: Aries, Leo, Sagittarius

Fire signs want to have a great party. Providing your guests with good
food is important but, truthfully, it's not the biggest priority. You instinctively know that eating is just one part of what makes an unforgettable event.

A lavish meal is most important to the Leo bride, who likes to reward
those who love her with the best of the best, as one Leo told me, "if
you're going to do it, do it right." With a classic yet bold taste, you
might choose filet mignon or salmon but pair it with an unusual veg-
etable. If you want to save money, skip the cocktails, instead having
carefully selected champagne and wine flowing all night.

Aries and Sag are more flexible. A sit-down dinner is nice, but you
might enjoy a buffet with many stations. With a good selection of
items, people are free to move about, change seats, and have seconds of
their favorite dishes. The classic open bar is perfect for the fun-loving
Aries and Sag who know how to have a good time and want to make
sure their guests do, too!

❑ ❑ Earth: Taurus, Virgo, Capricorn

Earth girls love good food. You look forward to this wonderful opportunity to share a delicious meal with those you love the most. You prefer well-served food that tastes both comforting and familiar. Choose a great caterer who makes nice portions of standard wedding dishes such as filet mignon, chicken, and salmon.

For a formal cocktail hour, make sure there are both passed hors d'oeuvres and stations of heartier fair for the foodies in your group. If budget is a concern, save money by limiting the choice of alcohol or just have wine and a champagne toast.

Many Earth brides like a less formal approach to their meal. As long as there are wholesome dishes prepared and presented well, you can just as easily choose platters of tasty appetizers or buffet-style service over the traditional sit-down meal.

For Taurus, the food has to taste great, it has to be practical for the Virgo, and for the Capricorn, of the highest quality. You like a good dessert, too. We all know everyone will be eating a great piece of cake, but you'll definitely want to make sure there's another tasty treat as well.

❑ ❑ Air: Gemini, Libra, Aquarius

Aquarius and Gemini girls love to experiment with food and your wedding is no different. You love to eat at hot new restaurants and you want your unique flavor palate reflected in the food on your big day. The cocktail hour is vital for the Aquarius and Gemini; unusual hors d'oeuvres and hip oddly named cocktails to sip is your idea of a good time. The sit-down dinner is just boring in comparison!

Do something unusual; instead of a three-course meal, serve platters of tapas. Go to your favorite bars and sample their most unusual cocktails, then serve them at your open bar—or if you're on a budget just choose two or three.

Libra likes the classic sit-down dinner, but may choose a lighter fare, such as fish and vegetables. What's important to a Libra is the presentation, the colors of the food, the garnish, the plate—you want fine food but taste comes in lower on the list! The gracious Libra host loves wine, champagne, and cocktails served in elegant long-stemmed glasses. Skip the hard liquor, you won't miss it anyway.

❑ ❑ Water: Cancer, Scorpio, Pisces

Water sign brides know how to choose food and drinks that will perfectly enhance the mood you are working so hard to create. Not an extravagant element, you don't need the most lavish and expensive catering on the planet, as long as your guests are nourished by the meal. You know the people you love are happy to celebrate your union and will enjoy whatever you feed them.

Out of all the Water signs, food is most important to the Cancer bride. The sign that rules the home knows that quality food nourishes the soul. A sit-down dinner with classic taste is perfect for the Crab. No outrageous spices or unusual dishes to throw off your guests. The traditional Cancer also enjoys traditional cocktails, wine, and a champagne toast.

The Scorpio and Pisces bride looks forward to making a statement and sharing your beliefs whenever you can. It's easy for you to choose a sumptuous vegetarian feast, organic food, or even arrange for a local homeless shelter to swing by after it's all over to take the leftovers.

Take a risk with your menu, consider serving food and drink from sexy, exotic locales with a decor to match.

■ Flowers

We've already discussed the floral design for your ceremony; now you get to build on that theme, bringing your unique vision to life for your party. Here are some insights to make that dream a reality.

❑❑ Fire: Aries, Leo, Sagittarius

Your love of bright colors and bold floral design is no surprise. When choosing flowers for your party, pass on the traditional-looking arrangements for something with a unique, powerful vibe.

A breakaway style centerpiece is perfect for all three Fire signs. Instead of having one common flower arrangement in the center of each table, several smaller overflowing clusters of flowers in differently shaped vases, interspersed with tons of romantic candles, will give your flowers a strong presence and distinctive look.

For Aries, choose sizable peonies and pillar candles. Leo, make it more traditional by opting for roses in frosted glass vases and votive candles. And Sag, choose hydrangeas and tweedias in terra-cotta pots with lots of greenery and tiny tea light accents.

A way for the Fire bride to make the reception your own is to create perfect flower accents to brighten up dull spaces. Get together with your bridesmaids and create small inexpensive globes bursting with fragrant flowers for the bathrooms and hallways. Aries Summer got together with her maid of honor and created gift box centerpieces out of Styrofoam, flower heads, and ribbon. "They were really pretty in the pictures," she says, and created great memories for her as well.

❑❑ Earth: Taurus, Virgo, Capricorn

Earth brides are fastidious when it comes to reception flowers. The blooms are such an important element that you'll focus a tremendous amount of attention on their style, color, and fragrance. Whether you are working within a tight budget or have more flexible spending power, they are going to look exactly as you envision them.

Virgo and Capricorn brides like a clean, crisp, understated look. A classic glass globe vase filled with beautiful white tulips and roses is both uncomplicated and beautiful. For a more sophisticated look, go for a low, wide frosted glass vase filled with unusual white blossoms and green accents encircled in votives.

Taurus girls just love lots of beautiful, colorful flowers. Budget-conscious Aviva ordered two professional arrangements for key places and then finished off the look with another six dozen lavender roses in borrowed vases.

Consider doing the flowers yourself with help from committed friends or family. Earth brides are serious about their do-it-yourself projects, taking on the most ambitious, artistic endeavors like a pro. Research online, find flower wholesalers, instructions, vases—everything you need. Start early and practice; by the time of the wedding, you might have another career!

❑❑ Air: Gemini, Libra, Aquarius

Air sign brides want their reception flowers to be light, airy, and totally modern; no heavy stone urns, no cascading bundles of bright colors, and definitely no flamboyant theatrics.

As the most classic of the Air brides, Libra likes beautiful soft colors in pretty arrangements of flowers like pale green hydrangeas, pink roses, and carnations in white ceramic pots for the center of your tables. Finish off the look with elegant tapered candles in small individual candleholders.

Aquarius and Gemini brides add an element of whimsy and geometry to the elegance. Aquarius, consider several tall orchids in square moss-covered galvanized steel pots surrounded on either side by neatly organized pillar candles.

Gemini, take a risk with an informal affair by placing yellow daffodils in mismatched vases purchased by scouring a million Sunday flea markets. For a more upscale choice, create a breakaway centerpiece with triangular tall glass vases of different-colored long-stemmed blooms.

Gemini Elizabeth recalls, "The florist knew that I was trying to be a bit untraditional, so the centerpieces on tables were combinations of flowers, including roses, and crazy fruits and vegetables stuck in the design like artichokes and limes."

☐☐ Water: Cancer, Scorpio, Pisces

Romance, romance, and more romance is the motivation for the Water sign's floral design; you just know how to use flowers to totally enhance the mood of your carefully chosen location. Pisces and Scorpio brides make bolder choices for their reception flowers, while the traditional Cancer bride takes a more understated approach.

Pisces and Scorpio, before choosing your party blooms, meditate on the theme or mood you wish to create and let your inspiration be your guide. Scorpio likes drama—a romanesque stone or iron pedestal filled with lush red anemones, roses, and red cascading amaranth is your perfect choice. The two-sided Pisces, on the other hand, will have a hard time deciding between the more passionate arrangements and the pretty pale ones, like French wire baskets filled with white calla lilies, lisianthus, and blush-colored roses.

Cancer brides are attracted to classic centerpieces; a trumpet vase of roses or calla lilies and tapered candle accents gives the perfect amount of sparkle without being ostentatious. One Cancer I spoke with wanted beauty on a budget: "We decided the flowers needed to be simple, so we went with clean Black Magic roses in a silver bowl. They were gorgeous."

▪ Music

Every bride and groom wants to have a great time at their wedding and the music is such a key element to making that happen. Whether you are into the classic big band or fun pop tunes, here are the perfect music ideas for your sign.

One Intricately Planned, Totally Carefree Wedding

When brides first get engaged, many think of having the sophisticated weddings they've always seen on TV; the elegant reception in a glamourous hall with delicious food and guests dressed in black tie.

These days, a perfectly designed event doesn't have to be a totally glam affair. Here's one bride whose well-planned wedding was a decidedly more down-to-earth fantasy.

From the beginning Kristye knew she wanted her day to be the wedding every girl dreams about. After all, being a Pisces, the fairy tale is in her astrological blood. But for her the story is one of country elegance. "I love country stuff, I love rustic, I love the simplicity." You can really feel the influence of her laid-back Sagittarius Rising as she speaks. "You can be a beautiful country girl and not have all the paint on your face and jewelry on your fingers."

Where else would a country bride and groom have their reception but in a barn? A barn so well decorated that guests said it reminded them of a scene from *Hope Floats*. As people entered, they were greeted with yellow roses, wagon wheels, and old butter churns. "We had candles everywhere, but it wasn't like you think of candles and weddings. We made chandeliers out of mason jars with candles in them." The ceiling was carefully draped with white fabric, above which hung candle jelly jars, twinkling like otherworldly stars.

Along with the carefully prepared decor was a smattering of family heirlooms, a must for the sentimental Water sign. The backdrop for the cake table was a picket fence draped with her grandmother's handmade quilt surrounded by hay bales and her grandfather's old tractor seats. Every decoration was perfectly executed to inspire the dream.

Besides a year of planning, the assistance of her invaluable Cancer wedding coordinator, Tina, and the support of Jeff, her wonderful Leo groom, just what went into transforming this earthy dance hall into a tiny slice of country heaven? Ten close friends and family, twenty hours, and 1,500 square feet of white material. "It was just beautiful," says Kristye.

One unforgettable day this dreamy Water sign will relive for the rest of her life.

❑❑ Fire: Aries, Leo, Sagittarius

We already know that Fire sign brides love to party, so going all out with the music is very important to you. If hiring a band or a DJ isn't a financial decision, first consider what type of music you like to dance to. For the elegant Leo that might mean a band while the fun-loving Aries and Sag go for the DJ.

Fire signs aren't likely to micromanage the song list, so hire someone you trust and hand them a short index of your favorites. The highbrow Leo might have a list of no-nos as well. The Aries and Sag will go for some crowd-pleasers, even if they are a bit on the wild side.

For Leo Mary Ellen, who wanted music that sounds exactly the way everyone listens to it, a DJ was the obvious choice. "We wanted to hear all different types of music, but we had some songs we didn't want him to play," she says. Tunes like "Celebration" and "We Are Family" made it onto their *absolutely not* list.

Fire signs surround themselves with friends who like to have a good time. If you choose classic music for your ceremony or cocktail hour, add some rocking tunes for your reception to give them a chance to show off. "The music was everything from the '60s, '70s, all the way up to Madonna and 'Love Shack,'" says Aries Summer. "People were really sweaty by the end of the night, all in their formal dresses," she says proudly.

▫️▫️ Earth: Taurus, Virgo, Capricorn

Earth brides like traditional music for their reception; everything from 1940s big band classics to the romance of Nat "King" Cole to the latest hit from Madonna. If money is no issue, the upscale sounds of a good band is the way to go, but plenty of budget-conscious Earth brides choose a DJ and have an awesome time.

For Virgo and Capricorn brides, creating the perfect song list is a wonderful project to keep you busy in the quiet months before crunch time. Start with your favorite CDs, check out song lists on wedding Web sites, download some great new favorites from iTunes, and, of course, talk to your DJ or bandleader.

Taurus girls are much more easygoing. Take an afternoon to research your favorites and make sure your hire knows exactly what your musical tastes are. Expressing your desires is *very* important; you might not want to micromanage the list, but if he inadvertently plays a song you can't stand, you'll get hot under the collar!

Since Earth signs love D.I.Y. projects, here's another one: If you are having an informal affair, instead of hiring musicians, buy a spiffy new iPod and create your own music program; you'll spin them better than a DJ and have a great new iPod as a wedding present when it's over.

☐ ☐ Air: Gemini, Libra, Aquarius

Air sign brides like an eclectic mix of music. You pride yourself on being in-the-know, sampling the latest sounds, techno-gadgets, and analyzing remixes. As a social party girl, it's important that your guests be up and dancing, but you also want to include your innovative taste in the mix.

A band is very appealing to the traditional Libra bride, who prefers the elegance and excitement of polished professional musicians— but they have to be a great band or else you'll be very upset by the sound. Aquarius and Gemini are more likely to choose a DJ over live music because your particular choices of tunes just sound better that way.

One easygoing Aquarius who preferred a DJ had a tiff with her Capricorn mother over a band. "The music I like is not generally played well by bands," she affirms, "but we found a DJ that satisfied her desire for old standards at the beginning of the wedding and would pick it up with more pop tunes toward the end." True to Aquarian form, she didn't care about much else, but the music was important to her: "I wasn't about to give in on that one."

☐ ☐ Water: Cancer, Scorpio, Pisces

Sound is an expression of the heart to Water sign brides, who take their reception music very seriously. Whether you choose a band or a DJ isn't as important as making sure every song is full of meaning. Work with your DJ or bandleader to fine-tune the perfect selections that will nurture the spirit of your guests and reflect who you are.

Integrating your culture into the music is a great way for these sentimental signs to feel complete. Of Middle Eastern decent, Cancer Leila did just that when she provided her DJ with tons of Arabic music. "I wanted half the night to be Arabic dancing and half American," she says. As a Pisces having a destination wedding, I brought a CD of the traditional Jewish Hora to our DJ in Scotland. I'm confident that was the first Scottish Hora ever performed in the six-hundred-year-old historic castle we rented!

Asking talented friends and family to sing creates the perfect memories for Water signs. Scorpio Lois asked her niece to sing Alicia Keys's "If I Ain't Got You." She recalls, "I didn't realize the impact of her singing, that it would make everybody cry, her voice is so beautiful."

■ First-Dance Selections and Styles

Your first dance is the perfect opportunity to come out in style and show the world who you are as a married couple. But these first dances aren't just about you. From the time you were a little girl, your dad's been dreaming of the special dance you'll share together. Before you choose standard first-dance tunes, discover the best dance styles for your sign—you may be surprised at what you find out!

❑❑ Fire: Aries, Leo, Sagittarius

Fire signs are courageous brides who want their first dance to make a big impression. Since you'll be the center of attention, choosing that perfect song with great rhythm and lyrics that highlight your individuality is very important.

All Fire signs should pass up classic love songs for something more upbeat and edgy. You love finding new adventures and new ways to express yourself; I'm sure you've taken dance lessons in the past, so there's no reason to play it safe now!

Aries wants a song that is both passionate and soulful, so consider dancing a spicy Latin salsa or an energetic swing. For a popular tune, check out Al Green's or Tina Turner's "Let's Stay Together." Leo has more highbrow taste. A modern fox-trot to Steve Tyrell's elegant and uptempo "Cheek to Cheek" is stylish yet classic; work with a professional for a completely polished look.

The easygoing Sag isn't likely to put on a show (unless you have an Aries, Leo, Gemini, or Libra Rising). You are most comfortable with something down-to-earth, such as a spontaneous twirl to U2's "All I Want Is You," or Percy Sledge's "When a Man Loves a Woman."

Pick a meaningful father-daughter dance and let it all hang loose. Stevie Wonder's "Isn't She Lovely" is a fun Fire favorite.

▢▢ Earth: Taurus, Virgo, Capricorn

An Earth bride likes classic dance music so it's no surprise that your first dance selection will be a traditional one. When it comes to making the perfect song choice, Earth girls know what moves their tender hearts and what shows them in the best light—you're not about to tackle a complicated routine unless you're sure you have the talent. And yes, you're great at summing up the effort to study something new, but unless dance lessons are one of your priorities, you may not want to allocate the precious resources to do it.

Unless you have a Fire or Air sign Rising, Taurus likes familiar classics. Go for an oldie like "It Had to Be You" by Frank Sinatra. Virgo wants to make sure the lyrics reflect her feelings perfectly; consider Sam Cooke's "You Send Me." Capricorn will either play up her conservative side or her ambitious one, like Andee, who surprised her Latin in-laws by performing a tango with her groom. Go for "I've Got My Love to Keep Me Warm" by Ella Fitzgerald, but only if you're willing to master the fox-trot so you can let it all hang out!

Tender and loving are the priorities for the Earth bride's father-daughter dance; "What a Wonderful World" by Louis Armstrong is the hands-down favorite.

❑❑ Air: Gemini, Libra, Aquarius

Air sign's first dances are going to be on the edgy, cheeky, and elegant side. Leave the slow love songs to your Earth friends and pick something a little unusual to highlight your unique style. Take advantage of the fact that you are the most graceful element in the zodiac and plan a routine that will delight your guests and make your parents smile.

The Libra bride wants an airy beautiful song so you can sweep down the dance floor like a modern-day Ginger Rogers. An old standard with a strong rhythm accompanied by some dance lessons will do the trick.

Nonconformist Aquarius and Gemini brides enjoy dancing to the beat of their own drum. Knowing you have carte blanche to choose a song to step out to is just thrilling. If you've got a playful personality, consider doing a swing to Count Basie or Duke Ellington. If you want something on the hip and cool side, "Ice Cream" by Sarah McLachlan is the way to go. Finally, if you're looking for a bold upbeat classic to ham it up to, choose "You're My First, My Last, My Everything" by Barry White.

An Air sign father-daughter dance that is both cheery and sentimental: "My Girl" from the Temptations.

❑❑ Water: Cancer, Scorpio, Pisces

The Water sign bride's first dance is going to be heartfelt and sentimental. To you, finding a meaningful song is your number-one priority, its style comes in a distant second. You may choose to take dance lessons with your sweetheart, but putting on a show isn't your motivation; it's the melody and lyrics that move you.

The Pisces bride's taste runs from passionate to angelic. For the romantic in you, choose "Unchained Melody" from the Righteous Brothers or "At Last" by Etta James. For lighter fare, consider Harry Connick, Jr.'s rendition of "It Had to Be You."

Cancer brides have more traditional leanings. A theme from your favorite movie, Broadway play, or an old standard will put you in the mood. "All I Ask of You" from *Phantom of the Opera* is a popular choice, as is "Love Is Here to Stay" from Billie Holiday.

Scorpio will go to the ends of the earth to find the song with lyrics that reflect your beliefs. Something like Joe Cocker's "You Are So Beautiful" is what you're looking for. The sentimental Water sign father-daughter dance is to Al Martino's "Daddy's Little Girl."

■ The Cake

The cake is one of the most common elements in a wedding and one of the most unique at the same time. Think about it, no bride and groom would get married without one and yet no two are alike! Whatever your cake budget, you can work with your baker to create one that perfectly complements your astrological personality. What should your cake reveal about you?

❑❑ Fire: Aries, Leo, Sagittarius

Fire signs are divided on their approach to wedding cake. Aries and Leo brides want their wedding cake to be dramatic and oversized, while the laid-back Sagittarius bride would be happy with anything but large and theatrical!

Aries and Leos have larger-than-life personalities, but that's not why you need to have a beautiful, unique, well-decorated wedding cake. You love the pageantry of weddings, the walk down the aisle, the first dance. The cake is one of these very important dramatic elements so you've got to make it count.

Sometimes you enjoy making spontaneous decisions, but in this case take your time. Research on the Internet, buy specialty cake books, and interview bakers. Think through all the possible choices—and sit down for tastings—before plunking down your deposit.

For a Sagittarius who is much more interested in location, this can be a low priority and a way to save money. Choose a smaller cake with simple decorations or add a fun cake topper to a plain one; by the time the cake comes out, people will be enjoying the party too much to notice.

◻◻ Earth: Taurus, Virgo, Capricorn

Earth brides love the traditions of weddings so you are looking forward to choosing a great design for your cake. Since all three of you are detail-oriented perfectionists—especially Virgo and Capricorn—it must fit into the style and theme of your day perfectly (or you might have a meltdown)! Earth signs love good food as well, so it's got to be made of the highest-quality ingredients and taste great, too.

Virgo and Capricorn are going to micromanage your way to a fantastic wedding cake, inside and out. You want a cake that looks beautiful yet understated, a classic three-tiered cake with smooth white fondant decorations of ribbon and pearl accents. Both Virgo and Capricorn have sophisticated tastes, so pass on custard or butter cream filling for layers of fresh fruit or raspberry mousse, which would better suit your style.

Taurus brides have the same seasoned taste, but like a more decorated cake with bolder colors. Add colorful handmade sugar or marzipan flowers to your well-proportioned cake, or try a soft translucent lilac-patterned lace made of butter cream and fondant.

◻◻ Air: Gemini, Libra, Aquarius

The cake is another way for an Air bride to show off your unique personality—you can't wait to design a special dessert to celebrate your marriage that is totally striking and modern! Libra will go for something beautiful and gracious; Aquarius and Gemini, something elegant and whimsical.

It's not just the look of the cake that is important to you. Air signs love sweets and have a very discerning palate. Take your time analyzing various tastes and talking to your baker before choosing a sophisticated blend of flavors that will end up as the foundation for this hip delight.

Libra, go for a white fondant with tasteful white or pale colored gum paste flower accents. Choose a delicate flavor combination of white cake and white chocolate mousse and creamy raspberry filling.

The sky's the limit for Aquarius and Gemini who have a great imagination and cutting-edge taste. Start with a whimsical, asymmetrical three- or four-tiered design. Surprise everyone by giving each tier a distinctive taste—such as carrot, sour-cream fudge, or white chocolate sponge cake layered with a different complementary filling. Elizabeth's very Gemini cake was ivory fondant with green stripes and shapes. "We liked the modern-looking geometric pattern," she says.

❑❑ Water: Cancer, Scorpio, Pisces

Water sign brides want their cake to look like wedding cake (for those great romantic photos) and taste as satisfying as a dessert in any four-star restaurant. Unless you have an Air sign Rising, you're not into experimenting with unusual shapes and flavors—why confuse the guests?

Cancer and Pisces want a traditional look and familiar taste; go for a beautiful two- or three-tiered white cake with chocolate butter cream. Decorate it with delicate ivory and white lacy royal icing and tiny pearl accents. You might consider using your parents' cake topper, if it's well preserved, to add sentimental value.

Besides the Cancer and Pisces famed sensitive stomachs, many Cancers love cooking and baking. Make sure to choose a top-notch baker that uses fresh, high-quality ingredients. You don't want to get sick, but in addition, there's nothing more embarrassing to you than a cake that looks good but tastes terrible.

Scorpio wants a cake to reflect your passionate tastes. Why feel coerced into a light, airy white cake with ivory fondant? Go for a rich chocolate fudge cake layered with chocolate ganache instead! Decorate it with dark chocolate butter cream and some beautiful jewel-toned marzipan flowers. It will look sexy and taste divine!

■ Toasts and Speeches

Should you follow tradition with the toasts and just have the best man, maid of honor, and father of the bride speak? Or should you leave a mic open for all to share? Are you comfortable with spontaneous expressions or do you fear what these key players might say? There are so many issues to think about when it comes to this heartfelt and potentially touchy subject. Before you make important decisions about these orations get some insight from your sign.

❑❑ **Fire: Aries, Leo, Sagittarius**

Fire signs love dramatic, meaningful expressions and gestures. To you, a perfect speech has a few laughs, a few tears, and a warm hug. On the day of the wedding, it'll be really important that key players give sincere toasts and say them loud enough for all to hear. Let your loved ones know that you are looking forward to these wonderful sentiments so that they can prepare them in advance.

With the toasts, it just doesn't work one-way. You love giving speeches as well, so plan a good one of your own. Thank your family, your in-laws, and your best friends, recalling wonderful memories that make each one feel special. If you're not comfortable standing up during your reception, then definitely make sure you say something at the rehearsal dinner.

Fire signs are great at creating the space for this kind of self-expression. Let your close friends and family know that you'd love them to share their thoughts and feelings. Summer and Tony, a fiery Aries-Sag couple, were surprised at the number of people who had heartfelt words for them. "The emotions that surged throughout the whole party were unexpected. People who weren't even slated to speak got up and started crying and saying these wonderful things," recalls Summer.

☐ ☐ Earth: Taurus, Virgo, Capricorn

Heartfelt speeches are a a vital part of every traditional wedding and you are looking forward to having them be a special part of yours. Seeing your dad stand up and welcome your new husband into the family with a kind word and a warm embrace will make your heart smile; having your best friend reminisce about all the fun things you've done together is priceless.

We already know Earth girls are very tender and loving, but there's a private side to you as well. Unless you have an Aquarius, Gemini, Aries, or Leo Moon or Rising, you're very happy to stick to tradition when it comes to the toasts; the best man, maid of honor, father of the bride, and father-in-law is enough for you.

Earth brides love reaching out one-on-one. You'd rather walk around from guest to guest, lovingly thanking each one with a hug or kiss than make a big speech of your own.

Spontaneity isn't a strong suit for Taurus, Virgo, and Capricorn brides, so you might shy away from the idea of letting too many people have their say. For Virgo and Capricorns, not being able to control the contents of the speeches can be unnerving if you don't quite trust your family members! Think this aspect through before planning the specifics.

☐ ☐ Air: Gemini, Libra, Aquarius

Speeches and toasts are vital to an Air sign bride. You love gathering people together for a great party and hearing them speak about it is very meaningful to you. You're looking forward to all the standard toasts—best man, maid of honor, and father of the bride, but to be honest, that's not quite enough for you!

Make a short list of close friends and family and find a way to incorporate them into the wedding's speeches. Invite them to say a few words at the rehearsal dinner or set up a plan with your DJ or bandleader to pepper the evening with toasts. Make sure you tell these VIPs ahead of time so that they can plan something funny and heartfelt.

Unless you have an Earth Rising sign and a Cancer or Scorpio Moon, you're not about to let your own wedding go by without making a surprise speech of your own. You want to thank everyone for coming, make some jokes, and say some wonderful things about your groom! This is especially true for Aquarius and Gemini brides, who dismiss most social conventions. The Libra bride may choose to make this speech at the rehearsal dinner if a formal affair precludes it.

❑ ❑ Water: Cancer, Scorpio, Pisces

Water sign brides are very comfortable with deep, heartfelt words of affection—but only in certain settings. Before you invite anyone to give any speeches or toasts, consider how big your wedding is going to be, who is going to be there, and how you might feel about showing so much vulnerability in front of a crowd.

Pisces can handle more spontaneous, funny, and potentially uncomfortable words than Cancer and Scorpio; not only do you get mortally embarrassed by having your deep thoughts, feelings, and experiences revealed, but once you're rattled it's hard to let it go without a little processing—and how can you do that in the middle of your party?

These toasts will either create sentimental moments that warm your heart forever or become disconcerting memories that you just will not be able to shake. Consider carefully who you ask to speak and don't feel obligated by certain relationships—or at the very least, prepare yourself ahead of time.

Nina, a Cancer, sums it up perfectly. "I always get worried about toasts because I think, 'Oh, no, what are they going to say? Are they going to make a fool out of me? You know, my grandparents are sitting here.'" Ruminations about potential disaster aside, "The toasts were fantastic," says Nina. But then again, we're only talking about the maid of honor and the best man. "We didn't let other people near the microphone," she reveals.

▪ Favors and Crafts

The last way you separate yourself from the bridal pack is by choosing what small gifts and keepsakes to give your guests. When in comes to expressing your creativity, the sky's the limit. Design perfect little reminders of your very special day on any budget.

Ready to Elope Yet?

At this point, you might be ready to throw in the towel, run off to some exotic place, and just do it. This idea runs through the head of every bride at one stressful point during their planning, but it takes a very unique astrological mind-set to actually do it.

Take Jennifer, whom you met earlier, and Stephen, a Scorpio and a Libra, two signs that have very definite ideas of what a wedding and marriage is all about. "We believe that the wedding is actually for the two of us getting married, not for the rest of the family, and because of that, we did it our way," says Jennifer.

They knocked around a couple of ideas before picking a weekend and choosing the kitschiest chapel in Las Vegas. Right before jumping on a plane, they e-mailed friends and family with the surprise news and a link to the chapel's Web cam.

At the appointed time, the chapel picked them up in a white limo (apparently the pink Cadillac was in the shop). They got married by Elvis, who made them vow "to love each other tender," before singing three romantic songs. They danced with two showgirls in hula skirts, the photographer took about thirty great photos, and they were back at their hotel in forty-five minutes.

It took an hour of planning at the most and they have wonderful memories. "I can't tell you how many people have told me, 'I wished we had eloped,' the whole experience was very relaxed and enjoyable," said Jenn. Stephen agrees: "We started off our marriage in a really wonderful way; the point was to have fun."

So how did these newlyweds celebrate their big day after exchanging rings? By going to the casino, of course. "Til we lost all our money," Stephen adds, laughing.

While you're at it, don't stop at the favors. If you enjoy crafty projects, consider creating little mementos to surround the guest book,
ladies' bathroom, or any outdoor spaces your guests may enjoy.

❑❑ Fire: Aries, Leo, Sagittarius

Fire signs love an opportunity to be creative but you're also spontaneous, so stop yourself from choosing the first favor that crosses your
path because you might change your mind and order a second set!

Many Fire signs tie these little gifts in with sentimental memories,
like where they got engaged or exchanged their first I love yous. You'll
choose what moves you, even if the favors don't fit the overall theme of
your wedding.

Beyond that, use your creativity to design personal touches if you
are on a budget. That's exactly what Summer, the Aries queen of crafting, did with her wedding. Not only did she make the flower centerpieces as I mentioned earlier, but she purchased gilded picture frames
that matched those on the wall of the hall, four for each table, and
placed various photos of her and Tony growing up as well as their parents' wedding photos. As she says, "They were pretty to look at and
had sentimental value."

Their guest book wins the prize, though. People wrote wonderful
words on small pieces of paper, took an instant photo, and placed these
mementos in little envelopes inside an album. How's that for something to bring you back?

❑❑ Earth: Taurus, Virgo, Capricorn

Earth brides are meticulous about their favors and crafts. You want
something that is practical, inexpensive, and fits in seamlessly with the
theme of your big day. A set of requirements that might drive other
signs batty, you see as a great challenge.

Giving something edible is common for Earth girls or brides with
Earth Risings who love to nurture people (Taurus) and can't stand

cheap tchotchkes (Virgo and Capricorn). Creating beautiful elaborate packaging is a must. Finding the exact ribbon in your center-pieces on sale, handcrafting the labels—you are most proud of the little details.

Earth girls love making their own favors; look for bride and groom cookie cutters and use an old family recipe to make delicious and un-forgettable take-home treats. Once it's wrapped in wedding-bell cellophane, labeled with a famous quote on love, and placed on each plate, it will add to the festive decor as well. Just make sure you have your photographer take some photos of your creation so you can remember all the hard work.

Andee, our ambitious creative Capricorn, shipped small rattan boxes to Hawaii, hand-enscribed each of the name labels, and filled them with—what else—chocolate-covered macadamia nuts!

❑ ❑ Air: Gemini, Libra, Aquarius

Air sign brides create unique, interesting favors for their guests. For the Air bride, it's very important to choose something that is both reflective of who you are and will make people's eyes light up. Libra will go for something beautiful, while Aquarius and Gemini tend toward something a little kitschy. Either way, you love thinking and analyzing, and will mull over many ideas, do research on the Internet, and perhaps visit many craft stores before making this decision.

Air brides are creative and forward-thinking yet dislike being bogged down with tons of tiny details. You're better off with an item you can order that's almost complete, then add a unique crafty touch, like a ribbon and label or some unusual wrap. Once you've analyzed your choices, you need something that offers pretty much instant grati-fication.

You are the same way with other crafty ideas; coming up with them is more fun than actually making them. If your visions of transforming the reception space involve too many detailed hours to complete, invite your Earth sign pals over to help.

Our bride with the Mexican reception had the tables overflowing with Mexican crafts including *puta* dolls, rattles of papier-mâché animals, balloons, and Mexican hats that her guests could shake and dance with, and then take home.

▢▢ Water: Cancer, Scorpio, Pisces

Out of all the zodiac, Water sign brides take the the most time and effort deciding on little details like the favors and crafty extras. You come across as perfectionists, but the true motivation is to create meaningful elements and lasting memories. Water brides make no decisions on automatic pilot!

To create the perfect favor, first think of items that have sentimental value to you, then find a way to incorporate them into the theme of the day. Pisces and Scorpio will create something with practicality and personal meaning, while Cancer might go for something more elegant and traditional.

You love making things by hand, so if you don't see the perfect item in any bridal mags, make them yourself! That is exactly what Cancer Leila did when she got together with the mother of a lifelong friend and created a romantic set of candles wrapped in little silk baggies. One said *love* in Arabic, one said *love* in English.

The favors are a great way to keep a nosy mother busy, if you can give up control. One Scorpio bride with an outdoor summer wedding got her mother involved by making gift bags filled with flip-flops, suntan lotion, bug repellant, tissues, mints, and a fan. "She had fun going around and finding these things and putting the bags together." And she stayed out of her daughter's hair!

What She Really Needs From You:
How to Be the Best Groom on the Planet!

No one is on their best behavior when wedding stress rears its ugly head. When the reception hall is double-booked, the favors get broken in the mail, or the florist forgets the cascading ivy, brides everywhere lose their minds. If your bride freaks-out along the way, knowing exactly how to respond—and how *not* to respond—can make your trip down the aisle a lot more enjoyable.

Take all the guesswork out of being a groom. Here's how to be there for her in the most supportive way possible.

ARIES BRIDE   Let her vent. When she's upset the first thing she wants to do is let it out. Whatever it is, listen and agree. Ask her what she plans to do about it. Never offer a solution without asking, "Want to know what I would do?"

TAURUS BRIDE   Show her tender loyalty. This bride gives in easily on practical matters, but if key players want their way for no good reason, she'll hold her ground. Let her know her desires are important and that you stand by her. Never make a deal without consulting her.

GEMINI BRIDE   Let her talk it through. Her brain is running a mile a minute and she's got a ton of nervous energy. Calm her down by listening and helping her organize her thoughts. Never put these important conversations off until later.

CANCER BRIDE   Always be there for her. She's a sensitive soul who is easily hurt and has a hard time making decisions. Never assume she's got everything under control without asking how she feels; give her a tender hug and she'll melt.

LEO BRIDE   Tell her how awesome she is. She can get indignant when people forget to treat her like the bride she is. Help her reclaim her dignity by letting her know how much you admire her. Never question her authority and always discuss planning choices in private.

VIRGO BRIDE Tell her she's doing an amazing job. Virgo brides are most comfortable crossing things off their list. She needs nothing more than to feel valued and appreciated. Never take all her efforts for granted, or her feelings will be hurt.

LIBRA BRIDE Be a team. Libra needs harmony. When a problem arises, it throws off that delicate balance. Come to the rescue by working things out together. Never leave her too much to do alone and never tell her she's crazy for getting upset.

SCORPIO BRIDE Let her have her space. This bride likes to do things on her own. When she's ready to talk, ask her how she's feeling and let her vent. Never check up on her or question her decisions—she might feel like you're questioning her soul.

SAGITTARIUS BRIDE Lighten her load. When the Sag bride has too many things on her list, she feels the walls closing in. Doing some of the work will allow her to breathe easy. Never tell her what to do, *ask;* she's very flexible.

CAPRICORN BRIDE Ask her what you can do to help. Capricorn brides will always let everyone think everything is under control. Take a small job so she can focus on the important things. Always appreciate her efforts and never question her authority—talk about things instead.

AQUARIUS BRIDE Let her know you understand. Aquarius brides let most things slide off their back. When something is important, she needs to know you support her decisions. Never force her to follow standard traditions; give her a good reason.

PISCES BRIDE Whatever it is, promise to take care of it. When the unexpected occurs, Fish can become inconsolable. Reassuring her that you're fixing the problem will immediately calm her down. Never leave her to handle big issues by herself, she needs backup.

Chapter *Eight*

Fast-forward to the days and weeks before your wedding. As you wrap up all the unfinished business, tie up loose ends, and fix last-minute glitches, you hold on to your sanity by realizing that once this is all over, you get to jet-set off to some relaxing locale to chill out and just be together.

I'm sure you've been thinking of your perfect honeymoon for as long as you've been engaged, but choosing a specific destination and unique activities can be a tough decision when there are so many choices out there. Yes, you want to get advice from family and friends who have been there and done that, but you've got to make sure your coworkers, parents, or travel agent don't try to talk you into a honeymoon that's just not right for you as a couple.

Staying true to your sign extends to the honeymoon, as well. Every member of the zodiac has very specific ideas of how they like to spend their time. From sunrise to sunset, here's your astro-guide. The perfect trip awaits your creation!

■ Choosing the Perfect Destination

Hawaii, Greece, Alaska, the Caribbean—let yourself imagine the possibilities. This is the time to get together with your fiancé, a great travel Web site, a honeymoon guide, or a stack of travel mags and consider what your dream vacation looks like. Only this time instead of starting from scratch, here are some tips and key words, courtesy of your birthday.

Since we're a combination of our Sun and Rising signs, read both to get a good idea of what makes your vacations tick. If you are reading this with your significant other, use the keywords for each Sun sign as your guide and find a locale that gives you everything you both need!

❏ ❏ Fire: Aries, Leo, Sagittarius

When a Fire sign thinks honeymoon, you think *big*. No matter where you choose to go, Aries and Leo want the red-carpet treatment—a magnificent room, a luxurious hot tub, upscale meals, and wonderful entertainment.

Sag thinks big in a down-to-earth way, looking for the most exotic spots on the planet where you can learn about a completely new culture, sleep somewhere cool, explore the area, and hang out with the locals.

Fire signs love beaches; consider Hawaii, Bora Bora, Thailand, or Rio de Janeiro. You crave constant excitement so pick a destination that has a lot going on, day and night. A quiet island might sound romantic but you'll go stir-crazy without things like a spa, casino, dinner cruise, and horseback riding to give your days variety.

If you plan to go island-hopping, save the smallest for last, when you've already had a chance to unwind and it won't be such a culture shock. Remember to pack a good book or some fun games to keep you busy on the beach.

Fire signs love risk-taking, athletic activities, and will seek out the most daring experiences to write home about. A honeymoon just wouldn't be a honeymoon without going shark or stingray feeding.

When doing your research, a good rule to go by is making sure there is at least one new adventure per day and one per night. You don't have to plan it in advance, you just want to make sure there's enough to enjoy while you're there. Being bored on this most special of vacations is one of the worst things a Fire sign could imagine.

❑ ❑ Earth: Taurus, Virgo, Capricorn

Earth signs want their honeymoon to feel like a honeymoon—no trekking halfway across the world to some exotic destination; no heart-pounding, risky activities; and no place that involves too much dirt and bugs. (Unless you have a Fire or Air sign Rising, then you might just be a little more adventurous than most!)

What you do like is a lovely hotel in a beautiful location with terrific amenities. Capricorn chooses total luxury, Virgos want perfection, while Taurus wants something more down-to-earth and comfortable.

Earth girls love being active and being outdoors but you're not big adventure enthusiasts, so choose a destination that has a smattering of different activities. You enjoy quaint shops and interesting museums as much as you like riding a bike through breathtaking scenery and swimming in a calm ocean.

The two things you definitely need are some quality food and entertainment. Well-prepared meals with delicious wines; a Broadway show, jazz club, or lively Irish pub is thrilling for Earth brides who are happy to cuddle all night at a back table, holding hands and people watching.

I know we're dreaming but even a fantasy comes with a price tag for an Earth bride—you just cannot feel romantic and carefree knowing that it's costing an arm and a leg. Your luxury and comfort must come with a good value.

So where can you find these things in one place? The Canadian Rockies, the picturesque coast of Maine, the south of France, or even Napa Valley. You also like to revisit familiar places that you love, so consider going back to a favorite spot and doing it five-star this time.

❑ ❑ Air: Gemini, Libra, Aquarius

Most other signs hear the word *honeymoon* and automatically think *Hawaii*, Air signs hear it and think *anywhere but Hawaii!* From Libra's luxury to the unconventional plans of Gemini and Aquarius, nothing is ordinary for this Air sign holiday. Instead of reading bridal magazines for common ideas, read travel mags instead. You'll find a host of interesting places that a honeymoon expert might never recommend.

On this great trip, Air gals would much prefer to do a ton of things quickly rather than take their time with any one pursuit. Make sure wherever you go there are many different activities, good photo ops, things to explore, and plenty of time to talk about it. (Over an exotic drink, of course!)

The one thing you like is space. Choose a hotel that has spacious rooms, big windows, and amazing views. Somewhere you can ride a gondola to the top of a mountain and see for miles as you dine on local fare. A place that no one has ever heard of is a plus. You love sharing your recently discovered secrets with friends and family; besides, going where everyone else goes is such a turnoff.

Libra likes gracious romantic activities; a museum one day, sailing the next; shopping, tanning, a nice balance of everything. A beautiful location with fine food and sophisticated entertainment is a must. Libra enjoys the gentle Caribbean as much as Paris so take your pick.

Because freedom-loving Gemini and Aquarius never follow the rules, for inspiration think, *Where have I always longed to go and how can I make this work?* Ecofriendly Thailand, for instance, where you can hike through jungles, feed elephants, visit Buddhist temples and windsurf maybe?

❑ ❑ Water: Cancer, Scorpio, Pisces

Water girls can simply not get enough romance. Whether you are choosing a warm tropical island, a beautiful resort in South America, or hopscotching the European countryside, you want your honeymoon to be nothing short of mythic.

If you want a beach, make sure it's the right beach. While Water signs love being around all forms of water (for obvious reasons!), you're not especially hearty souls. Unless you have a Fire sign Rising, you'd much rather enjoy a leisurely dip in an infinity pool than take on sports like white-water rafting or waterskiing.

Water signs enjoy being pampered (especially the Pisces) so choose a spot that has a spa. In addition, Cancer needs some delicious food, and Scorpio, good-natured, conscious people. You are all so sensitive to other people's moods that going to an overcrowded hot spot where the staff is rude, overworked, and underpaid might weigh more heavily on your mind than you realize.

Water brides love quaint shops, art galleries, and small mom-and-pop stores where you can support the local economy and bring back goodies for the people you love back home.

This trip is so vital to starting your marriage off right, you must find the absolute perfect place to begin your life together. To discover this once-in-a-lifetime destination, contemplate locations that tug at your heartstrings. Consider staying at a chateau in France, a palazzo in Italy, or taking a cruise around the Galapagos Islands. A honeymoon that's earth-friendly is good for your conscience and your heart.

Marriage for the Ultimate Adventurers: A Weddi-moon

When it comes to weddings, Sagittarius brides break the mold. Exploring the unknown is a priority for this fire sign. They're more likely to get excited about the globe-trotting honeymoon than posies and napkins.

Meet Kawana and Joe, a fun Sag-Gemini couple. "We're really low-maintenance kind of people," says Kawana. "Originally we were going to have a traditional wedding, but the more we talked about it, the more stressful it felt." Then she was talking to some friends who suggested getting married on the beach in Jamaica: "It was like a strike of lightning for me."

Once they made the decision, it was a month of stress-free planning and within four months they were at a beautiful all-inclusive resort on the beach with thirteen of their closest family members and friends.

Choose a destination wedding and you throw little details out the window. That's fine for Gemini and Sag, because what makes for great memories to these freedom-loving signs is the spontaneity and the ad-

venture. "The preacher had a really thick accent, we didn't understand a word he was saying. I was looking at Joe and he was nudging
me like, 'That's your part.'

"I was more concerned about my eyes. 'What are my eyes doing?'
I whispered. 'Forget about your eyes, this is your part.' I never wore
fake eyelashes before, and I didn't quite get them on right. So there we
were on the beach and they were flickering in the wind." Kawana
laughs but other brides might cry at that experience.

Resorts know how to please. After the ceremony, they had a lovely
reception with champagne, hors d'oeuvres, cake, and a horse-and-
buggy ride for the newlyweds.

For eleven days they went swimming, snorkeling, scuba diving,
trapezing. "I thought the best part was that everybody was on the
beach, hanging out and swimming before the wedding and again after
the wedding. We just put my grandmother right back in the same
hammock and we watched the sunset; it was just great."

■ Practical Decisions

Now we get a little more realistic (which is easier for some signs than
it is for others!). This is where we think about combining your dream
vacation with realistic issues to come up with *the* honeymoon. Each
sign has its own set of concerns, such things as budget, season, aller-
gies, length of vacation time, and access to travel.

Let's take a look at what's important for you to feel comfortable on
your first trip as a married couple.

❏ ❏ Fire: Aries, Leo, Sagittarius

The biggest concern for a Fire sign is choosing a place where you're going to have fun. When it comes to logistics, Sag and Aries are much
more flexible. If the first beach destination is too expensive or too far
away, you'll simply choose another one without skipping a beat.

Leos, on the other hand, want luxury and are willing to do whatever it takes to get it. You must have the best on your honeymoon even if that means working hard upon your return to pay it all off.

Aries and Sag on a budget would rather stay at a less expensive hotel and stretch your vacation for as long as you can. It's the opposite for Leo who can't imagine staying at a no-name hotel, no matter how decent it is. Packing it up two days earlier is well worth the trade of being treated like a queen while you're there.

Fire signs are not ones to play it safe. The possibility of bad weather won't automatically deter you from going where you've always wanted to go. After weighing all the options, you might just take your chances knowing that luck is on your side. Plus Fire signs are upbeat, optimistic people who manage to find adventure in everything, including walking in the rain and exploring indoor activities.

Big spenders, all of you can get carried away in local markets. If money is a concern, be aware of what you are spending and limit your shopping days.

❑❑ Earth: Taurus, Virgo, Capricorn

Earth girls love mulling over the practicalities of the honeymoon. Unless you have a Water sign Rising, you never get your heart set on a destination until you've done your homework.

First up is the budget; if you're choosing to spend your cash on a big wedding, you may decide to have a honeymoon in your own backyard. Research lovely mountain inns and beach town bed-and-breakfasts within driving distance. Earth brides are great at finding bargains (you don't pay full price for *anything*). Scour the Internet for destinations with off-season specials and get more for your dollar no matter where you go.

Earth signs are very careful planners; look into weather patterns and skip any place that may have delays or cancellations because of seasonal problems, and don't forget to buy vacation insurance. If you take your chances, you may end up sitting in the airport fuming that you've missed hours of your precious honeymoon.

Next thing on the Earth girl agenda is making sure that you can easily get where you are going without having to take a million planes, trains, and automobiles—and avoid the added costs of those transfers. You have a lot of patience, but sitting on a plane for fourteen hours, to then hop on a two-hour ferry can be very uncomfortable, especially if you only have a week. Find another slice of paradise to hang your hat; you can have a good time anywhere.

❑ ❑ Air: Gemini, Libra, Aquarius

You love to research and analyze the possibilities. Putting your choices side by side, looking at them logically, and figuring out which ones have what you are looking for is a joy for an Air sign. And, of course, we can't forget how much you like talking about it as well.

All that analyzing aside, there aren't too many practical issues that deter Air signs from going where you want to go. Call it luck, call it ingenuity, but Air signs always find a way.

Budget-conscious Air brides would rather do research than be grounded. You are great at uncovering that little-known secret travel Web site (and then passing it along to everyone you know). Eco- and humanitarian-minded Air brides will make sure they are not compromising their ideals just for a vacation as well.

Aquarius and Gemini just like to get on an airplane and go on a grand adventure. Vaccinations, visa requirements, international driver's licenses, nothing is a big deal to you. Libra, on the other hand, gets anxious about too much paperwork or a visit to the clinic, so stay in your hemisphere.

The last practicality on your agenda is simply making sure that you don't pick a destination or hotel that is too far away from all the action. You may want to relax but just the thought of feeling stuck sends shivers down your spine.

❑❑ Water: Cancer, Scorpio, Pisces

Water signs are not practical and compromising when it comes to your deepest desires. If a fairy-tale honeymoon is important to you, settling on a lesser one can be downright depressing. On the other hand, after spending all your dough on the wedding, money may be a concern.

Instead of trying to be realistic and then getting sad, get smart. Search for off-season deals, travel at odd times, or shorten your trip. Choose your dream location and skip the four-star digs for a condo rental, cook food from local markets rather than eating most meals out, and limit your purchases. Water signs don't need top-of-the-line luxury and pampering to have a good time; one spa treatment will make you feel like a million bucks and will not bust your bank.

Water signs do have sensitive stomachs. In fact, unless you've got an Earth Rising or Moon sign, Cancer and Pisces are prone to vulnerable constitutions in general. Keep this in mind when choosing a destination and err on the side of caution (you don't want to get sick on your honeymoon, so save the trip to South America for another time). Know what you can handle and don't let anyone misguidedly convince you otherwise. At the very least stock up on natural remedies before you go.

A Romantic Honeymoon Minus the Beach

When they hear the word *honeymoon,* most people think *beach,* but the truth is, not every sign likes that type of vacation. For Lois and Chris, a Scorpio-Pisces couple who honeymooned in Ireland, finding a new place to explore together, some place neither of them had been, was most important in choosing their destination.

"Everyone who has been to Ireland told us how friendly the people are, how beautiful the countryside is, that we would have such a great time," says Lois, who planned the itinerary by searching the Net and taking recommendations from friends.

The first stop on their two-week jaunt was a castle in the country-side. "It was a sprawling masterpiece and the grounds were unbeliev-ably gorgeous," something you'll find all over the lush isle. "We were so jet-lagged we slept a lot those first couple of days, but even sleeping we felt like a king and queen." Sounds like a fairy-tale adventure any Water sign newlywed would love!

The next stop was a hotel in Kenmare where they skipped the car and rode bikes around town. "We stumbled upon an ancient ceme-tery and spent a good hour reading tombstones," she reveals. "We were fascinated by the Celtic crosses."

Driven to find a deeper meaning, Water signs enjoy transporting themselves back in time with their rich imagination, something you just can't do on a beach. "One thing we can't forget are the stone cir-cles and other remnants of Druid and pagan culture. We thought we'd see old things because it was Europe, but some of those ruins from 2500 B.C. blew us away," recalls Lois.

Hard-core days of sightseeing were followed by relaxing days where they would venture out by foot to check out the local towns, eat lunch, and shop. "We didn't want to come home, it was really just so much fun," says Lois, who can't recommend the Emerald Isle enough. "Ireland is so green and so beautiful, the people are so kind; it was definitely the magic we were looking for." How positively Scorpio!

■ Romantic Activities for Day and Night

Whether you choose an exotic island adventure or a down-to-earth get-away, each sign has its own passions and interests (as well as activities that they can't stand). What appeals to you? Read up and you may just discover something about yourself that you didn't know!

❑❑ Fire: Aries, Leo, Sagittarius

We already know that Fire signs like edgy activities—there's only so much lying in the sun you can take. You love to try new things and have

a great story to tell later. Jet-skiing, parasailing, snowboarding—the
more exotic the the better.

By night Aries and Leo like just as much excitement. Dinner and
dancing, late-night clubbing, even karaoke is fun when there's champagne involved! Sag might mix in some mellower activities—hanging
out in a bar by the pool or a jazz club is just your style.

Avoid all activities that make you sit for too long or think too much.
Touring an old factory can be torture unless it's very interactive, and
keep any walks through botanical gardens short. On the other hand,
sex and shopping are two indoor sports you adore; focus your attention
in that direction on a rainy day.

Every sign should honor who they are before they commit to something. Almost every Fire sign I spoke with who honeymooned on a
beach went shark-feeding and loved it. Yet they *all* recalled that most
other people got scared when the sharks came around for lunch and
swam back to the boat. Earth or Water signs, perhaps, who should've
chosen to swim with the dolphins instead!

❏❏ Earth: Taurus, Virgo, Capricorn

Earth girls like to be active but don't like to be rushed. You enjoy meeting new people, but can't stand to hang out in large, loud crowds. Skip
the commercial tours and opt for activities like hiking up a volcanic
mountain, horseback riding in the hills, or walking through beautiful
manicured gardens.

You find swimming, sunning, and sipping at martinis pleasurable,
too, but just don't try to pack too much into each day or it won't feel
like a honeymoon to you.

Earth couples also enjoy arts and culture. Meandering through a famous museum, stopping at the "local bakery for a cup of café con leche and
to sample the croissants, and watching the locals go about their business
allows you to soak up all the little details of life that other signs may miss.

Skip the high-end shopping and head for the flea markets and local
artisans' co-op where you can bargain for one-of-a-kind works of art

and antique pieces you just can't find anywhere else. Coming home with that handwoven rug or stained-glass window will remind you of your first days together for the rest of your life.

At night, visit local theaters, jazz clubs, and four-star restaurants. Unless you have a Fire or Air sign Rising, you'd much rather linger over dessert than go clubbing until the wee hours. One night of dancing is enough to satisfy you.

☐☐ Air: Gemini, Libra, Aquarius

Air signs like to be busy, to constantly explore the environment and discover new things. You're looking forward to trying all the activities your destination has to offer, yet not in a particularly hearty way. Skip the hours and hours of outdoor activities other signs love so much and go for a little sampling of everything.

Instead of signing up for an all-day sailing and scuba excursion, go for a two-hour tour and follow that with a walk through the historic district, visiting art galleries and photographing quiet alleys as you learn about life in this foreign land. One of the most pleasurable things you can do is chat with some friendly locals and find out what they do on their off-hours. Even better still, have them show you around.

Air signs love hip, happening nightlife. Lounging in the back booth of a jazz club, listening to music, and chatting about your day, while you whisper sweet (and witty) nothings to each other is your idea of perfection. In addition, check out the local theater, comedy shows, dance clubs, and try every restaurant that has interesting food and drink on the menu.

Air gals love sleeping late, shopping, sunning, and sex, but even then variety is key. Switch up your schedule every day and pack it with tons of exciting things to keep your attention.

☐☐ Water: Cancer, Scorpio, Pisces

Water sign gals spend a ton of time researching and planning meaningful activities for both bride and groom. Not that you need to control every moment, you just want to make sure that you experience all the things you love on this most special of holidays.

First check out the local sights, everything from botanical gardens and museums to old historic homes. Soaking up the culture is vital to the sensitive Water bride. Sign up for a day or evening walking tour; you enjoy learning about architecture, historic events, and ghosts from well-trained tour guides.

Sentimental Water signs love purchasing the perfect keepsakes, so make a day of visiting flea markets and antique shops. Just remember to negotiate with vendors; sometimes when Water gals get their heart set on something, they'll hand over any amount to get it.

Come night, seek out quiet, romantic restaurants where you can sit next to each other and hold hands while sharing a bottle of wine. Get tickets to a play and go out for a late dessert. Unless you have a Fire or Air Rising, you won't need to be constantly on the go. Lounging around the hot tub and watching the sunset is one of the most thrilling experiences you can share!

Add some romantic outdoor activities as well. Sailing, rowboating, sledding, horseback or bike riding—nothing that will exhaust you or make you sweat too much; you don't want to feel like you've been to the gym, it's your honeymoon!

A Classic Honeymoon on a Budget

When Sari and Victor, a Libra and Aquarius, first started thinking about their honeymoon, they tossed around the idea of going to Greece but wanted to use airline miles and couldn't get the tickets. (A great idea for couples who have tons of miles and potentially empty pockets. You just might have to book the airline tickets the day after you book your reception site—especially if you're getting married in the summer.)

They discovered Aruba after watching ABC's bachelor, Charlie O'Connell, take three lovely ladies on their last date to the tropical paradise. As the island lies below the hurricane belt, it's a safe choice for a beach honeymoon in August.

"This was the first time that either one of us has gone on a significant vacation that we've paid for and planned ourselves, so it was a big deal," says careful Libra Sari. Once they settled on an island vacation, they decided to go for an all-inclusive so it would be ultra-relaxing. "We wanted adventure but we also wanted not to be always on the run to get our fun and adventure," Victor adds in true Aquarian fashion.

They took advantage of the resort's honeymoon package that included a romantic sunset dinner, and received a great off-roading excursion from one of his friends as a wedding gift. "That was an amazing day. We went in six Jeeps, everybody got to switch off driving, back-roading, going to the wild part of the island where the ocean was crashing," says Victor.

For some couples, contributing or paying for your wedding doesn't leave you with much to work with when it's all over. You could choose to stay close to home, postpone your grand getaway, or get creative. Air signs enjoy doing quirky things, Sari and Victor sat through two short time-share presentations and received two complimentary gifts that translated into free entertainment.

One was a scuba-snorkling hybrid called snuba diving and the other was casino chips, which was the perfect freebee for Sari. "I liked going to the casinos everyday," Sari reveals, "and we actually won quite a lot of money by the end of the trip." Sounds like the beginning of a lucky marriage to me!

▪ Adding the Perfect Surprises!

This is your opportunity to scrap all those *Let's Go!* guides for something fun and quirky. Using both of your sign's inner personalities as a guide, here are the extra touches you and your groom must have to make your honeymoon unforgettable.

❑ ❑ Fire: Aries, Leo, Sagittarius

Warm and loving partners, Fire sign brides and grooms love spontaneous displays of affection. Get creative with all the ways you can surprise your sweetheart with a hug and a kiss or an I love you. Take his hand in the middle of dinner and softly caress his fingers, grab him around the waist when you're walking down the street and whisper sweet things into his ear—these are the kinds of fun moments that will make a Fire sign honeymoon extra-spicy!

Fire sign brides and grooms love receiving fun, expensive (and sometimes outrageous) gifts. Buy him a pair of fun boxers to match that fabulous lingerie you've got packed. Surprise him with a picnic lunch in a beautiful secluded gorge (better yet if you have to take a romantic rowboat to get there!).

Another thing that will score big points with your Fire groom: Find out what types of sports and outdoor activities the hotel has to offer and sign yourselves up for a private lesson. He'll love to rappel into a canyon with a local guide but he'll be extra-thrilled to know you're coming along! Don't tell him about it until you are on the plane or arriving at the hotel!

❑ ❑ Earth: Taurus, Virgo, Capricorn

Earth sign brides and grooms love delicious food. Surprise him with a scrumptious room-service champagne breakfast your first day there (especially if you arrived late the night before). After sleeping in, treat him like a king. Give him a foot massage, run a relaxing bath, read him a gentle love poem you wrote just for the occasion, and don't leave the room until lunch!

Tender and devoted Earth brides and grooms love quiet time spent relaxing with their partners. If you're one who is constantly on the go, quietly plan a spa day for both of you. Go for a workout and a couple's massage and don't rush on to the next activity. Instead, sit around the spa's fireplace, sipping a cup of warm lemon water, holding hands, and smiling at each other. Private Earth grooms can have a hard time being pampered when it's not coming from their significant other, so don't schedule any bizarre exfoliation treatments or salt baths for him.

Earth brides and grooms love to be constantly touched and caressed, so hug him and tell him how *wonderful* he is—and remind him to do the same for you! Write him a love note and hide it in his luggage.

❏❏ Air: Gemini, Libra, Aquarius

Air brides and grooms just love being with their partners. Everything becomes an adventure when you do it together. From waiting in line at the airport to sipping champagne in the hot tub, there's always something to observe, chat, and laugh about.

Surprise your Air groom by discovering all the celebrities who have been to your honeymoon destination and reading the list on the plane. Make up fun games like "Top Ten Reasons I Love My Honey" over coffee at breakfast and make jokes about all the odd people you run across sitting in the hotel bar after dinner.

One of the best presents you can give an Air sign on their honeymoon, besides all that fun companionship, is a special day of activities designed for him and a special day for her. Research the most interesting sights off the beaten path, find unusual tour guides, cool restaurants, and put them together to make your special day. Plan things that he has never done before, such as ride in a hot air balloon or race dirt bikes, and finish off with a sunset dinner cruise.

If he doesn't have a videocamera, that would be the best surprise of all. Then he'll be busy spending his first few weeks as a married man editing a honeymoon movie on his computer.

❏❏ Water: Cancer, Scorpio, Pisces

There is nothing a Water sign bride or groom loves more than sweeping romantic gestures. Start off your honeymoon by writing love notes and hiding them in your groom's suitcases. Hold his hand through the entire airplane ride, and whisper sweet nothings into each other's ears often throughout the trip.

Committed Water signs are sentimental and love living among beautiful memories. Plan to surprise him with a nice camera. Make sure you can shoot in both color and black-and-white so you can take some nice artistic shots. Collect pamphlets from your favorite museums, business cards from restaurants, even the hotel bill, and then, after you get home, make a memory book you can look at often.

The best way to surprise a Water groom is to sneak away while you are having a romantic dinner and request they play meaningful music, like the song you danced to at your wedding. He'll recognize it right away without you even having to bring his attention to it!

Water grooms notice the small things. Remember to shop for a small gift for his mom and dad, help him pick out something special. Asking him what he wants to do, listening to him, and making him feel special are better than surprising him with any expensive gift.

■ ■

A heavenly honeymoon awaits your creation; and when you get back, a lifetime of companionship and love. Before I set you free to plan your big day, get a sneak peak into what life will be like when it's all over. Turn the page and see "Happily Ever After" for real.

Happily Ever *Afterword*

No bridal book would be complete without giving you a taste of married life. Yes, we've all read about Cinderella—but no one ever told us what happened after she found her Prince Charming! Unfortunately, there's no fairy-tale manual for learning how to live together, understand each other, and support one another.

In comes astrology. New brides everywhere face similar issues, but did you know that each sign tackles them in its own unique way? The zodiac can be a wonderful signpost to light your path. Use your sign's strengths and avoid the weaknesses as you navigate the world of newlywedded bliss. Here's how to harness your communication skills, understand your needs, and cope with your bad self!

■ The Aries Newlywed

Aries brides cannot wait to start their married life together—patience is in short supply when you're excited about something. To you, marriage is a new adventure, and you're looking forward to finding spicy fun things you can do with your husband and making your life together an interesting one.

To keep it fresh, set aside special date nights, find

hip restaurants, bars, and weekend activities to explore within your area, and pick something new every week. Make sure to include him when making plans so he doesn't feel bulldozed by all your dynamic energy.

On the flip side, needing constant excitement can be exhausting. Allow yourself time to chill in between all the fun, and teach your new husband how to take care of you in those moments. When Aries feels strongly about something (and when do you not?) you can get overheated pretty quickly. Take a deep breath, don't assume you're in for a battle, learn to process your feelings, and express them in a balanced way. Recognize that your security is not threatened by a disagreement.

■ The Taurus Newlywed

The Taurus newlywed knows that life is sweeter when you get to share it with a special mate. Showering your beloved with attention and setting up a lovely home together, these are the stuff of dreams for the Taurus woman. Loyal, tender, protective, and slow to anger, you are built for marriage.

Financial security is extremely important to you; keep this in mind when expanding your lives together. Visit a financial planner early on or read some good books on money management. Play it conservative with car loans, mortgages, and expensive items or you won't feel safe in your everyday life.

The dark side of Taurus is that you're stubborn! You like to be left alone to set up and run your home as you want to. Woe to the husband who changes anything without your knowing! Once upset, you can hold on to a grudge for days. Minimize this, catch your discomfort early, halt the changes, figure out how you can feel safe, and share those ideas. Most important, don't clam up and keep it in—communicate.

■ The Gemini Newlywed

Excited to get started on your new adventure, the Gemini newlywed is a restless being who needs constant mental stimulation. Unless your husband is an Air sign as well, you might want to give him a break occasionally! Plan fun activities that you two can share together, but also plan to spend fun time with friends and dive into hobbies close to home so that you have plenty of challenges to keep you busy.

Geminis enjoy marriage but don't take well to being domestic. Along with a wedding comes the standard responsibilities, such as making sure there's food to eat and a clean bed to sleep in. In order to be happy you have to find creative ways to share the chores and make old routines feel like new. If you're not vigilant about this early on, you might become bored and want to run.

The very worst thing for a Gemini is to feel misunderstood or unheard. When you sense a problem, don't let it get to the point of incessant chatter; take a moment to collect your feelings and express them in simple, logical terms your husband can understand.

■ The Cancer Newlywed

Cancer is the zodiac's nurturer, mother, and homemaker, so the idea of creating a wonderful home life for you and your new husband just thrills you. Home is not only a sanctuary for you, but a retreat for others as well, so make sure you make space for everyone you love. Inviting your parents, in-laws, brothers, sisters, nieces, and nephews into your home and nurturing those relationships is an important part of marriage.

Being extremely sensitive to others has its drawbacks. Cancers can magnify slights into big hurts and have a hard time letting go. Remember that no one is perfect and that people don't mean to hurt you—whether that be your husband, your parents, or your in-laws.

Cancers love being with their beloved but in order to have a healthy marriage you need to make the time to be alone (to process those deep feelings) and hang out with friends. Having an open and loving relationship is the lifeblood of Cancer women. If you run into a snag along the way, a good psychology or self-help book is comforting to your soul.

Something Every Newlywed Needs to Know

Geminis are known as the master communicators of the zodiac. It's a good thing we have one on hand to help newlywed couples master the art of conversation. You first met Elizabeth the chatty Gemini in chapter 5 after she and her husband, Eric, spent a gazillion hours crafting their ceremony. They spend just as much time engaged in healthy communication today, something that they've had to constantly work at.

"I think it's imperative to muster up enough courage to say exactly what you are feeling, the moment you realize an emotion, when you are still calm and rational," says Elizabeth. "It's really important to tell each other what you need, even if it sounds a little selfish," something women are particularly prone to thinking.

Early on in their relationship she realized that occasionally she would neglect to tell Eric how she was feeling but learned over time. Now she's very open about needing time to unwind and relax with no interruptions. "I think the most important part of communicating as a couple is to be careful with timing, the tone of your voice, and be careful to not let emotions build without trying to talk about your thoughts," often easier said than done when two people are first learning to live together.

Most of all she reminds us that it takes the sustained efforts of two. "We are becoming better and better at backing off and not pushing each other's buttons at the wrong time."

In the meantime, if you are too hot under the collar to have a meaningful conversation, she suggests that you go into another room and organize your thoughts. "During a couple of arguments, when I was starting to lose it, I drafted a whole list of things that I wanted to say. Just the act of writing calmed me down," says Elizabeth of this typical Gemini exercise.

On the positive side, this bride and groom rely on modern love notes to keep the dialogue fresh. "We still enjoy notes and letters from each other. We leave notes on the dry-erase board or sometimes tuck Post-it notes in each other's work bags." How sweet!

■ The Leo Newlywed

The Leo wife is loyal, dignified, and charming; a dynamic proud partner, a creative and loving mother. Natural leaders, Leos like to be the authority figure—whether in the boardroom or on the playground. You just love being the head of your household and running your family life.

But watch out! Nothing is too good for a Leo, her home, her husband, and her children. Yes, you want your brood to look like a million bucks and have a plethora of wonderful things but don't break your bank trying to do it!

Leos are proud, stubborn women. In relationships, you might have a hard time admitting a problem and asking for help. Identify what you need early on and use your creativity to find ways to rebalance your life; delegate some responsibilities to your devoted mate and go for a massage once in a while.

In the heat of the moment, the one thing your husband should never do is treat you without respect. The secret to your happiness is to receive a constant flow of loving attention—make sure your significant other knows this—you'll do just about anything when you're adored and appreciated.

■ The Virgo Newlywed

Practical, refined, and tender, the Virgo sweetheart cherishes the role of wife and mother. You love doing things for others in a gentle and nurturing way. Organizing your home, creating fun activities, and keeping everyone on schedule come naturally to this capable sign. Just make sure you don't get too caught up in needing perfection or you may inadvertently put spontaneity and fun on the back burner.

With Virgo, sometimes emotions don't get the attention they deserve. You'd much rather dive into a list of tasks than mull over how you feel, but that doesn't mean you don't get hurt. To keep your relationship fresh and healthy, don't hold your feelings back or minimize their importance, make sure you talk about them with each other on a regular basis.

You love improving yourself and others, which is one of your gifts, but be careful you don't take that to the extreme or your significant other may feel like you are picking on him. Virgos can be worriers; when you feel like beating yourself up, go find a project to tackle and that will calm you down!

■ The Libra Newlywed

As the ultimate partnership, Libra thrives in a beautiful, harmonious marriage. You enjoy treating each other with dignity and respect. Your home always looks like a page from the Brocade Home catalogue and you are always surrounded by charming, gracious friends and family.

Libra has an innate need to live in balance and harmony. As long as that balance is maintained, everything moves along sensationally. On the other hand, you can't stand unfairness of any sort. It's in your nature to hold a little upset inside to keep the peace but once the scales tip too much, you might just lose it. Be vigilant about expressing yourself in clear, gentle terms at the onset of any problems and they will go no farther.

As a newlywed, Libra enjoys pleasing her mate and you love being appreciated in return. Instead of expecting him to know how to comfort you, you might have to spell it out for him. Let your husband in on a little secret: A happy marriage is ensured by giving you tender encouragement, compliments, and love notes. You can overcome any hurdle life may bring just knowing that you are valued and appreciated.

■ The Scorpio Newlywed

Scorpio women wrap their mates in an intense embrace, making them feel loved, cherished, and protected. It can take a while for a Scorpio to open up to someone but once they know a secure relationship, their world is never quite the same again.

As a newlywed, you create a safe and private environment where you can explore all sides of your significant other—through long, romantic walks in the park to evenings in the bedroom. Whether you are making your home a greener place to live or studying up on your parenting skills, Scorpios have the ability to spend long hours on things that are vital to improving your lives together.

All of this intensity has its downside as well. When you feel misunderstood or isolated from your partner, you can easily get hurt and have a hard time letting it go. Recognize that he might not have even realized he hurt your feelings and find a way to safely vent your frustrations without stinging him.

Scorpios love diving into the unconscious thoughts, patterns, and motivations that make us tick—pick up a good relationship self-help book and let the fun begin!

One Bride, One Groom, One Terrific Kid— And One Huge Transition!

Sometimes marriage is not your typical boy-meets-girl story. Patty, an Aquarius, and Todd, an Aries, met on a windjammer sailing cruise in Grenada (yup, adventure, that about sums up these two signs). She was living in New York and he in Atlanta, when they fell hard and fast.

After a whirlwind, long-distance courtship, he proposed. Aries like to fly by the seat of their pants and for her part Aquarians can wrap their heads around change much more easily than most. Somewhere along the way he and his nine-year-old son moved to Arkansas and that's where this story gets interesting.

From the Big Apple, Patty begins planning a move to Arkansas and a wedding in her hometown in North Carolina. How does one go from sophisticated single to wonderful wife and stepmom without losing herself in the process?

"Give yourself plenty of time, whatever *time* is for you." Patty ponders, "I could've moved right away, but I wanted to have some time to myself as a single person to get my life in order; to say good-bye to my singlehood properly." A wise decision for this Aquarius, who was conscious of just how big an adjustment this was going to be.

The transition from single to married can be bumpy enough without moving a thousand miles and acquiring a stepson. She suggests making incremental changes. Moving south a few months before the big day gave them all a chance to get used to living together without the pressure.

"The hardest thing when I first moved here was for all of us to re-define our roles; we talked about it and talked about it and we kept talking until we figured it out." Aquarians enjoy finding solutions that work for everyone. "I think I've just gotten really lucky. Reagan is an exceptional kid who was ready to have a female influence in his life on a daily basis."

For Patty, having a home and family-oriented Cancer Rising also helps. "I think it's in every woman's nature to sacrifice personal stuff for the family but I had to keep reminding myself that was not going to help me in the long run." Something this forty-year-old says she might not have known had she married earlier in life.

Her biggest piece of advice for newly married pre-fab families is to get involved in the kids' lives. "We're doing things like taking golf lessons together," says this newlywed who loves her married life. "It's just great to have someone to share the responsibility, share the glory, share the ups, share the downs," she exclaims in oh-so-Aquarian fashion. "I highly recommend it!"

■ The Sagittarius Newlywed

Enthusiastic, optimistic, and adventurous—the Sag spirit just loves being in love! Nothing is more exciting to a Sagittarius than embarking on a new adventure. When you see your marriage as the ultimate learning, growing experience then every activity and chore becomes fun when you do it as a team. That said, you need a ton of variety—plan little trips, visits to museums, outdoor sports activities, and dates with other newlywed friends.

Sag women are wonderful partners. Your spiritual, philosophical nature supports open communication between each other and encourages him to become all that he can be. You can't stand unethical behavior from your significant other but there's never a problem too big for a Sag gal to handle. Sit down for some frank discussion where no subject is off limits, and soon you'll be ready to let whatever it is go.

When you're in the mood to be right, you seriously dislike having your beliefs questioned. You may exaggerate to get your point across or act a little holier-than-thou when you're feeling unsafe. Remember there are no right or wrong ways to do something—just different. Respect his beliefs and opinions.

■ The Capricorn Newlywed

Tender, loyal Capricorns are ambitious newlyweds who work hard to create a wonderful life for their partners and extended family. As a perfectionist, you always want the best of the best, although the practical side of you won't waste a lot of resources to achieve that status.

Capricorns take their new role very seriously but you have to be careful not to take the weight of the world on your shoulders as well. There's a difference between respecting your marriage and carrying the burden of home and family all by yourself. Yes, you are an independent woman, but realize it's a strength to ask for and expect help.

Your hardworking nature makes it a joy to organize activities and keep everyone on a schedule—you love to call the shots! To create a balanced relationship, allow your new husband to plan occasional romantic activities, fold laundry, and take care of you once in a while. If he doesn't know how to do this, teach him and then let him do his job!

Have a great life by having compassion for yourself and others, delegating responsibilities, and spending a little money on the luxuries of life.

■ The Aquarius Newlywed

The Aquarius newlywed never really settles down. Life after the wedding has to be just as exciting, or you'll get restless. Social Aquarians love constant adventures, so get busy planning fun things to do with your mate. You take your commitment seriously but you never quite give up your independence either. Hanging out with your friends is just as important to your well-being as it was before the ceremony.

Unless you have a Water Moon or Rising sign, you're put off by deep emotional arguments, choosing to think instead of feel. Use your strengths to analyze a situation in a detached and truthful manner and team up with your partner to find solutions that work best. You do like to mix it up once in a while by throwing out some shocking statement or odd behavior just to rile him up. You don't have to stop being you to be happily married, simply make sure you do your verbal sparring at appropriate times!

Rebellious Aquarians reinvent the institution of marriage. Learn to be a bit more interdependent, teach your husband how to support you, and yours will be an equal partnership.

■ The Pisces Newlywed

With constant affection, romantic activities, and a steady stream of love notes, a Pisces marriage is the stuff of legend. Fueled by your distaste of harsh reality, you create a loving home that is a respite from the world.

Pisces are so connected to their mates that it's sometimes hard to separate your feelings from his. It's important to avoid taking the weight of the world on your shoulders and to learn good coping skills—a great psychology or self-help book can work wonders for your spirit.

A healthy marriage is wonderful for the sensitive Fish, with a protective husband around to help you set boundaries and act as a gatekeeper to those who would take advantage of you. The biggest thing to remember is to avoid the common Pisces problem of trying to rescue him or put yourself into a position to need rescuing yourself!

The spiritual, mystical Pisces are great problem solvers. Since you can't stand when your significant other is upset at you, use your creativity to sidestep arguments and still be heard—just don't avoid sharing your feelings or you'll be putting stress on your body.

■ ■

A wedding is one thing, a marriage is something completely different. As you plan your wedding, prepare to be Mrs. Right by keeping your heart open and your feet planted firmly on the ground.

According to Reverend Susanna Stefanachi Macomb, interfaith minister and author of *Joining Hands and Hearts: Interfaith, Intercultural Wedding Celebrations, a Practical Guide for Couples,* the greatest myth she encounters is that brides and grooms think their wedding and marriage are going to be nothing but pure unadulterated joy. The reality is that family and friends are going to give opinions, complaints, and act out their own unresolved issues before and after the big day.

To keep those issues from hurting your relationship, discuss everything first and present a united front. "The wedding day is the birthday of your marriage. You are telling the world, especially your families, how you're going to operate as a couple," she affirms. Great words to live by as you lovingly plant the seeds of transition. "When you get married, the two of you form a nuclear family and that family must come first. Your spouse now comes before your parents."

Whether before or after the wedding, people learning to live together can have their ups and downs. "Couples don't even want to admit those feelings of discomfort because they think, 'We shouldn't be having these problems so early on in our marriage,'" Susanna contends. In truth, growing pains are normal and something to be worked through.

No matter what your sign, it's important to get to the underlying issue. "It's usually not that one's messy and one's neat, it's usually about respecting each other's needs and feelings. You have to be open and willing to work together to help each other feel comfortable." With love and commitment, your marriage will grow into a wonderful union. Many of the couples featured throughout this book revealed that they've never felt as safe as they do today.

In good times and bad, we can bring ourselves back to Reverend Macomb's powerful words. "You are together because it is together that you can manifest your full potential—that is, the magnificence that lies within each of you," she says with the grace of her Gemini Moon. "You are each other's springboard to the stars."

And, as we've seen, the stars are an enlightening tool to live by! Using astrology, you have planned a wonderful wedding, a romantic honeymoon, and laid the foundation for a successful marriage. May your life as Mr. and Mrs. always be as joyful and loving as your wedding day—and may you always read your horoscope.

Acknowledgments

■
■

This book would not have come into being without the assistance of so many wonderful people. First off, I have a tremendous amount of gratitude for my editor, Peter Joseph, who worked with me every step of the way to make this a most excellent book! A big hug and a kiss go out to my agent, Lisa Hagan, who in addition to being a terrific Pisces pal knows her stuff really well!

I'd also like to thank astrologer Heather Roan-Robbins for being a terrific sounding board—and for adding her amazing astrological knowledge, too. Bravo to musical genius Julia Gregory for guiding me through many musical selections. High-fives to the wonderful Denise Ashlynd for her research and transcription services as well as to my scheduling goddess and super-support person, Sue Hubbard Tarlton—without her I'd get nothing accomplished!

In addition, I appreciate the many people who generously gave their time, thoughts, words, and attention: Reverend Susanna Stefanachi Macomb, Chiera King, Maureen Jeffries, Sheryl Kayne, Jennifer Taber, Karli Stein; my parents, Harvey and Roberta Wolf; and my husband, Ed Lamadrid.

And most of all, I'd like to thank the many brides and grooms who shared the honest, heartfelt experiences that truly make this text come alive: Jeff and

Kristye Golly, Heather and Jamie Roan-Robbins, Tony Glazer and Summer Crockett Moore, Simi and Franz Ketterer, Lisa and Glen Stewart, Kawana Reed-Perricone and Joseph Perricone, Maureen and Gilbert Jeffries, Mark and Aviva Mitchell, Nina and Charles Mansfield, Shannon Duke and Jared Horton, Sari and Victor Erdos, Lois and Chris O'Neill, Andrea and Santiago Ferrer, Patty and Todd Mathes, Jennifer Lord-Bessen and Stephen Bessen, Wendy and Chris Jeffries, Eric and Elizabeth Bliss, Mary Ellen and John Ezelius, Dennie and Peter Visvardis, Leila Sbitani Hahn and Andrew Hahn, and Emily Garcia and Derek Grunewald.

Shannon Taggart

Pisces Stacey Wolf, a professional psychic astrologer for over fifteen years, is the author of *Psychic Living, Secrets of the Signs, Love Secrets of the Signs,* and *Get Psychic.* Stacey has appeared on numerous TV and radio shows, including *The View, Beyond with James Van Praagh, The Other Half, Late Show with David Letterman,* and ABC's *World News Now,* among many others. Stacey has been featured in *Cosmopolitan, Bridal Guide, Mademoiselle, J-14, Twist, American Woman, Woman's Own,* and *Fate* magazines, as well as the books *The 100 Top Psychics in America* and *Esoteric Guide to New York.* She is married to acupuncturist, Taurus, and all-around great guy Edward Lamadrid (www.integrative healthstudio.com), and lives in Manhattan.